'Lively and endearingly eccentric . . . There are no half measures with Miriam Margolyes'

Woman's Weekly

'Gloriously larger than life'

Observer

'A life worth immortalising . . . As irrepressible as ever, Margolyes's warmth and wit shines through'

Radio Times

'Crass, brash, rude, crude, funny and sad . . . delightful and surprising'

Good Housekeeping

'Flawless . . . Long may she reign!'

Herald

'Blisteringly honest and hugely entertaining'

Daily Record

'Both interesting and hilarious . . . full of life and vigour'

Irish Examiner

'Outrageous and outspoken, her life will induce guffaws as much as gasps'

i Paper

'An absolute hoot . . . naughty but nice . . . lyrical, natural and shoulder-shakingly hilarious . . . the main impression the reader is left with is of her kindness'

Guardian

Also by Miriam Margolyes

This Much is True

Born in Oxford, England, in 1941 and educated at Newnham College, Cambridge, MIRIAM MARGOLYES is an award-winning veteran of the stage and screen, and an internationally acclaimed voice artist and documentarian. Winner of the BAFTA Best Supporting Actress award for *The Age of Innocence*, she received an OBE in 2002 for Services to Drama. *This Much is True*, her long-awaited award-winning autobiography, was in the top ten for over a year. *Oh Miriam!* is her bestselling second book.

More Praise:

'Famously filthy, funny and phlegmatic . . . *Oh Miriam!* is Margolyes's manifesto for a fulfilled life . . . She loves to tell it straight. And the older she gets, the straighter she tells it'

Guardian

'Gleeful and deliciously unbridled . . . There is something heroic in her unruliness'

Observer

'Hilarious and frank, Miriam Margolyes spares no blushes, and the spotlight adores her for it . . . a legend, a living embodiment of British eccentricity'

Vogue

'Magnificent . . . [*Oh Miriam!* is] full of profanity and profundity. Its title comes from all the people who have ever exclaimed her name in every tone from horror to hilarity; and her unfiltered personality leaps off the page – honesty, kindness, generosity, sanity, erudition, outspokenness'

Irish Examiner

'Startling, thrillingly outspoken, provocative, potty-mouthed and exhilarating . . . Her personality is so likeable she can only leave you wanting more'

Daily Telegraph

'A force to be reckoned with'

Good Housekeeping

'This book is like Margolyes herself – outspoken, ebullient and unexpectedly wise'

Daily Express

'Pearls of wisdom on living a good life . . . a mix of eye-watering candour and engaging self-reflection'

Guardian

'*Oh Miriam!* risks the curse of the sequel, and pulls it off . . . A force of nature, a tour de *farce*. Bold, brave and bright, but also revealing, shocking and touching. Miriam is an icon, a cocksucker – and the star of her show'

Independent

'Superb . . . A one-off, a treasure, a fearless taker of no prisoners, Miriam Margolyes produces a laugh a minute and says what others dare not'

The Times

'Margolyes is a natural comedian, and the chuckle that seems embedded in her voice is delightfully cheering. But there is also something impressive about her clarity and quiet passion'

Financial Times

OH MIRIAM*!*

**Stories from an
Extraordinary Life**

Miriam
Margolyes

JOHN MURRAY

First published in Great Britain in 2023 by John Murray (Publishers)

This paperback edition published in 2024

1

Copyright © Miriam Margolyes 2023

The right of Miriam Margolyes to be identified as the Author
of the Work has been asserted by her in accordance with
the Copyright, Designs and Patents Act 1988.

A CIP catalogue record for this title is available from the British Library

B format ISBN 9781399803373
ebook ISBN 9781399803380

Typeset in Minion Pro by Hewer Text UK Ltd, Edinburgh
Printed and bound in Great Britain by Clays Ltd, Elcograf S.p.A.

John Murray policy is to use papers that are natural, renewable and
recyclable products and made from wood grown in sustainable forests.
The logging and manufacturing processes are expected to conform
to the environmental regulations of the country of origin.

Carmelite House
50 Victoria Embankment
London EC4Y 0DZ

www.johnmurraypress.co.uk

John Murray Press, part of Hodder & Stoughton Limited
An Hachette UK company

To H. A. S. – the person least likely to read this book

Contents

Contents

To be natural is such a very difficult pose to keep up.

Oscar Wilde, 1854–1900

Cast your bread upon the waters and it will come back sandwiches.

Ruth Walters (Mummy), 1905–74

Oh Miriam!

I was in the Lower Third at Oxford High Junior School in Bardwell Road, Oxford. Miss Willetts breezed in, ready for the fray.

'Right,' she said briskly.

'Left!' I immediately responded.

That was the quickest sending out I ever experienced.

———

I spent a great deal of time outside our headmistress Miss Stack's door, waiting to be summoned into her office. She would sigh as I strode in again, by then probably a little crestfallen: 'Oh Miriam, what is it this time?'

Hello

Here we are again, I can't believe it.

———

Well, you have to start somewhere. We all know 'The Second Book' is the 'sinker', where all the goodwill and success won by Book One disappears, and the dullness, the paucity of anecdotes, the weary recycling is eagerly seized upon and the book and the writer pitied and then obliterated. Please remember that I'm eighty-two and my memory palace is more of an attic, piled high and haphazardly with all kinds of things. I'll try my best to deliver an interesting read – and as before, it will be totally truthful.

What maddens me is when people think I must have made it up. NO, I DIDN'T. I did take my clothes off for Augustus John; I was bullied by some of the public schoolboys who ended up in Monty Python (aka Light Entertainment's Bullingdon Club); I was the Cadbury's Caramel Bunny and a PG Tips chimp – but I was also Queen Victoria, Mrs Mingott and Sister George. I might have forgotten some details and transposed a date or two by accident, but what I wrote, happened. For instance, in 1963, in the Edinburgh Festival I wasn't in *Ubu Roi*, dressed in Gerald Scarfe's life-size vulva costume, looking like an enormous pink conch shell, I was in the sequel – the year after. You know what they say: once a cunt, always a cunt.

Writing a memoir was not something I ever intended to do. I've never been able to remember my life. I've just lived it. I didn't know what else to do. I was always hopeless at learning my lines but I love telling stories. Covid helped; lockdown meant there was nothing much else to do. So, rather than headbutting it, I gently tickled my book into being. I talked to lots of friends and colleagues to jog the memory and things fell into place. And when I got an offer I couldn't refuse from the publisher, I thought, 'Let's go, girl!'

It's a disturbing thing, to tell the truth about yourself: I knew it had to be the truth. I didn't know how people would react. I've offended a lot of people in my life, and some may think I'm very rude, but when I examine what I've achieved, I feel pleased. I don't feel smug, however, because I'm not complete yet. I've still got a long way to go. And like that first book, this one I suspect is not something that every grandmother is going to want to read. (There is a chapter about what I learned from my grandmothers that I think mine would not have approved of.)

Heather still hasn't read *This Much is True* and I'm relieved. She gets really peeved, telling me that when she googles her name, all that comes up is 'partner of Miriam Margolyes' – as if the life and work of a distinguished historian of South East Asia is just a footnote to me.

As eighteen months ago, I'm sitting at the computer in La Casella, Montisi, and reflecting on my life. I thought this would be a peaceful period, but it isn't. For reasons which I will attempt to analyse, in the past decade I have become much more well known – even referred to as a 'National Treasure' or – more cruelly accurate – a 'National Trinket'. And the corollary of that is that I now receive appalling remarks in the comment pages of the *Daily Telegraph*, a nasty newspaper for nasty people I much enjoy reading. (I do get the *Guardian* online too.)

I have never been older or busier. Suddenly, I am overwhelmed with offers: documentaries, radio plays, theatre events (*The Addams Family*, to play Grandma), voice-overs, the whole range of work available to performers. And many films, all over the world, in New Zealand, in Prague, in Australia. I even had to turn down Marvel because the timing didn't work and the money wasn't enough.

Almost everyone I know seems to be setting up a podcast, and the requests hurtle in. I refuse most of them. I like podcasts, although I think of them as radio broadcasts, which is what they would have been called back in the days when I worked in the BBC Drama Repertory Company. But there comes a point when not only do I weary of the sound of my own voice, but I fear others will too. And I'd rather quit when I'm ahead.

I now spend much of my time on Zoom, a powerful, ubiquitous communications programme which the pandemic made essential. Our computers stare at each other; we often forget to turn on the video or the sound or both. 'Can you hear me?' we shout at each other, looking interestedly at the background, which can be a cheat or really the journalist's messy kitchen or study. I love it when the dog or the husband makes a fleeting appearance and proves that it's real after all.

Ruefully I remark to myself, 'What took you so long?' Why is it that now I am showered with the work which eluded me for so many years? I am not bitter; that would be a fool's reaction. I am grateful – it's late but it's there! I have reluctantly come to the conclusion that it's my potty mouth, my bodily effusions, my appearances on *The Graham Norton Show*, and the Cameo messages which someone (not me!) puts on TikTok, that have propelled me into an area of public scrutiny and made me more famous than I have any right to be. Don't think I'm grumbling. I'm just gobsmacked. I've never had such loving, appreciative responses to anything I've done. Now every day, people send me gifts, letters, emails, ask me to their parties, to read their books (and write something nice on the cover), tell me that I'm making a difference to their lives, that I've given them new hope, made them laugh, made them cry, made them read Dickens. That's the best of all. Perhaps the pandemic forced people who don't read much to find a book and then to write to me. Complete strangers share their sex secrets with me; it's touching and humbling and I'm extremely grateful, though seldom aroused.

I've been travelling around the country, partly because of my last book and partly because of my television series, and I've been bowled over by the way that the public, when they see me, try to envelop and embrace me. Sadly, I've had to keep them at arm's length – I wish it were otherwise but I'm so frightened of catching Covid. I brandish my walking stick like a weapon and often bellow 'STOP RIGHT THERE!' as they rush towards me. Outside the Queen's Hall in Edinburgh, I was forced to poke someone with my rubber-tipped ferule in his belly button, to make him stay back. It has been extraordinary to me to realise that, somehow, something in me has evoked a mass, loving trust in who I am. Assuming I was off air, I swore on my one – and probably only – excursion on the *Today* programme, talking about the iniquities of a particularly Teflon-coated Tory minister. My mortification was assuaged a little when friends later sent me news footage of a placard outside the Houses of Commons saying: MIRIAM SPEAKS FOR THE NATION.

I had thought my career was over. I'm semi-crippled now; usually that means you have to stop. And I don't think I can do theatre again unless I'm playing a character similarly disabled. I know Maggie and Eileen and Judi and Vanessa still tread the boards, and they're older than me – but they're fitter, bugger it, and good luck to them! However, I've told Lindy, my agent, to say I'm still available and I am.

The great thing with voice work is that you can do it sitting down, but before I went off to do a recent *Doctor Who* show on radio, I managed to throw in a fashion shoot. Yes, you read that correctly, and it still makes me hoot with laughter. *Vogue*, the most glamorous and important fashion magazine of them all, featured me in their July 2023 issue, and provided me with hair and make-up and a STYLIST. I didn't get to keep all the clothes, but just for a few hours, I was Barbara Goalen and Kate Moss and Twiggy all rolled into one. (More on this to follow.) Well, I wasn't them, but I was in their shoes, prancing around pretending I'm desirable. In case you don't know who Goalen was: when I was growing up in the forties and fifties, she was the leading model of the day; one of exceptional beauty and elegance. 'Her haughty demeanour, delicate bone-structure and wasp waist came to represent the height of glamour.' Somehow, I doubt that will be said in my *Guardian* obituary, but never mind. I made it into the fashion pages against formidable odds; I just wish Mummy and Cousin Buffy, owner of the smartest dress shop in Conduit Street in the 1970s, could know and *kvell*.

You never can tell what's going to happen. You have to be open to the moment, in real life as in acting. Death is probably around the corner, drat it – just when I've got going. But as long as I *carpe* a *diem*, so to speak, and don't shirk a chance, Life is there, for all of us. I can't avoid mentioning now the horrors of this government, how hard for everyone it's made just getting by, how shabby the morals have become, how ungenerous and unloving and unwelcoming our attitudes. But let's hope I live to vote in the election to come. Let's hope YOU do too and that you vote the way I'm telling you, which is basically: AVOID THE TORIES AT ALL COSTS.

So, is it just vanity that's making me write another book? It may well be. And then people might say, 'But what else have you got to say, Miriam?' Well, my response to that is: Just because I've written my autobiography, it doesn't mean that I'm dead; it doesn't mean I'm mute. I still have a life. I have thoughts. I want to find out *who I am*. I was pleased to discover how much I enjoyed putting pen to paper (or rather fingers to laptop keys); I didn't want to stop writing.

But enough pontificating. What is this book about? I know that it's about me and about my discoveries as I live. I've called it *Oh Miriam!* because this exclamation has been such a constant refrain in my life, said in all kinds of tones – laughs and surprised gasps sadly rather outweighing the orgasmic sighs (though there have been plenty of those too). I'm hoping for all those from you as you read on. My first book took a journey through my life; this one takes you through my heart and mind and the things I've learned and am still learning. I've written my own Vagina Monologue and my Tale of the Unexpected: as you'll see from the contents page, the following chapters range from 'Swearing is Good for You' to 'How to Stay Married' so you know what you're in for.

I don't want to hurt anyone, and I don't want to put anybody down. That's not the idea. But I will tell the truth, and sometimes the truth is painful. The public only sees you when you're up, so they think you're always up. But nobody is always up. Anybody who was, would either be insufferable or very stupid. Of course, I want to make you laugh, I want you to enjoy reading this book, but I hope the moments when I'm down might also be of use. I'm not climbing onto a soapbox here. I'm not trying to tell you how to live your life, just to tell you some stories from mine. I'm hoping that telling you about my thrills and spills will entertain you. I always have opinions – and people are always asking me for advice. When *This Morning* set me up as an agony aunt, I don't think even they expected my bluntly telling one viewer that she should leave her husband (he sounded such a pig) and another one that she should go on a diet. It is so important to tell it like it is. But it is always just as important to be kind.

After all, I've made it to eighty-two, mostly in one piece. Admittedly I did have a heart operation and my dentist recently discovered that my gag reflex was not up to scratch (probably all the cocks I sucked back in the day) but I'm still here. So off we go . . .

Getting to Know You

I've always loved talking to people. As a child, I used to talk about the housing shortage, obviously because I'd heard my parents talking about it. 'Of course,' I would announce to visitors to 'the hovel', 'we can't move from here because of the housing shortage.' And then I would hold forth to other children at playtime: 'You *do* know there's a housing shortage, don't you?'

Another of my favourite topics was *tsuris*. It's a Yiddish phrase that means 'ill fortune', 'bad luck', 'sadness'. When I first went on holiday to Kingsgate, near Broadstairs, with my parents, I was playing with the little girl next door in Percy Avenue and my mother heard me asking her, 'Do you have *tsuris*?'

'No,' she replied.

'Oh, we have plenty,' I said, perfectly mirroring the adult cadence.

———

Tsuris aside, there are not many similarities between me and Marcel Proust. He was a reclusive, droopingly moustachioed hypochondriac who spent many years in bed, writing one very long book.[*] I am an actress, documentarian and citizen of the world; while he drifted off into a fey

---

[*] I admit to not having read *À la recherche du temps perdu*; I keep starting it and then running out of puff . . .

reverie of the past every time he nibbled on a moist, buttery madeleine. Admittedly, I do find a large piece of cheesecake leaves me rather sleepy . . . but like me, he was fascinated by what made people tick. In 1886, a fourteen-year-old Proust discovered the 'confession album', which used a series of searching questions to build up a picture of the inside of someone's head. The questions were often used as dinner party entertainment or as a parlour game, an innocent precursor to Truth or Dare, and Spin the Bottle. He realised that it was a way to jump over the banality of small talk and dive straight into deep conversation, and he was right.

Here are thirty[*] of the questions Proust became obsessed by in 1890 – my answers are in CAPITALS:

1. **What is your idea of perfect happiness?** A REVERSAL OF BREXIT: I'm writing these words in our terracotta-tiled living room at La Casella, having just stoked the wood stove while our two enormous cats happily stalk around us. Heather's and my chief joy in life is to spend time here together. But along came BREXIT which has limited our time in the house we own. Freedom of movement? BOLLOCKS! We have to count the days, or be fined and branded as criminals. I will NEVER forgive those who voted for this insanity. The whole United Kingdom suffers in different ways. And my last years have been torn apart by the stupidity of it all. I want my life back.

2. **What is your greatest fear?** HAVING A STROKE: I don't remember where I was or how I got the news when Mummy

---

[*] In fact, he asked thirty-five – but these are the most interesting.

had her first stroke in 1968, but it changed my life for ever. I thought I would never smile again.

3. **What is the trait you most deplore in yourself?** LAZINESS: I was born a sloth and never exerted myself again – skiving off from games, curling up with a book or a woman whenever action was expected. I deserve my fate, now immobility has become the norm. I enjoy work, but activity, moving the body – never.

4. **What is the trait you most deplore in others?** MEANNESS: I watch myself keenly for any sign. Mummy was generous; even when, after her stroke, she could only use one hand, she would always grab an orange to give to her carer. Daddy was invariably mean. It may have stemmed from the poverty of his youth. But he would never take a taxi, always turned the lights off, sometimes if someone was still in the room. He guarded his cash, seldom gave tips, worried about money, never thought we had any, and feared complete economic collapse. I resolved never to be like him in that regard. I over-tip with anxiety. However, I do have a rather unpleasant trait. I love treating friends to restaurant meals: they can have much food as they want; but I won't pay for drinks. I rarely touch alcohol and I resent the restaurant mark-up. It's up to you what you drink, I'm not paying for it!

5. **Which living person do you most admire?** DAVID ATTENBOROUGH: I didn't want to admire a politician; they seem uniformly disgraceful. Sir David is a mensch: he's worked hard, he's witty, forthright, honest, and cares about the planet, animals and our responsibilities to each other. I've met him

once, briefly, and felt absurdly tongue-tied. I hope we meet again before we both pop our clogs.

6. **What is your greatest extravagance?** ICE CREAM: Coffee is my favourite flavour, although I don't drink coffee (it keeps me awake). Good ice cream never comes cheap, but it's worth it. I recommend Mullins Brasserie in Market Place, Margate for the best I have ever tasted, followed by Nardulli's on Clapham Common for the best in London, and Il Paradiso café, Trequanda, for the best in Italy. I know it's bad for me, but I love it.

7. **What is your current state of mind?** APPREHENSIVE: How can anyone not be, considering the state of the world? I've never known such a time, when truth is ignored, when fame is idolised, the planet under threat. And of course, my own fate awaits me; mortality stares me in the face every time I look in the mirror.

8. **What do you consider the most overrated virtue?** MODESTY: I think it's important to know your own worth; it's not conceited to claim excellence as long as you're right. It's pointless to hide your light under a bushel, or indeed anything. Be proud of your achievements. Trumpet them if necessary. And if you have lovely breasts, please share them.

9. **On what occasion do you lie?** AFTER A MEAL I HAVEN'T ENJOYED: Lying is a mug's game, you'll always be found out eventually. But when I'm a guest, it behoves me to say something tasted delicious, even if it didn't. It's not an important lie, no one will die because of it, and to say something tastes awful is just rude and depressing. I prefer to keep everyone happy and say 'Yumbo!'

10. **What do you most dislike about your appearance?** MY BELLY: I inherited my belly from my mother. I remember noticing when she did the vacuuming in the nude that her belly hung down and flopped about. And I thought, 'Oh that's awful. I'll make sure I never get to look like that.' Well, it's happened. I can't blame childbirth, as Mummy did. My belly was made all by myself, through years of over-eating and under-exercising. Now it's my overhanging nightmare – and I have to put up with it.

11. **Which living person do you most despise?** BENJAMIN NETANYAHU: There is no shortage of candidates for my Despised List. The decline of decency, honesty and justice in the world during my lifetime has been inexorable. And the nastiest of the current nasties is the Israeli prime minister, who should be in jail for breach of trust, accepting bribes, and fraud. The crime of his recent attempts to control judges in Israel is the most egregious. He is fanning the flames of conflict between Israelis and Palestinians and removing the chance of peace between them.

12. **What is the quality you most like in a person?** KINDNESS: Kindness is the quality I have come to value more than any other. Whatever the sex, recognition of others' humanity is crucial to civilisation. Without kindness we are worse than animals and we do not deserve to inherit the earth.

13. **Which words or phrases do you most overuse?** 'AS THE ACTRESS SAID TO THE BISHOP': That phrase has made me laugh ever since I first heard it. Sometimes changed to 'As the Art Mistress said to the Gardener' (which I believe

was popularised by Beryl Reid in the 1950s BBC radio comedy series *Educating Archie*), they both convey a medley of sexual games and mutually pleasing activities crossing all class boundaries, and never fail to raise a smile and a suspicion of naughtiness. Sex is often serious but it's possible to have fun with it too. Apparently, the French have their own version: '*Comme disait le hérisson en descendant d'une brosse à chaussure*' ('As the hedgehog said when getting off a shoe brush').

14. **What or who is the greatest love of your life?** HEATHER: My partner of fifty-four years does not want to appear in any of my books. She is naturally reticent and finds my habit of self-publicity one of the more irritating of my character traits. Be that as it may, she *is* the love of my life, the most constant factor of my life, and the source of the most intense pleasure, physically, mentally and emotionally. We are very different creatures: she is a scholar, I am an actress. But the breadth of her vision and the irony deep in her nature delight me. I am supremely satisfied. (When I read that to her she groaned and said, 'Couldn't you just delete that paragraph?')

15. **When and where were you happiest?** IN 2012, TOURING WITH *DICKENS' WOMEN*: 2012 was the bicentenary of Charles Dickens's birth. What better way to celebrate the occasion than a World Tour of my one-woman show *Dickens' Women*? Started in 1997 at the Edinburgh Festival, it was the joint creation of Sonia Fraser and myself. Richard Jordan, who had worked on the original West End production in 1993, took me around Britain and to America – then handed me to

Andrew McKinnon, who took me and John Martin my pianist, around Australia and New Zealand. It was the culmination of my life's dream. What larks, Pip! When Andrew died suddenly a few months ago, a light went out in my life.

16. **Which talent would you most like to have?** DISCIPLINE: I'm not sure it's a talent, but I need it more than any other. I have talent; I need discipline to harness and organise it. I am lazy, I procrastinate, I allow myself to fritter away the most precious thing there is – time! What a pity.

17. **If you could change one thing about yourself, what would it be?** A STRONGER BLADDER: A weak bladder is a pissing nuisance. It's something I've never valued or thought about, but every time I go out now, I have to check where the loo is. I am obliged to drink a lot of water because of my kidneys – oh the Organ Recital is so BORING! I just wish I'd done Pelvic Floor Exercises when I could.

18. **What do you consider your greatest achievement?** MY FRIENDS: I am ferociously proud of the friendships I have nurtured throughout my life, from kindergarten to the present day. They form the rock on which my life is structured, and they continue to sustain and delight me. Friendship is a serious thing and I take it seriously.

19. **If you were to die and come back as a person or a thing, what would it be?** QUEEN VICTORIA: For a long time, Queen Victoria has fascinated me. I have played her at least three times on TV: philanthropically in *Blackadder*, seriously in a documentary on the restoration of the Albert Memorial and comically in *The Windsors*.

20. **Where would you most like to live?** ITALY AND IRELAND: How odd that they're both Catholic countries! I do not find the Catholic faith at all attractive. But there's no doubt the people of both countries are intoxicatingly gorgeous. The scenery in which they live, the passion with which they eat and dance and laugh and drink, are impossible to resist.

21. **What is your most treasured possession?** MY CHERUB STATUE: He's a family heirloom, I suspect bought in an auction by my grandfather. It was in their garden for ages, then in Oxford – then I brought it to my London home. Made of the finest Carrara white marble, the boy Cupid crouches on the wings of two doves and reaches for his arrow. He stands on a plinth seven feet high and he needs six men to carry him. I once thought I would sell him. But, after I'd already struck a deal with an auction house, I found I couldn't bear to let him go. When I see him it means I'm home.

22. **What do you regard as the lowest depth of misery?** TO BE WITHOUT FRIENDS: It has not yet happened. I don't think I could cope.

23. **What is your favourite occupation?** TALKING TO AN AUDIENCE: There is nothing I enjoy more than to have someone to talk to. I look forward to book tours, to hospital waiting rooms, anywhere where I have people who are prepared to engage with me in conversation. It is a delight, it never fails. It could be called flirting on a grand scale.

24. **What is your most marked characteristic?** FRIENDLINESS: I have always expected to be liked. I am unafraid of new contacts; my round face is a friendly one, so people seem unafraid of me. I project guilelessness – little do they know!

25. **What do you most value in your friends?** LOYALTY: You might think show business is a murky world of betrayal and falsity. Not so. The overriding quality I have found in my friends in the profession is a steadfast loyalty. I demand it – and I offer it in return.

26. **Who is your hero of fiction?** JANE EYRE: 'I am no bird and no net ensnares me. I am a free human being with an independent will.'

27. **What is it that you most dislike?** TORIES.

28. **What is your greatest regret?** BEING EIGHTY-TWO . . . and still fat.

29. **How would you like to die?** QUICKLY.

30. **What is your motto?** CARPE DIEM: Seize the Day. Don't waste a second, plunge into life and savour every moment. It's over in a trice, this is not the Dress Rehearsal: this is it!

When Did You Have Your First Fuck?

My first week at Cambridge, I attended a crowded meet-and-greet at the ADC, where you forced your way through the frenzied throng very purposefully towards me, to my alarm (*me? Why me?*). When you reached me, you said, without further introduction, 'Do you think the Queen has periods?!' It's still the oddest opening remark I've ever experienced. (Classic Miriam, as I later realized. What did I reply? I've no idea. Speechless probably. But it made its mark. I never forgot it.)

Carey Harrison

Carey Harrison (son of Rex) was one of my first directors and is still a firm friend. Over sixty years later my preferred method for breaking the ice hasn't changed much.

I have always asked lots of questions. My technique is friendly but direct; I go for the jugular and ask the questions I think people don't want to answer. I've always thought that what people want to hide provides the key to their character. But conversely, there are things people love to talk about – and sex, a universal obsession, is one of them. Thus, a good question to start balls rolling is: 'When did you have your first fuck?'

I watch the face very closely as I ask. Sometimes people pretend to have forgotten, or perhaps they genuinely don't remember. Sometimes they smirk slightly, and I know the memory is there and pleasurable. But if their eyes fill with tears, I quickly move on to another subject.

Conversation has certain jobs to perform; to be able to talk entertainingly is essential, but so also is *to listen*. Some people think of conversation as a tug of war; I don't. First of all, everybody must be equal and be listened to . . . and the next thing is to show off! To dazzle and confound my audience is my hope.

Conversation is both an art and a pleasure. Women and girls have the best conversations, roaming discursively around their inner lives and their longings. I learned so much from the talks I had with my mother, lying in bed next to her, staring at the ceiling and knowing I could ask anything. It's like that with Heather now. Our conversations, after fifty-four years together, are as interesting and surprising as they ever were. We don't talk about sex, though. Our conversations range across politics, history, philosophy, music, books, death.

Men, however, are different; I don't really know what men talk about. I don't know if they have longings. In 2022, I was thrilled to be chosen as the subject of Alan Yentob's BBC TV *Imagine* programme. But even when Mr Yentob was supposed to be asking *me* the questions, I couldn't stop myself from grilling *him*. When we were in my kitchen and he was cooking liver and onions for me on camera, I asked him, 'When did you have your first fuck?' Though clearly embarrassed, he did answer that it was when he was fifteen. Then he said, 'I don't think we'll put that in the programme.' But they did.

Jay Rayner reminded me of the first time we met; his mother, my great friend Claire, had invited me to a family dinner. I sat down at their kitchen table, looked under it, and said to his brother, Adam: 'Darling, what enormous feet you have. Do you have a huge cock?'

I can't help myself, it's natural rudery. But it's not *just* that. I also truly believe it relaxes people, because they unite in being appalled. You can define it either as nosiness and impertinence, or as evincing a genuine interest in people. Of course, I realise it *does* upset some, and that disturbs me, because I really don't want to make them uncomfortable. But there is a thrill in getting a totally unrehearsed reaction. You learn more about the people you are talking to. And I was genuinely curious.

Documentaries give me the opportunity to engage fully, talking, questioning, learning. It never occurred to me that you could get paid for being nosy. I now realise I've always been a documentarian. As soon as I've met people, I've always asked them *everything* I could. Age has only increased my curiosity and the urgency of satisfying it. I'm aware that my time is limited; especially now.

I don't want to ignore gossip. Gossip, as long as it's not malicious, is fun and a great linker-upper of people. To have 'inside information' and to share it does give a frisson of pleasure. But I think there are good questions and bad questions. Good questions get conversation flowing, they unplug the cork of good manners or natural reticence; bad ones stop any promising discourse in its tracks.

Money, sex, religion and politics are the things that we are encouraged to omit from polite conversation. People shy away from these topics, frightened to cause arguments or heighten disagreements. It's a very English characteristic, to demur and sidestep when conversations become focused. But to me it's meat and drink. I think they are *exactly* the headings we should make a beeline for. It's refreshing at dinner parties to handle the real things; in the end, I've found that people are always glad they did. I mean, these are the things that *matter* – I'd be happy talking about nothing else.

For instance, I've always been happy to talk about money. I love money and I want everyone to have what they deserve. I'm a trade union member, it's in the workers' interests to have accurate information, so I've always talked about my income with my colleagues and asked them what *they* earn, because it helps us all to establish what we *should* get.

'Are you Jewish?' is another question I am often asking, though only if my 'Jewdar' has been alerted – by someone's looks, their voice or, most often, their surname. Sometimes people bristle, but I am just trying to connect.

Exploring my conversational gambits has got me thinking about the evolution of language and when the idea of the interrogative came into being. Did the question come later as our human brains grew more complex? Think of cavemen, grunting: 'Kill . . . Eat . . . Fire . . .' At what point do you think they said, '*Why* is there no food?' or '*What* do you want to eat?' or '*Where's* the fire?' Most communication is still made in the form of statements. Socrates, bless him, was possibly the first documentarian. He made dialogue important. And it is a wonderful thing – the awareness of another mind and sensibility stimulating one's own responses to the world about us. Questions demand answers. Asking a question is not just accepting someone else's statements: it's probing, curious, *interested*. It's one of the foundations of Jewish education; we call it *pilpul*. And I remember, at Cambridge, Dr Leavis explaining to us that a foundation of intellectual discourse was the 'Yes . . . but . . .' response. Q&A is the most basic acknowledgement of the 'I and Thou' – the awareness that we live in the world with other people.

Proust's questions are not bad as conversation starters I suppose, but several are a little on the genteel side for my liking, and I'm not sure that the ensuing chat would be *that* fruitful or riveting. So I decided to draw up an alternative 'Miriam's Questionnaire' with twenty-five of *my* sort of questions:

1. When did you have your first fuck?
2. How long do you want to live?
3. Your biggest mistake?
4. Your greatest triumph?
5. What enrages you about modern life?
6. The greatest sin?
7. Is religion useful?
8. Should inequality of income be abolished?
9. Create an alternative Ten Commandments.
10. Is space travel a waste of space?
11. Who should define madness?
12. Should cunnilingus be taught in schools?
13. Do you prefer to look forwards or backwards?
14. Best Jewish joke?
15. Would you change sex?
16. Why did you marry your partner?
17. Are you born in the wrong century?
18. Are you antisemitic?
19. Should obesity be a punishable offence? (Daddy thought so.)
20. Is the Country always better than the City?
21. Has America's legacy bettered or worsened human happiness?
22. What's the greatest compliment you've been given?
23. Was it justified?
24. What laws have you broken?
25. Who benefits most from anal sex?

I can't promise that you'll find my answers to *all* these in the pages that follow. I've always hated being too predictable. But I hope these offer jump-leads for conversations of the most galvanising and enjoyable kind.

How *Not* to Play
Grandmother's Footsteps

M any of my friends who are grandmothers insist on looking after their various grandchildren. The joy this gives them is deepened by the knowledge that at the end of the day, they can hand back the squalling infant and the house is theirs again. And that when the children grow up, my friends can rely on constant IT support. Alas, I have to pay someone to do that.

I'll never be a grandmother because I never had children, but I did have two fine examples of my own. What I learned from my grandmothers was where I wanted to follow them and where I didn't. My grandmothers were both products of their times and yet different in every way. My mother had a poor opinion of my father's family which was entirely reciprocated. She would probably admit she married (quite deliberately) above her station; and the Margolyes family agreed. After my parents' wedding in London in 1930, I don't think they ever met again. The Margolyeses never ceased to believe in, and sometimes to voice, their superiority. They felt 'a cut above'. But they did have something in common. Mummy's father was a furniture salesman and so was Grandma Margolyes's father. But Grandpa Margolyes had gone up in the world since then and owned a substantial jewellery business.

Grandma Margolyes (we never said 'Granny'; it was always 'Grandma') was born Rebecca Turiansky in 1874 in Odessa, then

Russia, now Ukraine, and died in Glasgow in 1959. Grandma Walters (always so designated to distinguish one from the other) was born in 1864 in Gowers Walk, Whitechapel, in the East End of London, dying in 1953. What different journeys they had made in their lives, one geographical, one merely from rags to riches, but because they were such different people, with profoundly different attitudes to life and the world around them, the example they showed me is varied and occasionally puzzling.

They were both, of course, Jewish, but born into two entirely different Jewish worlds. Although Grandma Margolyes left her homeland as a toddler – carried across Europe in her mother's arms until they came to the port of Leith in about 1877 and got off the boat because they thought it was New York – her birthplace came along with her and never left.

She seemed always afraid: afraid of dogs, afraid of people, afraid of poverty, afraid of being thought ignorant. She saw the world beyond as a threatening, unfriendly place, where people hated you because you were Jewish and would come in the night, set the dogs on you, and burn down your house if you didn't flee. Unlike Cossack Russia, Scotland wasn't a hostile place. There was little antisemitism there (not enough Jews!), but she was fearful nonetheless.

She married Grandpa Margolyes in 1897 in Edinburgh, where her father had his thriving furniture shop. They moved to Glasgow, had four children, whom she brought up lovingly but strictly, and she remained innocent and unworldly all her life. She wasn't a capable woman in the way that the women on my mother's side were. She wouldn't have dreamed of running a business or doing any of the things that Mummy and Grandma Walters had done. She believed women should open their legs (once married, of course) but not their mouths, should marry early and procreate, keep the dietary laws of the Jewish faith, go to synagogue regularly and live in a Jewish bubble.

Her husband, Philip Margolyes, had climbed from real poverty into middle-class merchant prosperity. By 1928, he had become a well-known, highly respected businessman, and a founding President of the Pollokshields Synagogue. He was certainly richer than anyone else in the family; they'd always been peasants in a small Belarussian *shtetl* called Amdur, about seven miles from the Polish border.

While Mummy recognised that Daddy's family *were* a cut above her, she also thought they were mean, and despised them for it. She used to say, 'They've got short arms and deep pockets.' There is the cliché that the Scots are a little bit 'careful'. So, to be Scottish *and* Jewish, well, it's a double whammy. I choose not to follow that example.

Grandma Margolyes looked a bit like the Grandma in the Giles cartoon for the *Daily Express*, but she was much less combative. She was little in stature, as was Daddy, not fat but rather round, and always dressed in black like Queen Victoria. She often wore a little hat and had a somewhat rasping voice, with a throaty Yiddish 'r' underlying her strong Southside Glasgow accent. I am often requested to demonstrate this, which I relish doing – partly because it brings her definitively back to me, and partly because everyone else who used to speak like that is dead. My grandmother never went to the shop; she stayed at home in Aytoun Road, where her daughter, Eva, looked after her. Her vision of the world was therefore restricted, and I think she found my confident mother terrifying. She'd never met a woman who could sing and dance, and strongly disapproved.

Her primary expression was always one of deep disapprobation. You see, by upbringing my grandmother was an Edinburgh Jew; she wasn't a Glasgow Jew and she always had a hankering for Morningside. And as you know, Edinburgh people are famously snobbish, censorious. There is a famous joke about a woman going into Jenners department store, once known as the 'Harrods of the North', on Princes Street. A lady goes up to her and asks, 'Are you not Mrs McTavish?' At which the woman rolls her eyes and says, 'Och, no! Quite the reverse!'

With me, Grandma Margolyes was warm and loving, but she was always limited, inhibited, trammelled. She didn't know how to express emotion and would have found any outpouring of feeling rather suspect. In character, she was kind but narrow-minded, forever expecting the worst. She was always pleased to see me and interested in what I was doing. But she had no concept of what kind of a person I was. She came from another century.

She did love me. I know that. She was always affectionate but clearly puzzled by my confidence and by my unruly hair. To be fair, almost every adult I met seemed to have a compulsion to get out a comb and Kirby grips to try to control the explosion on my head. It never worked! (English manufacturers Kirby, Beard & Co. Ltd. of Birmingham made hairpins similar to the bobby pin, before the bobby pin's invention.) She was confounded, too, by my loudness. She was always concerned with other people's opinion. Whenever I spoke, she'd look round to see if anybody had heard what I'd said and how they had reacted. She worried about what the neighbours would say; which is absolutely *not* what I've inherited. I don't give a flying fig what the neighbours think. (I wrote 'fig' there to please Grandma Margolyes's memory.) In many ways I have defined myself, albeit negatively, against her example. I loved my summers in Glasgow with her, but I always knew I didn't want to live her life, imprisoned in respectability and unable to speak my mind or choose my own path. Her lack of generosity left me determined to give without stint. Her example gave me the courage to be different.

Grandma Walters, whom I got to know much better – because in 1952 she came to live with us in the New House (409 Banbury Road, Oxford) – was a completely different personality, and if I am honest, a more welcome addition to my world. She was trim, elegant, with excellent posture. She had poise and always took a pride in her appearance; she chose her clothes with care. She wore cream silk blouses with pearl brooches at the neck and long black skirts. Her voice was sweet and clear, her manner confident and outgoing, her ability to show love apparently never-ending.

Flora Walters (née Posner) was born in Whitechapel into a poor but respectable family. Like most Jewish immigrants, her parents were desperate to educate their children. And despite their lowly circumstances, Mummy's side wasn't mean. The Posners were exuberant, generous, lovers of music, dancing and theatre, in stark contrast to my father's family, who wouldn't recognise Art if it got up and bit them. When Mummy told Daddy she wanted a permanent seat at the theatre, Daddy, utterly puzzled, said, 'Whatever for?'

Flora followed her elder sister Miriam (after whom I am named), and became a teacher at the Jews' Free School in Bell Lane, known as the Eton of the East End, a school where many famous Jewish families, who were later to become enormously rich, had educated their children. She was a woman of power and influence, accustomed to an authority she naturally possessed. Like Mummy, Grandma Walters was an achiever, somebody who had run a house and a business, and did things. She encouraged Mummy to have dancing, ballet and elocution lessons, and they went to the theatre and music hall, often together – but becoming a professional actress was out of the question. Grandma had an agenda for her daughter: to catch a Jewish doctor. Not to find a career.

I was just five when her husband, my grandpa Sigismund ('Siggi') Sidney Walters, died but I remember him clearly. He had amazing charm; he was handsome and *immensely* seductive. I afterwards discovered he was a serial adulterer and had at least one illegitimate child. It was an enormous family secret that I only found out two years ago. But I think it was known in the family. I remember my cousin Buffy saying, 'Oh yes, he was a real ladies' man. You know, Miriam, he used to have them in the stockroom at the back.' My grandma must have seen the way her husband behaved with women. But despite everything she adored him.

I only knew her as an old lady, in her late eighties, but she never spoke about it. The official line was that he was a wonderful man and everybody adored him and I think that was true. I am sure his infidelity hurt her. Her expression was often sad in repose and she could be quite sharp and bitter, but when she looked at me, her lined face had sweetness in it. I always knew I was her favourite grandchild. Admittedly, there wasn't a huge amount of competition, as Auntie Gusta's offspring, Jack, Doris and Buffy, her three other grandchildren, clearly found her a trial. She had been living with their family in the 'big house' in Hampstead, 94 Platt's Lane, since Siggi's death in 1946. I vividly remember visiting with my parents as a young girl and seeing her struggling to walk downstairs, while my three cousins laughed and made disrespectful, pushing gestures behind her. I was young but I was shocked. I knew that was cruel and wrong.

When Gusta died aged fifty following a heart operation, it was obvious Grandma Walters couldn't stay in Hampstead any more. Mummy had always intended that she would live with us in the new house on Banbury Road, and one of the four bedrooms had been designed for her, with a fitted handbasin. But Grandma's arrival proved tough on my parents. The Margolyeses may have thought Mummy was 'common', but Grandma Walters deeply disapproved of my father. Mummy told me how, as they were leaving for the synagogue on the morning of her marriage to Daddy on 26 June 1930, instead of the expected blessing, Grandma Flora had rather nastily said, 'Well, Ruth. You've made your bed; now you must lie on it.'

But when Grandma developed bowel cancer very soon after joining us in Oxford, Mummy couldn't have been more loving and tender – and she was certainly tested. Grandma was demanding; she had a little brass bell on her bedside table that she used to summon my mother; she rang it all the time, expecting instant service – and she got it.

I grew up too fast for her. She disapproved of my burgeoning breasts and was shocked when I started my periods at eleven – a further sign of precociousness. Precociousness was a bad thing; a sign not of cleverness but smugness. My parents and Grandma disapproved strongly, but they could hardly blame me for menstruating early. It was a somewhat embarrassing recurring subject at mealtimes, and the lengthy discussions between Mummy and Grandma on how to make sanitary towels went on and on – long after an embarrassed Daddy had left the table.

Like Grandma, I have always lived surrounded by much-loved things redolent of the past. Her furniture from the big house in Underhill Road, where she had lived with Grandpa Walters, came with her to Oxford: wonderful old-fashioned wardrobes with floor-length mirrors in each door, hanging brass rails inside and substantial drawers with ornate brass handles between the cupboards. Her clothes came too: masses of Edwardian dresses smelling of mothballs, in fine fabrics with mother-of-pearl buttons. When, many years later, in a burst of spring-cleaning, I donated some of them to the theatrical costumiers Cosprop, they were ecstatic. They loved the feather boas, long black dresses with lace collars and the fox-fur stole, with bright eyes.

She was generous. I was her darling; she was constantly giving me little presents: jewellery, books, hankies, items of clothing. I hope I was loving back – I think I was. One gift I always remember was a gold and pearl brooch in the shape of a star. When she handed it to me, she said, 'Now you are the star of Oxford.' I have it still. I wish she could know I ended up going to Buckingham Palace and that I have earned the right to have a gold star on my dressing-room door.

What You Really Learn at School

Some people are not interested in scholarship; they think philosophy's a waste of time. Idiots! I counter that by saying I'd never fuck anyone without a PhD. (Haven't kept to that, I must confess.) It is entirely true that Heather's brain power and learning are key reasons I love her so much. I have an exaggerated degree of respect for intellectuality. However, while I did get into Cambridge, I chose theatre (or rather theatre chose me) and that was that. I was in twenty productions in my three-year course: this displeased the college authorities, and they threatened to take my Exhibition away, rightly fearing that learning lines crowded out all the other learning I should have been doing. I've been trying to catch up ever since.

My parents' very different upbringings left both determined that I should have the best possible education. The first of his family to go to university, Daddy had benefited from a scholarship to Hutchesons', a famous grammar school – so much so that he became the Dux (Latin for 'leader') of Hux, and won a place to study medicine at Glasgow University. When he was called up aged eighteen to fight in the Great War, his jeweller father, terrified that his beloved son would die in the killing fields of Flanders, went to see the Commanding Officer with a large uncut diamond in his pocket. He made the officer an offer he couldn't refuse, and the diamond stayed with the officer, and Daddy's name was taken off the draft. He went on to become an excellent doctor. Yes – it was bribery, but I'm proud that my grandfather was prepared to risk his good name to save his son's life. Mummy, however, had left school at fourteen to work in her mother's Peckham dress shop, and for all her psychological perspicacity and business acumen, keenly felt her own lack of conventional education, socially and intellectually, and wanted me to have all the chances she didn't have. They scrimped and saved to pay for me to go to Oxford High School for Girls, where the children of the college dons were pupils, and so I did. It was and is a very particular school. Everybody who went there in my day talks like me, not an accent you hear much now. I can still name every girl in my class and my closest friends there are still my friends – seventy years on.

The High School took in bright girls from every background and provided a wider social education, in many ways England was (and is) still in the grip of class, and my beloved OHS was equally in thrall. There was intense snobbery, but I didn't realise that until many years later, because I was one of the snobs. The 'County girls' were so-called because they had won scholarships offered by Oxfordshire County and as a consequence were seen as socially a bit beneath us 'City girls'. As the years passed, I have become closer to the County girls. I think it's vital to cross barriers which stop us appreciating the differences between us. Mind you, Oxford hasn't changed; it's still a hotbed of class and intellectual snobbery.

The school's obsession at the time was 'to show promise'. Everything that you could do to 'show promise' was a good thing. I decided that 'ambivalent' and 'ambiguous' were potent words, and sprinkled them at every opportunity in my essays to signify that I had a fizzing intellectual mind.

The Bible says: 'In the beginning was the word.' And for me, it was. Joan Plowright told me one of my favourite stories about first words.

When we were filming *I Love You to Death* in America, Larry Kasdan, the director, gave a terrific pool party and we all wanted to hear Joan's stories about her life with Sir Laurence Olivier. She has a delightful narrative style, slightly lingering on the words, relishing and pointing them like poetry:

> Princess Margaret had been angling to get to know us better for ages, but Larry [Olivier] liked a bit of peace and quiet. Eventually, of course, I had to ask her over. She came in, looked around the whole house, went upstairs, narrowly missing Peter O'Toole (drunk as usual on the landing). We settled in the living room and I offered her a nice tea. Conversation was a bit stilted, until she saw that Dr Spock book on the coffee table. We both had sons of about the same age. She perked up and asked me what my son's first words had been. I said, 'Oh, I don't really know, "Mama" I should think.' And then Princess Margaret, smiling with superiority, said, '*My* son's first word was CHANDELIER!' Not much you can say to that!

I had acquired a love of literature as soon as I was able to read. Once at school, that passion was well nourished. Miss Bartholomew, Miss Gummer, Miss Gilbert, even our fearsome headmistress Miss Stack (who had a passion for Robert Browning), were outstanding teachers; their joy in sharing their enthusiasm reached us all, setting me up for life.

It was a conventional grammar school education, so naturally our English lessons focused on Shakespeare and the nineteenth-century classics. As I told Queen Elizabeth at a British Book Week celebration at Buckingham Palace, 'We are so lucky to be English, Your Majesty.

After all, we have the greatest literature in the world.'* I can still vividly remember reading *Jane Eyre* and nearly exploding with pleasure at the line 'Reader, I married him'. And I still get overexcited at the first chapter of *Bleak House*, surely one of the best openings of any novel:

> LONDON. Michaelmas Term lately over, and the Lord Chancellor sitting in Lincoln's Inn Hall. Implacable November weather. As much mud in the streets, as if the waters had but newly retired from the face of the earth, and it would not be wonderful to meet a Megalosaurus, forty feet long or so, waddling like an elephantine lizard up Holborn Hill.

And you're there! Dickens commands 'Come here!' and pulls you into the book. I weep and I laugh and it grips me. The best literature has that effect on you. I want everyone to go back to the great books and enjoy them. These little slices of literature have stayed with me since my schooldays; they continue to stimulate my brain and I munch over them, like delicious leftovers. They are for everyone, not just for the educated classes. Dickens was in fact the last great artist to be appreciated by *all* classes, probably until Elvis came along!

At school, I wasn't initially engaged by grammar, but I became more interested as the nuts and bolts of language, the punctuation and the tenses, allowed me to see the structure of English, how grammar allows you to express *exactly* what you're thinking. I'm still thrilled by the gerund to this day. It was a revelation to learn that 'the gerund

---

* Shortly afterwards she told me sternly to be quiet but it wasn't because she disagreed.

takes the genitive'. Let me explain that. When you say, 'I was surprised at him going to India,' it really should be: 'I was surprised at *his* going to India.' Do you see? It's somehow sweeter that way, slips more easily off the tongue. 'I was surprised at him going . . .' doesn't sound right. It's not what I want. I'm always correcting people and I say, 'Don't forget the gerund takes the genitive!' and they look blank and say, 'What? What?' And then I explain. And then they say, 'Oh, fuck off!'

My love affair with that doomed punctuation mark, the apostrophe, continues to this day. I repeat again my mantra for explaining when to use it: 'An apostrophe is a tombstone for a dead letter.' I make children repeat that over and over again. It works because of the power of the word 'tombstone'. As you say it, you see the tombstone rear up into the shape of an apostrophe.

So, I fell in love with both the English language and literature at school, and I never lost that love. But the French language was a different matter entirely. I missed the first two classes because I was ill. Consequently, I failed to grasp that all French nouns were either masculine or feminine, and that really stymied the rest of my French education. When I joined the class on my return, I didn't understand what they were talking about, and I never caught up. French never felt like a language which people spoke, that's the trouble. It was a school subject: it was just on paper; I didn't see it as a living language, so there was no French flair and as a result France wasn't a country that interested me at all. My family never strayed further than the white-cliffed edge of Kent; whereas my friends went abroad in the holidays, so France and French had a reality for them. I say '*Quel dommage*', which means 'what a pity' – and my genuine regret at this missed opportunity gives a Gallic depth to my shrug.

While the word might have been there from the beginning, maths and I had parted company at birth. I have no maths anywhere in my system. I suppose I could recite some of my times tables now, but truthfully, numbers and I are not friends. I'm innumerate. It was always such a struggle. My father was good at maths, though, so any time there had to be calculations at home, working out Mummy's rental income for example, Daddy was always required to do them because I couldn't and neither could Mummy. She used to say, 'I can make money. But I can't count it.' And I'm the same.

At school our maths teacher was Miss Jackson, a delightful woman of humour and some sharpness, although I didn't realise that until I got older. Maths was the opposite of sexy (despite all the possibilities offered by multiplication). Miss Jackson saw straight through my pranks and tricks; she was the one who kicked me when I had a sham fainting fit and lay on the ground in a mock swoon, whilst the other teachers ran around in panic. When she said, 'Miriam, you're dreadful at maths – there's no point in pretending – and I don't think arithmetic is worth doing either,' I knew that it was hopeless and I dropped maths from my life from that moment.

You had to have a science in order to continue to A level. We were obliged to do physics, but I gave that up as soon as I could. I didn't understand what was going on and didn't pay much attention, to be honest. I can't remember *anything* to do with physics except 'surface tension' and there was something called a Bunsen burner, but that actually may have been in chemistry. Otherwise, the subject passed me by.

Biology did grab my attention, although I'm glad to say we never had to dissect a frog. The only piece of information that I retain from biology, though, apart from a film about how babies are made, to which we were glued but which was in fact very boring – is the word 'spirogyra'. I believe it's a primitive cell-structure creature, but I loved the word so much I have never forgotten it. In the film about insemination, or whatever they would've called it, I don't remember any humans appearing – certainly we were not shown a naked person or anything too inflaming. It was simply diagrams and circles and arrows. The fact that *we* might have anything to do with the topic of the film was never even mentioned: sex and insemination was something taking place out there in an 'adult world', which had no reference to *us*. And that's really all that biology means to me to this day.

Other than that unsatisfactory insemination film, sex education at my school, or indeed at home, was non-existent. It was in the bike sheds that we all learned about sex – the only information I was given was by people of my own age. Because of the class divide between the County girls and we City girls (who were the swots), the lipstick and petticoat girls from the County were the prime source of all sexual knowledge. Swots knew nothing about anything below the waist, but we were still deeply interested. As we got to sixteen or seventeen, *everybody* was comparing notes in the bike sheds. Carol Reay (who's now dead, alas) was the authority on sexual intercourse and a smashing person. Carol was 'experienced' and rather envied for her frequent 'goes' at intercourse. We hung on her every pronouncement. 'Always take some Vaseline with you,' she advised. We were baffled but immensely curious. But that's enough for now about between the legs – I do want *something* here to be situated between the ears.

History always fascinated me. But the history we were taught at school was on a very narrow canvas: in essence, it was a colourful

'Kings and Queens' history of England. The ruling classes were always noble and the peasants revolting. It was about maintaining the *status quo*, our map of the world was firmly painted in the red of the British Empire. There was no mention that anything about the Empire might have been a bad thing. A lot of people are furious that Alan Cumming has returned his OBE. I'm not returning mine (because I'm just so pleased to have it and, also, I love King Charles, who presented it to me and it would be a smack in the face to say 'No, I don't want it. Have it back') – but I do understand Alan's position.

Realising that the Martyrs' Memorial at St Giles' that we often walked past marked the actual spot where Cranmer, Ridley and Latimer had been burned at the stake by Bloody Mary (the only monarch to have had a stiff drink named after her) gave history a ghoulish intensity. Queen Elizabeth I was always a favourite and we loved hearing about her and frisky Mary, Queen of Scots, and imagining what had been in the Casket Letters, whether they ever met and what did they think of each other. The French Revolution shocked us; the liberation of it, the overthrow of an unjust regime, seemed less impressive than the violence and depravity of the mob. We were given a Scarlet Pimpernel view of the Revolution – tragic aristocrats rumbling in their tumbrils; the ferocity of a crazed Robespierre slicing through the French nobility with his focused Reign of Terror. The ideals of the Revolution passed us by: our sympathies were with the royals all the way, especially the Sun King, Louis XIV, who, in many ways had set the royal juggernaut thundering towards the guillotine: we thought he was sexy and divine.

I was bewildered by the Whigs and the Tories. I still haven't got them quite sorted out, but I remember the Corn Laws and the riots and Peterloo. And I've always had a pash on Queen Victoria. For one thing, she was almost exactly my height (4ft 10ins) so even her clothes would have fitted me perfectly. But it is her character rather than her physique that inspires me. Her passions and wilfulness and enthusiasms are endearing. Her vivacity and intelligence leap off the pages of her letters and journals; her courage, good sense and sexual joy deserve wider appreciation. The Age to which she gave her name will forever fully engage my attention.

So, it was all Anglocentric, and aristo-centric – and not much else made it through. I wasn't seduced by America. I wasn't interested in the New World. I shared Dickens's view expressed in 1849: 'This is not the republic of my Imagination.' And we accepted without question our teachers' conventional attitudes towards Russia and Communism. Our family doctor, Dr Gillett, was rumoured to have Russian sympathies, for example, and it was a Bad Thing. And, of course, people talked about my great friend Liz Hodgkin's parents being Reds (which they were until the Hungarian revolution of 1956); my parents lowered their voice when they added, 'I think they're Communists.' For right-wing Oxford, Dorothy Hodgkin's Nobel Prize (she remains the only British woman to have won one in science to this day) was more than cancelled out by her left-wing beliefs but not for me. I always wanted to know more. The lively discussions round their family dinner table made me realise that history and politics were insolubly linked, if not one and the same. I renounced the Tories on the spot (and have never looked back).

Geography was with Miss Turpin, and I liked her. She was tall and plain and spinsterish and had a wry sense of humour, but she wasn't a particularly good teacher. She wore the same dull-brown tweed skirt suit every day, her shapeless legs shrouded in thick lisle stockings. For that reason, perhaps, I have retained little knowledge of the subject. However, she was an excellent form mistress of the Lower Fourth, when we were at our most boisterous, as she was a ferocious disciplinarian. She once remarked how clever my friend Catherine Pasternak Slater was. I said, somewhat cheekily, 'Do you think she's cleverer than you are, Miss Turpin?' and she replied, '*Much* cleverer!' I was amazed that a teacher would admit to such a thing but she was right, of course. There was a strong feeling that we were an exceptional year. We always felt that too.

I didn't attend scripture, which is what we called religious education, unless it was a lesson on the Old Testament. Mummy had insisted that I should not be taught the New Testament and the school obeyed her scripture strictures. In some ways that is a pity because the Christian imagery used by many of the great writers can be baffling to a Jewish reader. I still have to swot up on the Apostles and the famous bits in Book Two (that's what I always call the New Testament). I only know that Peter forswore Christ three times before the cocks crowed. And about Judas and his thirty pieces of silver. All the other disciples slightly blur into one. And, of course, there was dear old Jesus. I've got a soft spot for Jesus. Or Joshua Ben Joseph as he would have been called then. He always sounded like a nice young carpenter; a caring, decent bloke and a firm Socialist to boot. Though packed with churches, the Oxford I grew up in would have sent him packing without a thought.

Whenever we behaved badly, we were sent to detention or, the ultimate deterrent, to the headmistress's room. My reports at the end of term always said: 'Miriam must try harder and must pay less attention to what's going on around her and more attention to the lesson in hand.' I couldn't help seeking an audience and playing to the gallery.

My behaviour improved as time went by, however. I didn't get into trouble as much after the Lower Fourth. Being elected a prefect calmed me down; it was a clever ploy, kill or cure. I became (and still remain) dictatorial and bossy. I have never feared Authority – I answered back. I always felt I was the equal of anyone: headmistress or factory foreman. I later had a vacation job in the Frank Cooper's jam and marmalade factory on Botley Road, where the punishment for insubordination was being sent to the horseradish-sauce section. It certainly made your eyes water.

Dame Maggie Smith also went to OHS, but because she's five years older, we never met. We shared an elocution teacher, Mary Plowman, whose star pupil she had been (Maggie has always been a tough act to follow). Mummy was determined I should have the cut-crystal tones she could never acquire and I did. She entered me for poetry recital competitions all over the country, at which I excelled. Although the clarity of my diction stood me in good stead for whatever productions the school was putting on, Drama was seen as a frivolous distraction and not something to be taken seriously: Miss Stack fully shared Daddy's dismissal of acting as a profession.

Thankfully, however, times have changed. Some years back, a later headmistress telephoned to ask for my help. She wanted me to talk to Maggie, with whom I had worked on the Harry Potter films, and ask her to come to Oxford and open a small theatre in the school buildings.

I tentatively approached her: 'Maggie, Oxford High School has asked me to find out if you'd come back and open the new buildings and a theatre space which they want to name after you.'

She glared: 'NO! No, I don't want to do that. I can't think of anything ghastlier. I loathed that school. It was so snobbish. I'm never going back there.'

She stared hard at me with her bright blue eyes. 'Why don't YOU do it? You'd like that, wouldn't you? Tell them you'll do it instead.'

When I reported Maggie's refusal back to the headmistress, there was a slightly tense pause and then she said, 'Well, um . . . Would you consider opening the studio, Miriam?'

Like a shot I said, 'Oh yes, of course. If you're sure.'

Maggie was entirely right. I knew I was the second choice, but I didn't give a hoot. Knowing that my beloved old school has named a proper little theatre space after me is a joyous thing, a bubble of pure pride and happiness. It makes me think about all the unexpected things my education gave me, not a lot on paper if I'm entirely honest, but so much in my heart and head. I may never have blossomed into the dedicated scholar I longed to be, but I learned so much about life and how to live it. I made friendships that last to this day; and best of all, now, however outrageously I behave, no one sends me into horseradish.

Breast is Best

It was the end of an extremely long and hot day on the production of *The Age of Innocence* before shooting started. Nineteenth-century American high society was a complicated new world to recreate, and Martin Scorsese and his extended crew were grimly determined to get every aspect of their production spot-on. The vast cast list was a roll call of amazing acting talent – and me. Daniel Day Lewis and Michelle Pfeiffer and Winona Ryder were the stars whom I hadn't yet met. It was Serious Hollywood and I was delighted (and more than a little nervous) to be there.

Since 6 a.m. that morning, the crew had watched a long succession of actors parade across the podium for hair and make-up approval. Actor followed actor and hour followed hour. I was the very last one, facing an exhausted workforce. By now their faces were polite but lined with fatigue. I felt it was my duty to raise their spirits. So, I fell back on my well-tried remedy for the flagging male – and female. (Thank goodness I wasn't yet in the complex corsets of my costume!) 'It's Miriam Margolyes playing Mrs Mingott,' I said. 'And you deserve these.'

And without further ado, I pulled up my maroon 'Dickens' Universe' T-shirt and my proud and thrusting breasts, released from any confining brassiere (I have always hated confinement) cascaded out of my clothes, in a snowy Victoria Falls of mammarial magnificence which stunned Martin Scorsese and the assembled crew; firstly into a dazed silence and then into roars of laughter and – it must be said – gratitude. Breasts never fail!*

Martin Scorsese has never forgotten it either. Many years later, he said to me, 'I remember that hair and make-up parade most particularly.'

———

For me breasts must be at the forefront, as indeed they are! It's either bums or tits, isn't it? And I'm most definitely tits.

My breasts arrived early and flourished like the green bay tree. I rushed into puberty long before anyone else at school and my sewing mistress was astonished to discover that in the Lower Fourth, I sported a 36B bust measurement.

'Good heavens, Miriam,' she gasped, 'you're the same size as me!'

Twelve was the breasts' coming-out party. That's when everything started to blossom as it does in May. And I remember the American soldier, slightly drunk in Cornmarket one day, who admiringly made a beeline for that bust and caressed it, to my mixed horror and delight, until his friends pulled him away.

My breasts were urgent. I always had holes in the flimsy wool of my school jumper because the nipples pushed through. My nipples were like bullets. I remember Miss Maddron (our head of French), who was herself quite a short person, had an uninterrupted view. As she was no taller than the smallest child, they were bang on her eye level. Her comment was crisp but kind: 'Oh Miriam, I think you'd better get your

---

* And I won a BAFTA for that film!

jersey mended.' It was a constant feature of my school life – two nipple-shaped holes forever requiring a stern darn.

I was extremely anxious not to have to wear a bra, however. Under my clothes in winter, Mummy had already forced me to wear a curious stiff, cotton undergarment called a Liberty bodice. This was mainly just to keep you warm, but the effect of it was quite the opposite of liberty. It was restricting and I have never liked to be restricted in any way. It resembled a thick vest with little rubber buttons on each side at the bottom where you were supposed to attach stockings, but I never had stockings. I wore knee socks. And huge, navy-blue, cotton knickers. I've always liked capacious knickers, never elasticated round the leg. In the early days, they had a small pocket for a hankie. Would that they still did.

Mummy and Grandma Walters, who had just come to live with us, kept bringing up the subject of my needing a bra. (As I said, she disapproved of my precociousness, even where my breasts were concerned.) Grandma said to Mummy, 'I think it's high time Miriam wore a brassiere. You *must* take her to get one, Ruth.' To me she said, even more firmly, 'You're a little lady now, Miriam. You *must* have a brassiere.' Of course, I never was a little lady. Never little and never a lady. It was much more fun being a boisterous hoyden.

I have never been sporty but I used my body as a weapon to great effect. My one skill on the hockey pitch was to befuddle my opponents and make them laugh. I was always lifting my gym shirt to expose my naked breasts. My aim was to make them lose sight of the ball and then WHAM! That was my chance to score as they doubled up with hysterical laughter. GOAL!! Grandma Margolyes would have been scandalised. For her the body was an enemy. And she wouldn't have approved of anyone showing themselves naked or flashing their tits – unthinkable. I knew I was being naughty when I exposed myself, but I was only shocking to entertain – as Miss Maddron said, 'You were naughty, Miriam, but you were never wicked.' I hope and believe that that is still true.

Finally, though, my mother ignored my protests and dragged me for a fitting at Elliston & Cavell's department store in town, where our neighbour, Miss Swinhoe, was in charge of corsetry. It's one of the few times when I can remember being utterly embarrassed. I had to strip, and stood there, red-faced, in my knickers as various bras were proffered. I remember Miss Swinhoe being continually astonished at the capacity required to encase my flourishing breasts. As she brought out one brassiere after the other, she would say, 'Oh dear, that's not going to go round.' It was a hideous experience for all concerned. I hated the flesh-coloured Berlei bra Miss Swinhoe eventually selected and I came out of Elliston's, sweating, tearful and humiliated. The Berlei advertisement read like this: 'It lifts you . . . cradles you . . . holds you firmly, separately, without a hint of strain. You'll be enchanted to see a new, perfectly beautiful you.' Bollocks!

My breasts continued to burgeon throughout my adolescence and I quickly learned that they were desirable. Like every woman blessed with embonpoint, I have often experienced my breasts being spoken to rather than my face. All the men (and women too) I've ever known sexually have wanted to fondle and play with them and suck on my nipples. It was Major Harding (aptly named), a retired Army officer living in North Oxford, who taught me one favourite amatory technique: my breasts were perfect for holding an erect penis, exerting a little friction until the desired ejaculation took place. I felt my repertoire of love really increased under his kindly instruction. I wanted to please and I did – often. I felt in control of everything and was never in danger. Army discipline is sometimes to be admired. So, at Cambridge and beyond, I found that to squeeze a penis between my globes of glory always resulted in cries of 'Encore!'

I'm glad up to a point that I had big breasts. Up to a point, as I say, because there have been occasions when they got in the way. Before I wore a bra, when I had to run on the hockey field or to catch a bus, for example, I nearly knocked myself out. When I joined the BBC Drama Repertory Company, and later in my voice-over career, I discovered that large breasts are not microphone-friendly – that's the only time really when breasts were an enemy. I remember when I went to record my first commercial voice-over with John Wood at his studios in Soho, I was in my little sound booth running through the script and John was alarmed by a resounding bang.

'What the fuck's that?' he cried.

I explained that it was the thud of my breasts hitting the table, where for comfort I'd decided to park them. Dear John Wood. I promised I would try not to repeat that mistake, but given the size of my bosom it has been a perennial problem since, because anything which interposes between yourself and the microphone is a foe. After that I just tried to get them out of the way. I soon learned that I had to move the breasts in one direction and my mouth the other.

Later, when I worked in television comedy, my breasts served as a rather useful in-built prop. In a sketch for *A Kick Up the Eighties* (more on which later), I played a buttoned-up secretary. Sirens are going off everywhere. Tracey Ullman rushes urgently into the rather dull-looking office I'm working in: 'It's the four-minute warning. It's time to do all the things you always wanted to do, before it's too late.'

I know exactly what this prim secretary in her pussy-bow blouse has always longed to do. I stop typing and immediately reach back and undo my bra, let my breasts luxuriously bounce free and smile beatifically, totally happy.

And in *Blackadder*, I relished the opportunity to play Lady Whiteadder and turn other breasts into comedy:

[*Edmund walks in with a pair of false breasts on. Percy makes coughing noises to try and alert him.*]

Lady Whiteadder: What he is trying to tell you is that you appear to be wearing a pair of devil's dumplings!

[*Blackadder looks down, notices the breasts, and promptly places them around his head.*]

Blackadder: Oh, my God, my ear muffs have fallen down! Would you like a pair? It's getting rather cold.

History's first turnip-based plotline, Ben Elton and Richard Curtis's script, was far ahead of its time. As I write (over thirty years later), a charmless Tory minister is trying to encourage reluctant Britons into eating more of our least inspiring vegetable. Lady Whiteadder, a true turnip obsessive, would have been right behind her.

The wardrobe mistress encased me in a plain, shapeless coarse linen habit, a rather austere matching hood, my only adornment a very large wooden cross hanging between my bosoms. Although it was long ago, sometimes people still shout 'Devil's dumplings!' at me in the street. (Do try not to.)

It has, however, been some years since I last flashed my bosom at an audience. I don't regret my breasts. I *can't* regret them. And now, of course, there they are, down by my ankles because gravity wins in the end. But they're so much a part of me that when I draw a portrait of myself (I think it comes under the heading of 'primitive' or 'naive' art), which I sometimes like to do, my breasts form the greater part of my body – just a circle with two dots for nipples and a face atop, crowned with a tangle of hair, and no neck! I have faced the truth.

Teenage Kicks

I was thirteen when my hero Winston Churchill resigned as Prime Minister on 5 April 1955. On a school trip to the Houses of Parliament I'd seen a shambling old man totter into the hallway. It was Sir Winston, looking stooped and tired and every day of his eighty years. I was shocked, I didn't realise age could defeat you. When you're young, the idea of age never enters your head, you never think it possible *you* will stoop and totter, forget things and piss yourself. Well . . . just wait a bit!

Later that year, in September, Nabokov's *Lolita* was published in Paris. I didn't read it until later in my teens. I didn't need to – in a sense I had already tasted the love juice of elderly men perving over me. I was lucky; they were kindly and appreciative, so when I did come to read it, I felt I'd already had a better deal from the penis than Lolita.

My parents always warned me about 'strangers' but the danger of the predatory male was closer to home than they thought. I made friends with many of my father's patients and as it turned out, two were serious gropers. But the odd thing is that I wasn't frightened. I had always been surrounded by love and I assumed the gropers' attraction to me was about *me* and not about their paedophile needs. On Coronation night, I wasn't quite yet a teenager but during a pause in the ceremony we were watching on our lovely neighbour Mrs Harwood's television, I was beckoned upstairs to look at the fireworks opposite, and as I stared through the window, the man behind me suddenly inserted his hands down my sleeves and squeezed my unexpectedly large breasts. He swung me around and pressed a squirmy tongue down my throat and slathered wetly on my lips. 'Yuck. Euuuuwww!' I responded and wiped my mouth clean energetically. 'Didn't you like that?' he asked, surprised. 'NO! It was horrible,' I said and we rejoined the Coronation downstairs. I may have been Milly-Molested-Mandy but no damage was done.

Being an only child is a curious fate. It cuts you off from your generation, so that my closest observations were linked to my parents. And then came school. Polio and pregnancy were probably the biggest threats to my happiness – well, they were certainly my parents' chief anxieties. The need to get into Oxbridge loomed large and that was the focus of my school efforts. My background was safe, Daddy was a doctor; he had a proper job, we had enough money, we could pass muster in a middle-class group. But if I drill down into who I was at that age I must acknowledge that it was what people thought of you, or rather, what you thought they thought, that mattered.

Perhaps the best thing about being a teenager is stopping being one, leaving behind the pimples and rages and anxieties besetting the years between thirteen and nineteen. But my teen years were so protected, so hemmed in by my parent's solicitude and my friends' warmth, that I felt little of the seismic physical and mental changes the youngsters today seem to experience. I left school still a child in many ways; probably that's what my parents decided was best.

She seems impossibly far away, the Miriam of then. I look at old photos and realise that from some angles, I was beautiful. I never knew it then. Perhaps looking forward to my sapphic self, I always resisted the trappings of being a girl. I preferred wearing trousers, rejected make-up, didn't enjoy clothes shopping, hated wearing a bra and couldn't get a boyfriend until gentle Shyam Malhotra fancied me when I was collecting for the blind in Cornmarket.

I was a somewhat aggressive charity-collector (they are referred to as 'chuggers' nowadays). I didn't wait for passers-by to drop a penny in the slot: I boldly blocked their passage down the street and said directly, but in a friendly manner, 'Please, will you help the blind?' They didn't have the gall to say 'No', and I became Oxford's top collector several years running. I was seventeen, busty of course, but probably dressed like a schoolgirl – socks and sandals for sure. Shyam was a postgraduate from India, studying for a further degree at the university, I forget which college. He was stout, smooth-skinned, smooth-tongued and very well-behaved. He asked if he could take me out; I said, 'You'll have to ask my father.' I knew I didn't fancy him, there was no groin twitch, but he was pleasant and it was a first date. My friends had all had them and I wanted to catch up.

I told him to return at the end of my stint that Saturday morning when Daddy came to collect me. I didn't really expect to see him again. To my surprise, Shyam duly appeared and approached my father. 'May I take your daughter out?' he said formally. 'I'd like to take her to the pictures.' Daddy asked him a bit about himself and said, 'Yes, you may take Miriam to the pictures, but you must bring her home at nine o'clock.' Those were racist times. I am proud that Daddy didn't even think to mention that Shyam was Indian; his time as a medic in Asia left him with great respect for Indians. The race was immaterial. Class and education, however, were another matter. I remember many years later, the wonderful novelist Angela Carter, my neighbour in Clapham, falling in love with her handsome builder and marrying him. I don't think Daddy would have stood for that. Had Shyam been a handyman, in Daddy's eyes an uncultured 'oik', he would have sent him packing. But he was an Oxford postgraduate, educated, personable and from a good family. So, Shyam and I went to the pictures, all very decorous and he brought me home at nine o'clock. We had several dates, but then it petered out. I hope he had a happy life; he was an utterly decent bloke.

I tried to think what I remember about those days when I was a different person and I thought it would be wise to ask a current teenager about what it was like. I spoke to Ella, the granddaughter of one of my closest friends. I was surprised by her poise and thoughtfulness. When people asked me questions when I was thirteen, it was usually 'What do you want to be when you leave school?' or 'Have you got a boyfriend yet?' I still remembered the contempt I had felt for such questions then, so instead I asked Ella what worried her. Her answer surprised me. Because it was exactly the same as mine, when I was thirteen. I worried about passing exams. But there the similarity ended. She explained that the future of the planet caused her much anxiety. She didn't think or talk about boys, but she did FaceTime and text her friends every night after homework and she liked a singer, Billie Eilish. She suggested I listen to her song 'Happier Than Ever'. I did: and it's one of the saddest things I've ever heard.

It's clear that anxiety balloons when you become a teenager. I worried about whether I was liked; whether I belonged; I never thought about the environment or about my future. We were that lucky group growing up after the end of the Second World War, who knew we would get a job, have a place in university, and our economic paths seemed clear and unthreatened. But my psychology was rooted in insecurity. Britain had just about won the war but my parents were refugees from the Blitz. Mummy told me I was conceived in their basement bomb-shelter in Plaistow during an air raid and I was familiar with the murder of the six million and the piles of corpses in the camps. Anne Frank's diary of her life as a teenager in hiding from the Nazis, published in English in 1952, brought the horror into a domestic setting. So I preferred to immerse myself in the safety of Dorita Fairlie Bruce's 'Dimsie' books. First published in 1921, Dimsie's world was an enclosed, largely female one, set in a boarding school on the Kent coast; it was one I felt I knew and would be comfy in.

School was my world and I was perfectly happy to engage with it fully. At the weekends, I would make plans with my friends, Catherine and Anna, to see a film, often at the Scala in Walton Street, go for a walk, or have tea in each other's houses. We didn't have mobile phones to spend hours gawping at social media. We looked at faces rather than screens. We read voraciously, shared books, went to the library together and took trips to Stratford to see a play at the Shakespeare Memorial Theatre. It was the time of milk bars, burgeoning teenage rebellion and rock 'n' roll, but not for us. We spent our spare time rummaging through the stock at Blackwell's and various second-hand bookshops in Oxford. Of course, we must have talked about sex as I got further into my teens. But the group I went around with were slow to develop and, as I said, Sex Talk came mostly from

Carol Reay and the other county scholarship girls in the bike sheds at school.

I didn't really enjoy holidays because I missed my friends so much. They often went abroad. Not once, throughout my entire time at school, did we leave the UK as a family. Mummy had bought two cottages in Minster-in-Thanet and every summer we went there, sometimes bringing a school friend with us for a week. There were no motorways then, it was an all-day journey, perhaps stopping either at Lyons Corner House, the flagship tea-rooms at Marble Arch, or more daringly, at the kosher restaurant, Bloom's, next door to Whitechapel tube station, famous for salt beef sandwiches and the rudest waiters in London.

I had finally learned to swim despite the polio fears, and Daddy would drive us to spend days on the beach at Birchington, Ramsgate and Margate. We did exactly what all the holidaymakers did – ate ice cream at Morelli's, went to Dreamland, gambled on the penny machines, watched the Punch and Judy shows (still going on at Broadstairs beach to this day, although with rather less wife-beating and baby-murdering and rather more sausages). And I always took part in the end-of-the-pier talent competition, usually reciting a poem and usually winning.

> Here comes the elephant,
> Swaying along,
> With his cargo of children,
> All singing a song . . .*

---

* 'The Elephant' by Herbert Asquith.

There were donkeys to ride on the beach; I remember even then being especially watchful that they were properly fed and watered. Sometimes, we made friends with other Jewish families; they're easy to spot – it takes one to know one – but if there were boys, I was shy and hung back. Mummy had no such qualms and we would have fish and chip suppers with pleasant Jewish people from North London whom we never saw again.

The Minster cottages were in Sheriffs Court Lane. They've been gussied up since I sold them in 1977 but it was fun when we used to drive there in the Daimler. The big drawback as far as I was concerned were the cherry orchards opposite. The cherries were delicious, but every morning at 4 a.m. the bird scarers were activated and woke me. They were set to go off automatically every five minutes and sounded like gunfire. I found it impossible to go back to sleep and lay angrily awake, staring up at the very low ceiling and thinking, 'My life is a hell.'

My hobbies were sedentary and solitary and all about glue. I collected stamps and had several albums. I would soak envelopes until the stamps came off and then use transparent hinges to stick them in. None of my friends seemed to do it, so I'd go to the little room next to the kitchen called 'The Den' and soak and stick stamps in for hours. My other hobby was collecting pictures of the Queen from newspapers, cutting them out and sticking them with glue onto the walls of The Den. It was covered with royalty; harmless enough but somehow a little sad.

I wasn't sporty at all. I never played tennis at the weekend or joined a running group. I didn't do Guides: my parents didn't approve; according to Mummy, 'Jewish girls don't sleep on the ground.' I didn't go youth-hostelling, as my friends Hilary Fletcher, Juliet Vernede, Liz Parnell, Margaret Stewart or Liz Hodgkin all did. They cycled around the Cotswolds and still do from time to time.

So, what *did* I do at the weekends? Precious little, it seems; I read, went for walks, but mostly spent time with Mummy. I was her rentals cleaner (she built a property empire, owning about seven houses which she rented out to students, and was considered the best landlord in Oxford) and Daddy would drop us off at whichever flat was in changeover and I would hoover and sweep and wipe the windows. I enjoyed it, Mummy would sing music-hall songs to me in her strong mezzo-soprano voice ('Sally, *Salleee*, pride of our alley, you're more than the whole world to me', or 'You are my honeysuckle, I am the bee') and then back to our house for lunch, which Mummy cooked and Daddy was served first. I remember how furious that made me, his assumption of being given whatever he wanted. He always started before anyone and then was ready for seconds before Mummy had sat down. I was determined to make him wait, or get him to serve himself. We talked about the news of the day or about things that worried my parents; they always seemed to be struggling with something. Life was a constant fight, over the will case for many years (see 'Family Matters' below), over my father's surgery being pulled down to build Pergamon Press, arguments about getting a new partner, selling the car, discussions which often ended in rows and tears. Mummy always gave good row – she was frighteningly emotional, and when she lashed out at Daddy and said horrible, terrible things, I would rush out of the room and take refuge in historical novels. I had eventually graduated from Dimsie and now read authors like Georgette Heyer and Margaret Irwin: 'In the brightness of the Queen's chamber, he took her.' I think that might have been the beginning of some sexual awareness; it was certainly more Sex than History. My parents absolutely refused to have a television set and probably they were right. It would have taken over communication, as it has proved since, and frankly, our home life was colourful enough.

I followed my own path; popular culture passed me by. Music for me was Mummy's taste in opera and music hall; I knew more about Marie Lloyd and Gertie Gitana than Buddy Holly. But when something interested me, I went for it and no one could stop me; I bulldozed through any objections from Mummy and Daddy. I had a vision of myself as a sturdy, tanned pioneer in an orange grove, so I went to Israel on my own to work on a kibbutz for a summer at the end of my teens. There were various predators along the way: such as the purser who expected me to pay for a better cabin with sex, but I wasn't having any of it and came back home *intacta*. When I wanted to meet Augustus John after seeing him on TV in *Face to Face*, I wrote and offered to model for him at no cost. Mummy and Daddy meekly drove me hours across England to his Fordingbridge studio in the New Forest and left me alone with the artist notorious for his sexual appetite and many illegitimate children – and it came to pass that I took my clothes off and climbed a ladder and he stroked his great beard and nodded appreciatively. 'Your skin takes the light,' he growled in his old-man voice. And I purred with pleasure.

I was protected by my confidence that no one would hurt me, by my innocence which was genuine, and I think also by a certain wildness, barely contained, which stopped people from 'messing' with me. They guessed I would retaliate. And, of course, because I was fat – which even then was not considered attractive. I didn't bother about my looks, certainly not the way kids do now. I liked my face, I never looked at my body – and if I could advise teens today, I would say: Try not to worry about what you look like. You're YOUNG! You lucky fuckers. Enjoy it! Just keep clean, keep reading and travel while you can.

How to Make Friends . . . and Keep Them

My father was deeply serious: sometimes I laughed at him for it. I asked him once, 'Daddy, why don't you have any friends?' He said, 'Friends? Friends are people who drag you down.' Well, Daddy was right about many things but he was wrong about that.

As I grew up, I often wondered, 'Why don't they have friends?' Because my parents didn't. Once we shut the front door, it was just us. Mummy had lots of acquaintances. She was sociable and hospitable, open and generous, but she didn't have proper conversations with people. After her sister Gusta died she didn't have anyone to talk to whom she trusted. She called the three of us her 'fortress family'. I think we became her defence against the dangers of engaging with other people. Being a Jew in the first half of the twentieth century didn't encourage trust, but my parents wanted me to have everything that they never had.

My fortress has always been my friends. My friendships validate my sense of self. I am still in touch with the bunch of girls I went to school with seventy years ago. Even when we haven't seen each other for a long time, immediately I hear those unmistakeable Oxford High School tones, it's as if we'd never been apart. We return to intimacy in a heartbeat. I think women are better at this than men. I blame the deep-seated male fear of emotion or any situation where tears might suddenly flow. Men clap each other on the back awkwardly, but women advance with arms wide-open and hug and hug. Women are sublime. No wonder I am a lesbian.

———

My first book was not just a list of cock-suckings, it was a roll call of friendship, rewarding and infinitely fulfilling. But now, so many of my friends are dying and have died that I am beginning to feel like a lonely, stout promontory surrounded by corpses. I don't want that. I want my friends. I need them to be alive and kicking. Maybe I shouldn't see myself as a promontory, but as something rather more like Reykjavík harbour, where the volcano is perpetually making new land. Because it is possible, indeed essential, to make new friends even when you're old.

I love meeting new people. When there's a park bench for example, or on a train, most go out of their way to avoid sitting next to complete strangers. But I make a beeline for the seat where someone's already sitting. I long for human communion. That to me is Holy Communion. And that is why ever since I was eleven years old in the playground at Oxford High School, asking the strange new girl, Katerina Clark, 'Will you be my friend?', I have tried to fill my life with others – and make them my friends. I'm constantly meeting people and thinking, 'Oh, I want them for keeps. I can't let go of them now, I'm going to snaffle them.'

My joy in friendship has always been motivated by a violent and uncontrollable curiosity – I want to know who they are. Talking, listening and learning what it's like to look at life through the eyes of another soul. That is thrilling.

I've talked about my groin twitch if I fancy someone. Well, when I meet someone and I want to be their *friend*, there is a brain twitch. I get joy from their company; when I talk to people and laugh with them, it's like a flower opening in the sun. I say to them, 'I want you in my life. Don't go away. If you don't want that, you'd better say so now, otherwise it's going to get embarrassing.' And luckily, so far no one has ever said, 'Miriam, stop right there. NO, I don't want to be in your life.'

Social scientist Robin Dunbar has a theory about how many friends you can have. He says that you can only have five *really* close friends. Well, that's ridiculous! Remember, I am an actress. When you're working with people in the theatre and television and so on, you're on stage or in rehearsal, at the theatre or on set, night after night after night. You're obliged to cover the emotional ground and get close. You can be years working with someone in an office or a bank before you say, 'I've got a colostomy bag,' or whatever secret it is. But in the theatre, too much information is absolutely essential.

One of the ways that acting works is that you need to expose yourself. You must immediately be open to the person with whom you're working. In ordinary life you try *not* to reveal yourself: you cover up. And that is considered good manners because you don't want to go *bleurgh* over everybody. Most normal people can't handle that but, in the theatre, you expect to be intimate immediately. Part of the pleasure of friendship is to be confident in exposing yourself. This is the funny thing about Heather; she is very contained, but it's the kind of containment that makes you want to know more, whereas some would say, with me, *it's the opposite*: you'd prefer to know less, because so much is available so quickly. I remember Susan Andrews (my Newnham friend) exploding, 'Give me some *space*, Miriam.' I was puzzled. I thought, 'What is she talking about? Why is she so cross? Am I standing too close to her?' I just didn't understand. I do now.

I tend to make at least one new friend during every single production, documentary job or whatever recording work I take on – which is why my phone contains a list of 11,739 names. I can't jettison people. I'm greedy. I want to keep *everybody*. I like to keep in touch with all my friends, to see them face to face when I can, and when I can't, I love talking on the phone, using FaceTime or WhatsApp whenever possible. I want to see their faces.

During the long months of the first lockdown, holed up in Clapham, what I missed most was people. I longed for human contact – so much so, that I used to sit on my front steps and call out to those walking past. I would ask my neighbours where they were going and strike up conversations of surprising intimacy with complete strangers. My favourite targets were dog owners, old people and cripples – all people who couldn't move fast enough. I am a recent cripple and I always like hearing mobility-scooter stories. If it were a couple, I asked if they were lovers or just friends and that often led to further tasty revelations. However, I hope the pleasant Indian gentleman whom I accused of being Jewish has forgiven me. In fairness, he *did* look Jewish! That helped me through the loneliness of lockdown.

Some, however, went the other way, which is not good for your mental health. We need the friction of others. We need reaction. The human dialogue is 'I and thou' – and that dialogue must continue. Not just with close friends and family, but also the aimless chat that you'd have with somebody when you buy a newspaper or ice cream – that's important too. During Covid, all that stopped completely. Everyday interaction was interrupted. This particularly affected heterosexual men, because they tend to have those very unspecific conversations about football rather than about their emotions. To say that men have an exterior emotional life and women an interior one is a massive generalisation, I realise. But because there was *no* football during the pandemic and the pubs were all shut, these men no longer had the means to talk to each other. And they still haven't recovered, poor souls.

The first step to being a good friend is to listen and to be interested in the other person. Friendship must be give-and-take, not 'Me, Me, Me, Me, and now back to Me!' And if you're listening to your friend and you get very bored, well, you must just say so. I often say to people, 'Did you know you're being a bit boring?' And if the other person gets very offended or the conversation stops right there, you just have to say, 'Oh come on, it doesn't mean *you* are boring, it just means you're *being* boring.' Then you go and give them a hug.

Friendship means you can be entirely *yourself* with that person; they know you and they still like you. People have remarked I possess a childlike quality. I'm not sure that they always mean it in a positive way – my beloved therapist called me 'a talented toddler' and that *wasn't* a compliment. But there's certainly an unfiltered honesty children have that I share. People often tell me they relish my directness. In my communication with others, I never ask for permission. I state what is on my mind pungently but politely. And they, in return, must tell me truthfully what is on their mind. I hope I am good at receiving the blunt truth from my friends. I prefer it. I want to feel that if I ask, 'What did you think of the book?' they could reply, 'Miriam, I didn't really like it. I think you're clever, but it's not what I wanted it to be.' In fact, nobody's ever said that, but if they did, I hope I wouldn't be offended at all.

You can't be friends with someone who lies to you. Truth is essential in friendship. Sometimes you need to choose your moment. When you go backstage after a show, you can't immediately say, 'Christ, what happened there?' When Carol Macready didn't like something I'd been in, she would say, 'It was fine, Miriam. Let's talk tomorrow.' And I knew there were things to be addressed. My blood didn't turn to ice, because I trust her. She's a good critic, she wasn't trying to destroy me: she was trying to help. She knows about things. Sometimes people might say, 'I hated the play, but I loved you.' Which is fair enough.

Truthfulness in friendship goes hand in hand with trust. You have to believe that you will each keep the confidences that you share with each other; that they're not going to talk about you behind your back, or betray and hurt you, and vice versa.

Some people, alas, are great fun to be with, but they can suddenly get up and bite you – they cannot resist the cruel dart. It's difficult to relax with somebody like that. In my book, those people are not a true friend but a 'frenemy'. My definition of a true friend is someone who delights in and brings out the best in you, and when you're in their presence, you feel enriched and happy. A frenemy, conversely, somehow revels in your weak points, is unreliable and says spiky and negative things, leaving you dissatisfied with yourself. Nobody needs that kind of person in their life; Mummy always said, 'Stay away from jealous people.'

In turn, you must be careful with your words. You certainly don't want to turn into anyone else's idea of a frenemy. However, you can and must be honest, so long as you aren't *planning* to say something purposefully nasty to them. If you seize the moment, and it comes out wrong, well, it's a crime of passion rather than premeditated murder. For example, smells are tricky. Nobody wants to smell and everybody's frightened that they *might*. Our good friend Peter's brother has very whiffy feet, and I remember dropping my pencil under the table and bending to pick it up, blurting, 'Christ! Your feet stink!' There was a chilly pause. I think I gave him a bit of a turn, but honestly his feet gave *me* a bit of a turn. And the key thing is that we're still friends.

One of the *most* difficult things is to tell someone that their breath smells. Everybody has bad breath sometimes and they aren't always aware of it. When I played Madame Morrible in *Wicked*, my make-up artist and now close friend, Sandra 'Biddy' O'Brien, at first just took very deep breaths and desperately hoped I'd give up my raw onion habit. But when I started popping garlic cloves too, she cracked and said, 'OK, Miriam, one of us has got to go.' I didn't know what I had done to upset her. And then she said, 'You've got to stop with that garlic. It's killing me. Can't you see that I am literally blue in the face when I try to do your lipstick?' I would have never thought that my breath could be so bad that it makes people in the vicinity reel. I hadn't realised that anyone could dislike the smell of alliums, and I have always warned people ever since.

In the late sixties, I was in a play with an Irish actor who was the sweetest man you could imagine. But, alas, he really did reek. It was a tiny auditorium, the actors were very close to the audience and people used to stagger out, fighting to breathe. It was painful. There was a company meeting without him and it was decided I was probably the best person to broach the subject.

In the restaurant, I sat next to him (hard enough with the smell!) and I said very quietly, 'Darling, I've been meaning to say this but never knew how to tell you. Look, we fat people – you're fat and I'm fat – we have to be super-careful about personal freshness. It's so easy to get smelly because being fat makes us sweat.' His expression darkened. I nervously continued: 'There's no easy way to say this, darling, but what about having a shower before coming into work?' It didn't go down well. He was so angry, he picked up the bowl of cling peaches which was our dessert and hurled it at the restaurant wall, storming out angrily as the ripe fruit slowly slithered down. He never spoke to me again. But it had to be done. And I'd always rather know; wouldn't you?

If you can help someone, always do it. In the ladies' room of Jenners department store in Edinburgh, I remember seeing a very respectable lady emerge from the lavatory with her dress tucked into her knickers, trail of toilet paper still attached. She was blithely exiting into the busy store; the whole queue said nothing, they were too transfixed with horror. I rushed up and shouted, 'STOP!' She turned round, somewhat indignantly, and I babbled, 'Sorry, but your dress is still in your knickers.' She tottered backwards. 'Oh, my God!' she gasped. 'Oh, my God! Just imagine if I'd gone out there!' After sorting herself, she clutched my hand with relief and, almost tearfully thanked me over and over again for saving her from what would have been a hideous Walk of Shame. Those chilly Edinburgh matrons can be so unforgiving. That was my *mitzvah* (Hebrew for a 'pious duty') for the day.

Another delicate area in a friendship are secrets. What do you do if you find out, for example, that a friend's husband or wife is having an affair? That's a difficult ethical dilemma. In the first instance, what I would probably do is tell the offending party that I know. I would say, 'I want to tell you something. I know that you've been pursuing this person. I'm not going to tell, but I want you to know that I know. Stop it immediately. And don't do it again.' So far it's always worked.

Then, of course, there are the friends that drain you. The needy ones. The ones who, when they visit, leave you utterly depleted, while they, on the other hand, go home invigorated. When I see them, although my face wants to go 'Oh, Christ . . .', I force a wide smile, take a deep breath, and say, 'I'm so glad to see you. Come 'ere and I'll give you a hug.' I try to give them as much love and confidence and arms around as I can muster. If I can make them feel wanted, it's a *mitzvah* and might leave them less needy and more able to deal with life.

The key thing is to be clear about boundaries. Once I've talked and listened, either in person or on the telephone, I say, always truthfully, 'Now look, I've got to stop right now. I've got to deal with emails,' or 'write the book,' or 'get ready to go out. Let's talk tomorrow.' I cut it off quite quickly. But the next day, I *do* talk to them again because I'm aware people might be hurting. I see it as my job to cheer them up and give them a bit of hope.

Then there are the moments that go the other way. When sex rears its head – or there is an inkling of its happening – between friends, it can also be a bit of a dilemma. Most of the time, if you're lucky, the feeling goes away and amicable relations can resume again. Otherwise, you must make an agreement not to let any twiddliness derail the friendship. It's not worth the risk.

Religion is another sticking point. A few precious friends I really care about *are* religious. But I just step carefully over that topic avoiding it whenever it arises, like cowpats in a field. If you are my friend, you are always my friend. Friendship is a responsibility; it's a serious commitment and a serious obligation. But it must go both ways. A friend is someone you can ring at any time and say, 'I'm really low. I need you to hear me and help me a bit.' And then, thank God, they will.

Always Talk About Sex

Before I became an established actress, I was known for my work as a voice artist. I have quite a high girlish voice but I found that I can deepen it for the purposes of sex. I once recorded what I call 'take-home wanking tapes', such as *Sexy Sonia: Leaves from My Schoolgirl Diary*. These were audio tapes for sale in sex shops. One day, I went into Ann Summers's shop in Soho to check the sales of my tape, telling the man behind the counter I was Sexy Sonia. He looked aghast and told me to keep my voice down; he didn't want people to know Sexy Sonia was in reality this fat, loud, rather unattractive lady. But it was too good a story to keep to myself and I think that it might have eventually prompted my being asked to voice the Cadbury's Caramel Bunny because, I suppose, sex sells. The *Edinburgh Evening News* voted the Caramel Bunny the third sexiest cartoon character of all time, and while that is undoubted evidence that their readers don't get out much, I'm not complaining.

Hey, Mr Beaver, why are you beavering around? Haven't you heard of Cadbury's Caramel? See, as the thick Cadbury's milk chocolate melts with that dreamy caramel, you just have to take things really easy. [*The lovestruck beaver has chewed all the way through a tree, ignoring the angry squirrels whose home he has destroyed.*] Looks like somebody else could do with some. Take it easy with Cadbury's Caramel.

Richard Herring confessed to me that it still got him hot under the collar all these years later ... And chocolate has its place in the repertoire of love.

My friend Jane Hamilton generously shared this story with me about her first encounter. It was at a shooting-party weekend (her family was Scottish upper class). In the glorious if blustery glens, whisky was downed and some charming conversation exchanged. One thing led to another and that night the ghillie overcame Jane's maidenly resistance. However, in the throes of passion he proved a comically inept lover. Flailing about, after repeated proddings, his willie waving in the frigid Highland bedroom, he mournfully wailed, 'Oh, Janey, Janey, I cannae find yer entrance.'

I have always loved talking about sex. As I'm quite short (and worse, usually sitting down), groins always loom close. You can't see much of a vagina; it keeps itself to itself. More's the pity. But the penis is so obvious and unmissable, dangling there. Even now, I check which way a cock is hanging, where the tell-tale bulge is: I examine the front of a man's trousers trying to place its position exactly. Where is it? What's it doing? Dressing to the left or the right? It's a game no one will admit to playing, but I bet everyone does. I have a violent curiosity about people and I discovered in my teens that sex is a fascinating shortcut to communion. In the words of Mae West, 'Good girls go to heaven but bad girls go everywhere.'

Learning about sex for me was rather like learning to drive. I started with the basic vehicles while picking up the skills of gear-stick control, and once I'd developed the proficiency, I had the confidence to take any car I fancied for a test-drive. At Cambridge I lived in a securely female world (my college, Newnham, did not admit men, and still doesn't), surrounded by wonderful women of great beauty, intelligence and sensitivity. My friends provided all the deep emotional sustenance I needed but they seemed so affected by men: I couldn't understand why. The joy for me was that you didn't need to engage intellectually with these simple creatures. For me men were always more of an impulse-buy, a source of instant gratification, not to be taken seriously.

As I cycled down King's Parade one day in the 1960s, my eye was taken by a handsome young GI in a nearby open-topped car. He had boy-next-door looks: glossy blond hair, bright blue eyes and those amazing American teeth. He must have been stationed at the nearby Alconbury base. I pulled up alongside him at a traffic light, smiled, and said: 'If you follow me to my college, I'll suck you off.' I knew that good manners required a girl to say clearly what was on offer. He accepted with surprised delight, went off to park his car and then we met up again at the Porters' Lodge. We walked in pleasant silence up the stairs to my room. The actual encounter was decorous rather than passionate. He was clean and I was expert and there was little casual conversation before battle was joined (well, hardly battle, but you know what I mean). I asked him where he came from and he replied politely, 'Texas, ma'am.' He told me about his brothers and sisters, I explained I was an only child and then out popped his member and we were off! The real joy for me was telling my friends about it the next morning in every ridiculous detail. And they were in convulsions.

I've always found it odd that no one talks about it. You might think from the deafening silence that I was the only girl sucking men off in Cambridge in the 1960s – I was not. I'm just the only one prepared to talk about it. My parents had laid it on very thick, 'You mustn't sleep with anybody because you will get pregnant and it will be a shocking thing and it'll make us terribly sad and it'll be horrible and you mustn't do it.' And I thought, 'Right, well, I mustn't do that.' Penis entry was out of bounds. But when you're young, it's absolutely natural that you are moist. You have feelings. The sap is rising. Your clitoris swells and all those physiological things happen, and if you can't sleep with somebody you have to do something else. As a good Jewish girl, it seemed clear that I should suck and not fuck. So that's what I did. I knew Mummy would've been very shocked. But that's how it started – there were various knobs bobbing around in my adolescence – I was fairly proficient by the time I went up to Cambridge and I continued with it until well into my twenties.

I didn't know I was a lesbian then: I just thought I hadn't met the right man yet. I found men slightly ridiculous, but their phallic inability to hide excitement was rather touching, and being desired was thrilling in its own way. I've always loved an appreciative audience. And an upstanding ovation!

I've never consulted a rabbinical authority on what is proper for Jewish girls. And it's too late now! I'm told that some Orthodox couples have sex through a hole in a sheet, making procreation the key activity rather than enjoyment. I hope it isn't true – sheets are so expensive these days. I just want everyone to have a good time and be sure to clean up afterwards.

I didn't and still don't have a technique, or anything like that. You just deal with the matter at (or in) hand. Interestingly though, once I was on a boat going from Gozo to Valletta (trying to catch up with Pat Gallimore and my suitcase – more on that in *This Much is True*), when the fisherman whipped out his prick, it never occurred to me to suck him off. From the beginning, I knew it was a wrist job. The hard part was steering the boat with one hand and giving him release with the other. But then I am a very good driver.

I honestly don't understand why people are so shocked. To quote an American professor (female) I had an affair with, it's just a part of 'the wide repertoire of love'. I have no preferences where penises are concerned. It's how they're used that matters. It's possible I've handled more than most lesbians, but it's quite a time since I had a sight of one and I'm just fine with that. If you happen to meet me, please don't pop one out because I will report you. Some silly chaps think all they have to do is expose themselves and women will collapse with longing. Not so. This is summed up by the recent phenomenon known as the 'dick pic' where men, unasked, send pictures of their dangling appendages by text because they think it's provocative and exciting.

Take it from me, whenever I started a relationship in the days before Heather, I would always make it clear how important foreplay was. I think it's crucial. And if they don't 'do' foreplay, get rid of them.

I used to leave a list on the kitchen table, to remind a potential lover about the order in which my body liked to be touched. Number One: TITS FIRST. My breasts had to be wooed before I was. Only much later on did below-the-waist excitements feature. I like a slow boil and those frenzied romantic shedding of clothes in films always worried me. Suppose you rip off an important button? What nonsense.

Don't Drop the Forceps

The close friendships I made at Cambridge set me up for life. One of those friends is Mike Newell. Then, he was a very tall, very thin boy, with a delicate, girlish complexion. He blushed easily, had dancing sparkling eyes and imperishable energy and optimism. We had worked together at the ADC, the university's Amateur Dramatic Club theatre; and then, against some criticism, he picked me to be Judith Bliss in Noël Coward's *Hay Fever* in 1963, when I should have been revising for my Finals. It was an amazing success and from my first joke – 'I've been pruning the calceolarias' – the play was mine. There was no way I could not choose acting as a career after that. Hard to believe it's over sixty years ago. (But I keep saying that about everything. You learn as you get old, that it happens suddenly, without warning.)

I duly went into the theatre and Mike into film directing, but we remained in touch despite his living always in North London and my being a committed South Londoner. (I wonder if that is another piece of my mother's influence embedded in me. She lived in Camberwell, Dulwich and Peckham all her single life and loved the Horniman Museum and Underhill Road and the Camberwell Palace Theatre.)

It's hard to write about friends, as they deserve a measure of privacy I think, but Mike and his wife, the remarkable actress Bernice Stegers, share a love of laughter, and when they laugh at me, it's still flattering. Bernice is a tremendous hostess and cook, their parties are riotous and generous; I hear her deep, growly voice gurgling with humour, I see her large flashing, black eyes. Even now, in her seventies, she projects vaginal promise – lucky Mike! He's always known how to pick the right woman for the part.

So, when he offered me a role in his directorial debut, *The Awakening*, in 1979, I accepted like a shot. I knew he'd also cast me because I was a friend and friends are needed on a film set. (On Kenneth Branagh's directorial debut *Dead Again*, the whole crew refused to do anything he told them to do. Although I was playing a medium, I didn't see it coming and I was flabbergasted when he went for the nuclear option and sacked the lot of them. It was very brave but meant he had to start again from scratch.) Mike trusted that I'd roll up my sleeves and get on with it and I knew I'd have fun playing the somewhat camp role of the Egyptian gynaecologist, Dr Kadira.

The Omen had a lot to answer for. Now everyone was desperate to make a film about an evil baby with occult power (ours was possessed by the spirit of a malevolent Egyptian queen), but this one was going to be filmed on location and I would be joining a fine cast which included Susannah York, Jill Townsend and Charlton Heston. Charlton, whom we all called Chuck, was the star. He was immensely tall with steely blue eyes. His face and body craggy and weathered. Although he'd played Moses twenty-three years before, he still looked so much like a Patriarch that every time he opened his mouth it felt like Commandments were going to issue forth, rather than the pleasant and somewhat banal things that he said. I liked him. His charming wife, Lydia, accompanied him. They were devoted and sweet together. Of course, his increasingly right-wing politics (he'd supported Nixon) and his position on gun control was anathema to me, but that was never mentioned. My impression was that he was a kindly bloke, polite and relaxed. And as he was 6ft 3ins, to my 4ft11 ins, Mike explained that every time we were in a shot together, I would have to stand on a box.

My gynaecological task was to deliver the infant Margaret, our film's evil centre. On *The Awakening*, my scenes were mostly in a hospital, and more specifically in the operating theatre of a labour ward. But I did have one scene somewhere outside with Chuck, where my box wasn't enough to equalise our stature and I remember their digging trenches for him to stand in. My first line was, of course in an Egyptian accent (all the *r*'s slightly aspirated), 'Your wife is suffering from postpartum depression.' Slightly different from the 'calceolarias' line, but I managed to make her sound professional.

The accent was easy enough to achieve – harder was the competence in midwifery my role required. I was woefully ill-equipped for the latter. I'd never had a baby; I'd never delivered a baby; I'd never even held a baby – let alone a devil baby – and I didn't know how to use the stainless-steel obstetric forceps supplied to me by the props department. They looked so much like scissors that I thought they were operated in a similar way. I didn't realise that there was no central screw; instead, the person who's handling them holds them together by putting his or her finger in one hole and his/her thumb in the other. This is a lot trickier than it sounds, because if you open your hand too wide, the two bits of forceps fall apart. So, each time Mike said, 'Action!' and I set about delivering Jill Townsend's baby, my forceps clattered to the floor. After a few ruined takes, they sent for a real midwife to teach me how to use this contraption.

'How long have you been doing this?' I asked.

'Twenty-five years,' she replied.

'Well, I've been doing it for seven minutes. I think you can cut me a bit of slack.'

Giving birth, based purely on my dramatic involvement in the labour ward, seems to me a very undignified process. I've never wanted children but people who have them tell me that once you have had the baby you forget the agony. (Sounds like a scam to me.) Luckily, no babies (or vaginas) were hurt in the making of this film. Many years later, I was in *Call the Midwife*, and even then I escaped the nitty-gritty of midwifery. Thankfully I was the Mother Superior standing at the bedside of the mother-to-be, proffering wisdom, advice and tea, but thankfully, not forceps.

The aim of my scene in *The Awakening*, obviously, was to make it realistic, but my other overwhelming purpose was to protect Jill Townsend from revealing any part of her crotch. She wasn't naked, she did have a stout pair of knickers, but Jill was worried about having her nether regions exposed to the camera and to the interested spectators, who are always hanging around a film set. We carefully arranged her clothes and I had to poke my head under a canopy of something that was supposed to be surgical. Put simply, I had to interpose my body, which was quite interposable, to protect her modesty. And so there I was, under the canopy, shoving my head up between her legs, and I thought the situation needed lightening. So I popped my head out just before I dived in and said roguishly, 'You do know I'm a lesbian?' Then I pulled the baby from under the canopy and, just before Mike could say 'It's a wrap', promptly dropped the forceps with a clang on the floor.

It was immediately after this film that Jill decided to give up acting. She was later quoted as saying, 'I remember being at the top of this pyramid at four a.m. so they could get a shot with the sun coming up and, as it did, I looked around and asked myself, "Why am I doing this?" ' Thank goodness it wasn't my peering up her skirts that put her off the movies.

Mike later told me he didn't think *The Awakening* was very good – his actual words were 'utterly terrible'. The film's shoutline was: 'The Evil One Must Not Live Again'. And as it was not a success – mission accomplished! But Egypt more than lived up to my expectations. We all stayed in the luxurious Nile Hilton and we had long cast dinners together in the velvet Cairo nights. On our days off, I explored the city and its monuments with Jill. My first sight of the pyramids was so overwhelming, I burst into tears. Their immensity, rising out of the flat desert took all words away. Now we think of the cruelty the slaves suffered, toiling away in the brutal heat to build a memorial for a pharaoh. Millennia later they convince all who look on them that Man is a very small thing.

I particularly loved shopping in the souk, because my buxomness was seen as a Good Thing and vocally admired everywhere I went. My spirits lifted every time the salesmen said, 'Madam, you are worth a thousand camels.' High praise, which helped when bargaining for spices and trinkets. And wherever you went in Egypt, people said, 'Oh, you are from England. You are welcome.' Such a contrast to the way that people in England welcome those from Egypt. It's an uncomfortable realisation.

The best thing I took away from *The Awakening* was my friendship with Susannah York. On the face of it, it might seem an unlikely pairing but although she was effortlessly beautiful and came from a patrician Scottish background, Susannah wasn't remotely interested in wealth. She was a genuine Socialist and we bonded through our politics. She cared passionately about those who had less and worked unstintingly to help refugees and charities. She was always planning fundraisers and protests. Like me, she was a South Londoner; her happy, light-filled Wandsworth family house, full of her children Sasha and Orlando, was close to mine and we saw each other a lot. Deservedly nominated for an Oscar for *They Shoot Horses, Don't They?* – the 1969 film about a Depression-era dance marathon, she did memorable work in film, TV and latterly, in theatre. When the film parts were less interesting, she simply toured with independent productions. When she died in 2011 far too young, the critic Michael Billington, wrote in the *Observer*: 'In her richly fulfilled later career, she proved that she was a real actor of extraordinary emotional range, not just a movie star.'

And then in the domino effect of friends begetting friends, a woman Susannah introduced me to went on to change my life even more: Angie, her wonderful assistant, who came to work for me too. How can I describe Angie? She was short, a little 'butch' in style, with a soft voice, decided opinions (she continued to vote Tory despite Susannah's and my entreaties); she was loveable, stubborn and utterly loyal. Modern technology defeated her; I forced her to use the computer in my office but she never liked it; our main arguments were always about it. She loved her red VW Polo, cats, watching horse racing and picking out the winners. And she made the best scrambled eggs I've ever tasted. Angie knew the pancreatic cancer diagnosed shortly after her retirement would kill her but she absolutely refused to accept chemotherapy, despite having been a smoker all her life. She said; 'How can I accept chemo when I've campaigned always for natural medicine?' Susannah spoke movingly at Angie's funeral in the lovely church in Hurley, where she is buried. Her parents had run the newsagent's shop there and after retiring at sixty, she bought a caravan and lived there until she died in her sleep one spring day. She was an entirely good person and one of the central props of my life. I only wish she could have heard Susannah's speech. It would have made her happy.

So you see, the knock-on effects of doing Mike's horror film in Egypt lasted a long time. Often you don't realise that everything has consequences, everything links up. Life is a kind of chain. You're introduced by somebody to somebody else and then to somebody else. And that's how friendships happen, how love affairs begin and end. Every acting job I have embarked on, each role I inhabit, has tentacles, which have reached out into my life, long after the performance itself has ended.

Grandpa Walters and Mummy on her wedding day.

Grandma didn't approve of Daddy, and said so, but she was wrong.
I love this picture of him and Mummy still smiling away, many years later.

Move over Shirley Temple! I've always adored an admiring audience.

I have never been afraid of the scene-stealing abilities of animals, even enormous stuffed dogs.

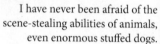

Here comes the fortress family on holiday in Broadstairs.

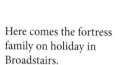

Dancing in a 'Smoker' (a special televised performance) with the Footlights. At least THIS cast spoke to me. From left: Eric Idle, me, David Gooderson, John Cameron, Susan Hanson and Graeme Garden.

I am somewhere in this scrum for Marlene Dietrich in Golders Green in 1966. 'Du warst wunderbar,' I called out to her. Her face lit up, and she bent down from the car and kissed me.

'Oh you are AWFUL!' with lovely Kenneth Williams, the saddest funny man I've ever met in *Oh Get On With It!* in 1976. Lance Percival was on a more even keel.

My breasts have always been the butt of jokes. Playing turnip-obsessive Puritan Lady Whiteadder finally gave me the chance to turn other tits into gags.

THEY THOUGHT THEY HAD
BURIED HER FOREVER!

ΧΕΝΘΑΙΣ ΝΑΚΕΝΔΑΙΝΑ
THE AWAKENING

A ROBERT SOLO PRODUCTION
CHARLTON HESTON
"THE AWAKENING" SUSANNAH YORK
JILL TOWNSEND AND STEPHANIE ZIMBALIST
SCREENPLAY BY ALLAN SCOTT AND CHRIS BRYANT AND CLIVE EXTON
MUSIC BY CLAUDE BOLLING ASSOCIATE PRODUCER HARRY BENN CONDUCTED BY ANDREW SCHEINMAN
AND MARTIN SHAFER PRODUCED BY ROBERT SOLO DIRECTED BY MIKE NEWELL

Let it not be said that I
have not suffered for my art:
whether in the deserts of
Egypt in *The Awakening* (1980) . . .

. . . having doors slammed on my head
by Steve Martin's psychopathic dentist
in *Little Shop of Horrors* (1986) . . .

. . . or living in a
fridge and being fed
cockroaches by Steve
Buscemi in *Ed and His
Dead Mother* (1993).

My stint as the voice of the Cadbury's Caramel Bunny showed me that chocolate has its place in the repertoire of love . . .

. . . It became something rather more sinister – and unexpected – in 'Fat Chance' with Sheila Gish and John Castle in 1980.

The closest I've ever come to playing football was in *A Kick Up the Eighties* with Roger Sloman, Richard Stilgoe, Tracey Ullman and Ron Bain (1981).

I discovered Dickens aged eleven and his books have continued to enrich my life. Filming documentaries about him and my one-woman show *Dickens' Women* still take me all over the world.

I have played many of his characters –
Flora Finching (left) and Betsey Trotwood (right) are particular favourites.

Not all the fallout from swearing on the *Today* programme (sorry again, Martha and Justin) was negative. Roll on that general election!

What joy for the second naughtiest girl at OHS to return, not into detention but as a 'wise Elder', listened to with rapt attention. '*Nunc inoblita celebrare tempus*' (the first line of the school song): 'Now is the time to celebrate'.

Try Everything Once

One of my mottos has always been 'Try Everything Once'. You must grab life by both proverbial horns, take risks, gobble – or at the very least have a nibble – at all the wondrous experiences it has to offer. What's the worst that can happen? You don't like something? Well, don't try it again. But when I say 'all' life offers, of course, I make certain exceptions. As a Jew, in honour of my parents and my roots, I have never eaten bacon or shellfish; nor have I ever had anal sex. That, most emphatically, is *not* on my to-do list. Everything else is up for grabs. Live life to the full. Seize the day and go for it. Just enjoy yourself.

As a young actress keen to get on, I rarely turned down work, no matter how unappealing, which is why my lengthy back catalogue is full of unexpected cult 'gems'. I find myself heralded in such unlikely disasters as *The Apple*, *Morons from Outer Space* and *Ed and his Dead Mother*. One of the more questionable joys of writing this book was diving back into these jobs. It's a good thing I've always enjoyed rummaging around in junk shops.

The Apple (1980) was an absolute turkey. If you look it up on the internet, it's gone down as 'Could this be the worst film ever made?' And I think it probably was. I blame Menahem Golan, our director, who was a horrible man; nasty, demanding – a bully.

It started badly and got worse. It was filmed in the famous Babelsberg Studio in Berlin. The descent into Berlin Tegel Airport was bumpy and alarming. The landing was shocking – *I hate* flying; on this occasion I was *absolutely* certain I was going to die. When I came through Customs, I was a nervous wreck, yet I was given no time to collect myself. Menahem insisted I had to go from the airport straight into a taxi and to the set. Somewhat alarmingly, the driver took me not to Babelsberg, but a desolate field in the Grunewald Forest. There I was hurtled into a strange costume (the film was set in a time in the future, supposedly 1994) and suddenly a crane appeared, manned by a platoon of army officers. I was attached to a harness and unceremoniously winched 60 feet or more into the sky, where I hovered like a stranded albatross for many hours. It was uncomfortable, nerve-racking, indeed horrifying. The additional anxiety was provided by the certainty that all below could stare uninterruptedly into my crotch.

Later, I had a stand-up row with Menahem Golan about my ordeal. I was quite surprised he didn't sack me on the spot. Unfortunately, he didn't. Maybe he realised I would have been delighted.

In truth, I remember nothing of the plot. It was a musical of sorts, meant to be like *The Rocky Horror Picture Show* based on the story of Adam and Eve in the Garden of Eden, but in a modern setting. Nor can I tell you anything about my role in the film except that I know I was in it – I just *wished* I hadn't been – and that I played a landlady. It's a role I could have brought much more to but the confused script got so much wrong. Mummy was a land*lord*, I'd like to stress. The landlady in *The Apple* was a strange, ugly near-witch who babbled and screamed – unlike Mummy, who did babble and scream, but only at home. She was always a consummate professional to her tenants. I don't think Mummy would have been proud of me in this role or of the film.

The only good thing I have to say about it is that I was among a lovely cast: Joss Ackland (as Mr Topps/Hippie Leader) is a divine creature. I adored Catherine Mary Stewart and George Gilmour, the two young actors who played the lovers Alphie and Bibi. Best of all was meeting the Polish-born actor Vladek Sheybal, who was excellent as the devilish, all-singing and dancing Mr Boogalow. He was great fun, ironic, slightly mysterious and had an extraordinary life and career. You may remember him as the villain Kronsteen, the sinister chess grandmaster in *From Russia with Love*, the second Bond film, starring Sean Connery.

I didn't attend the premiere of *The Apple* at the Montreal Film Festival. It was a fiasco: the normally well-behaved Festival audience hated it so much that they hurled the promotional vinyl records (now a sought-after collector's item, of course) at the screen and bellowed insults at the cowering Golan. He was convinced it was a masterpiece. He was wrong.

Another uncomfortable role was playing the dental nurse-cum-punchbag in *Little Shop of Horrors* (1986) at Pinewood. Steve Martin was the psychopathic dentist; yes, he was undeniably brilliant, but horrid to me. It was a vile experience. During my only musical number ('Dentist!') I was hit all day by doors opening in my face; repeatedly punched, slapped and knocked down by an unlovely and unapologetic Steve Martin – perhaps he was method acting – and came home grumpy with a splitting headache. Let it not be said that I have never suffered in the name of Art. When I later played the pixie-nanny to a changeling princess in *Merlin* (according to one review) I was 'able to take an exceptional amount of damage from Merlin's staff' in my final duel with the wizard. After that, I decided to be the striker, not the strikee.

———

Grumpiness continued as a theme in many of my more bill-paying roles, whether as the cave-dwelling 'Smelly Photocopier Lady' in *The Hitchhiker's Guide to the Galaxy* or the ticket girl in *Electric Dreams*. *Morons from Outer Space* (1985) was another low point. A haggard Jimmy Nail showed up late for work one morning, unrepentantly vomit-stained. What a charmer!

Later, when I was living in LA, I was cast in *Ed and His Dead Mother* (released in the UK as *Bon Appetit, Mama*). It is a silly film, but dear to me because that's where I met Steve Buscemi. Back then he was nobody and *I* was nobody, and we had lots of fun. We were the stars: Steve played the eponymous Ed, and his dead mother was . . . *me*.

The script was absurd. Ed can't get over the death of his mother, Mabel. When a mysterious guy enters his store, introducing himself as a rep from the Happy People Corporation and offers to resurrect her for $1000, Ed leaps at the opportunity. Arriving home, I take up residence in the refrigerator and, to stay alive, must feed on a couple of live cockroaches every evening. It wasn't a large fridge so who could blame my character going a little off the rails. It's not long before I am swearing like a trooper, jumping over 9-foot fences and scaring the neighbours, chasing dogs and cats, wielding a carving knife and chainsaw on a ride-on mower. In short, Ed has no choice but to snuff me out

– but I am determined not to die again and go on a killing rampage. Finally, he manages to decapitate me and buries me a second time – but not before my severed head reanimates and bites him on the lip as he leans in to give me the final kiss.

The role needed a menacing wackiness, but casting directors in Hollywood have always seen me as over the top, excessive and larger than life. Steve Buscemi is a brilliant actor and we had a delightful rapport. For somebody who's being terrorised by me in the form of a murderous living corpse, he was unerringly sweet – knocked spots off Steve Martin. He remains to this day the only person who has ever fed me cockroaches, and he did so with love and the utmost politeness.

However, not all my memories are so warm. In one scene, shot at night, I had to be buried up to my neck in the earth. It was bitterly cold and I can remember being furious, frozen to the bone, to find my trailer icy and dark after the long hours of filming. I just said, 'I require hot soup immediately.' I got it. Sometimes you need to be very direct; polite but clear.

Even worse was when they had to take a full cast of my head, post decapitation. I had to have my entire head completely covered in plaster of Paris. I couldn't see, hear or speak, and could only breathe through a straw. I was so terrified that I had to clutch the hand of the make-up artist who was applying the thick, viscous gunk. I was probably only incommunicado for no more than fifteen minutes while the substance hardened, but once it was cracked open and I was able to see the light again, I knew exactly how people who were buried alive must feel. And I swore afterwards that I would never ever do anything like it again and I never have.

Bad Habits

I've never taken recreational drugs and I don't gamble. I used to – until I found out that you can lose. After that, I stopped. Mummy continued to have a flutter on the Grand National; of course Daddy never gambled at all. He would say in his most pompous voice, 'A doctor doesn't gamble.'

At home, we never had alcohol around; it wasn't something that Jewish people did. When I went to university in 1960, I was all agog and ready for anything – and sherry parties were all the rage. That seemed to be how you entertained people in the Gentile world. So, in my first term I was extremely excited to be asked to a sherry party. The brand that everybody served was Tío Pepe, a dry amontillado. (Tío Pepe translates as 'Uncle Pete', which has a rather less sophisticated and very Gentile ring to it.) The only wine I'd tried before was Palwin No 10, the Israeli *kiddush* or communion wine, because one is obliged to drink four glasses at a Passover *Seder*. Palwin – like its American equivalent, Manischewitz – was more like sticky cough mixture than wine, so Jews seldom drink too much. At Jewish weddings, for instance, it's all about the food and how much of it you can put away. There's a lot of farting and very little drinking.

So there I was, at my first Cambridge sherry party – a proper social gathering. The sherry was a clear brown liquid, slightly viscous and it was served in a small glass, the size of an egg cup. I swirled a mouthful and liked it. A lot. Every time I drank, I refilled my glass immediately.

I rapidly became aware that I was not in full control; I could hear myself talking and laughing even more loudly than usual. Naturally, I felt I was hysterically funny, that my wit was flashing, positively ricocheting, round the room, although I may have been the only one noticing it. Rather than slowing down, I speeded up and I kept knocking back glass after glass of Tío Pepe. In the end, I drank SEVENTEEN (I know, because I counted them), which is probably a whole bottle of sherry, perhaps more.

Not long after that seventeenth sherry, I realised that I was going to be violently sick. I knew enough to know I'd better do that in private rather than in front of my peers, so I asked a friend to take me to a nearby lavatory. It was an attractive lavatory, with a substantial wooden two-tiered seat, which I raised, and a lovely Victorian design of leaves and flowers, possibly even an original Thomas Crapper. I had plenty of time to commit its curves to memory as I spent the next two hours there on my knees retching, staring down into the toilet bowl, every so often spewing copiously. Having sunk to my knees I couldn't get up again. I was immersing myself in the new experience of complete intoxication. I gazed into the porcelain, absently admiring the pattern; and every now and then kind friends continued to make courtesy calls to make sure that I hadn't passed out.

Later, I asked a few people, 'What was I like? Did I make a total fool of myself?'

'No, no, Miriam. You were great!'

But I wasn't great. Of course, I didn't have to drink seventeen glasses; one can be amusing without incoherence. What is the point of drinking if it just makes you hideously sick? I gave up sherry there and then. Once was enough. And I've never been drunk since that day.

That said, I do enjoy a gin and tonic. (Four cubes of ice, a slice of lemon, and let the gin cover the ice. Add tonic to taste.) It always amuses me when gin is referred to as 'Mother's Ruin', as it was indeed Mummy's failsafe solution to period pains. But I'd hardly call it a vice because, for me, one is enough.

Before I nod off, which happens *very* quickly when I drink alcohol, the gin gets me a bit giddy. My inhibitions are lowered; my internal sensor gets a bit wobbly – in truth it's not sharp at all. But I know what's happening. I'm perfectly aware of the perilous process. I feel stunningly amusing. The delicious gin enhances me so I use words like jewels; I juggle them in the air. I'm witty and delightful. And I say to everybody, 'Grab these pearls while you can! Because in about twenty minutes, I will be asleep.'

Unfortunately, acting is a drinking profession, and a lot of actors *do* drink heavily. Fear is the spur. We have to remember our lines, increasingly hard as we age. We know critics are out there on the first nights, pouncing on our mistakes, possibly ending our careers. We risk our professional lives every time we step on a stage. No wonder some of us need drink to start the ball rolling. Towards the end of his life, Sir Laurence Olivier used to beg to be pushed on stage. 'Push me, PUSH ME!' he roared in the wings, such was his terror. For what actors do is so rare, so difficult and perilous that they cannot help but be in knots about it. They've had to learn their words; they have to know their blocking and their moves; they have to be in character. They have to offer the audience a new reality. Then they must do it precisely, on time, when the curtain goes up, with that sigh it has, whether they like it or not. And they have to do it again and again, absolutely on cue and always perfectly, night after night. Some grow to feel that if they're not slightly pissed, the magic isn't there – they won't be able to deliver. Commonly, it starts as a pre-stage stiffener in the dressing room to get ready. But then the problem comes when you can't do without it. I would hate that. I don't want to be addicted to anything. I don't want anything that I imbibe or eat, to change me in any way. And when I think about being in thrall to something like whisky, or cocaine or heroin, I shiver with horror. Addictions are a terrible thing because you're enslaved by something external over which you have no power.

When I was young, Wilfrid Lawson was a wonderful actor: he was also a legendary drunk, apparently the only actor Peter O'Toole (another drunk) had ever admired. He inspired anecdotes. When someone pointed out that his stage name was the same as Sir Wilfrid Lawson, the great temperance advocate, his response was prompt: 'I'll drink to that.' Arriving on stage the worse for drink was not unusual, but on one particular night it was more than usually noticeable, and the heckling audience was not slow to point this out. Rolling a reddened eye at his tormentors, Lawson promised, 'If you think I'm pissed, wait until you see the Duke of Buckingham.' But there's another story that captures his deadpan wit best.

Late one afternoon, an actor just back from an extended tour of the provinces bumped into Lawson on Shaftesbury Avenue. Since it was 5.30 or so, the old friends rapidly repaired to a pub to celebrate.

'I'm out of touch. What's on that's good?'

Lawson got fresh drinks. 'They say that so-and-so's pretty fair.'

'Can we get tickets tonight?'

'I believe we might,' said Lawson.

They had a few more drinks, and went on to the theatre. It was close to curtain time, but they did manage to get two seats up in the gods.

The lights went down and the curtain came up. The play went on for ten minutes or so, at which point Lawson turned to his friend and whispered, 'Something very interesting is about to happen.'

'What's that?'

'Well . . . when that woman there onstage has finished dressing, I'm coming on . . .'

By the time I met Wilfrid in the 1960s he was too unreliable to work on stage, so we acted together in the more forgiving medium of radio. On his more sober days he was great company and very funny. We played a game where we tried to make each other laugh out loud on air. During one recording, he passed me a little note saying, 'Whenever I look at you, Miriam, you're always exploring some orifice or other.' I kept that note for years. It is true – I enjoy nose-picking more than any nice Jewish girl should.

While he was sitting in a post-prandial alcoholic fog (he would have never drunk on air), I dealt with my nerves by forever biting on my fingers, picking my nose or my ears, or fiddling with my hair. I still do it now. I particularly love picking my nose when I'm sitting at traffic lights. Then I like to explore and dig, thinking of my finger as a kind of trowel, and really excavate into the nostril. One of my favourite prizes is the snot that sometimes hardens at the back of the nose. When I get the hardened nugget out, it's a triumph, and I take care not to drop it so it can be fully examined. Some people eat it: I don't. But I do like to see it and then I flick it away.

These are things we all do to a certain extent. You could say a bad habit, like beauty, is in the eye of the beholder. I have a leaning; you have a peccadillo; they have a revolting habit. It is said that cleanliness is next to godliness, and I suppose I do hold with that to a certain extent. A daily shower is essential: I have a horror of being stinky. However, I think children today live lives that are *too* clean. Consequently, they're not getting enough bacteria to build up their immune systems. As I always adhere to the five-second rule – you can eat off the floor, as long as it hasn't been there for longer than five seconds – my bacteria quotient always remains at a healthy level. It can only be helped by all the raw onion and garlic I have always consumed as well.

I don't have many vices but the ones I lay claim to, I have rather badly. Of the four 'mortal sins' – Murder, Adultery, Blasphemy and Idolatry – I am guilty of two. (I leave you to work out which.) Of the seven deadly sins – Pride, Greed, Wrath, Envy, Lust, Gluttony and Sloth – for me, Gluttony is the main one, followed pantingly close by Lust and, lazily, by Sloth. Gluttony is eating to excess, which I have done all my life. My drug of choice is cheesecake. Jews have a word for it (to *fress*) and I don't really, in my heart, think it's a vice; I see it as an essential pleasure, because the word 'enough' is for me the sin – it's a killjoy, a party-pooper, an anti-life, finger-wagging blight on the world. I used to hoover up any food left on anyone's plate, leftovers were an eternal challenge to me to finish, and I enjoyed multiple helpings of everything, especially latkes (Jewish potato fritters), coffee ice cream and Bendicks Bittermints. I can't now eat as much as I want to – my eyes have become bigger than my tummy and I run out of space before all the food on the table has been consumed. There is every reason to limit food intake for health, but none I can think of to limit it otherwise. Quantity *is* quality, more is better, distention better than cure, and mastication a sublime pleasure.

Once at the BBC canteen on the top floor of the dear 'Acton Hilton' rehearsal rooms, I noticed a large amount of food left on the plate opposite where I sat. No one was there to eat it, so I did. Shortly after I folded my knife and fork, I was unnerved when the owner of the dinner returned from the lavatory, still hungry. I confessed immediately and I bought him a replacement. I may be greedy but I know how to behave.

Award ceremonies offer gorgeous opportunities for Gluttony. Often people don't show up for the hors d'oeuvres and I consume several helpings at one sitting before the unfortunate celebrities finally arrive to find less food than the menu had led them to expect. The first courses are always the tastiest – four plates are the most I've ever snaffled at one sitting – because by the time you get to the meat and two veg, the shine has gone off. (So often the case . . .) I would advise those who attend frequent award ceremonies never to be late. Best advice: avoid sitting on my table – if you want a full meal.

I don't cook myself, but am the happiest and most appreciative of dinner guests. When invited some years ago to a joyous house party at Sandringham, I made such a song and dance about the deliciousness, the freshness, the variety of the food, that the kitchen staff prepared for me a take-home gluttony feedbag, full of duck and venison and wonderful vegetables, so I could continue to gourmandise when I reached Clapham. His Majesty is a superb host and a keen provider of the very best in culinary taste. One of the footmen came to see me on my book tour last year, and sent a trug backstage piled high with amazing pink and purple onions. My rider is not complicated: give me good brown bread, butter, smoked salmon, freshly chopped onion and Big Tom tomato juice and I'm satisfied.

As far as Lust goes, well . . . there is quite enough smut elsewhere in this book, so moving swiftly on . . .

I like to use dental floss twice – that's not mentioned in the Bible so

I think it's OK for me to downgrade it as a vice, but I admit it could be seen as a rather unpleasant habit. The sins that are left don't concern me much. For me, Pride is not a sin. Mummy always said: 'Be proud of who you are; take a pride in your appearance.' I love Gay Pride. Envy is a waste of time: I don't go in for that, it makes you bitter, and bitterness is the end of talent – and also of happiness, I would say. Wrath and Sloth I have been guilty of, particularly the latter. I am deeply, irrevocably lazy and I am ashamed of myself, but if someone needs me, I'm there.

The Jewish festival I still observe and have done since I was thirteen, is Yom Kippur, when Jews are given the opportunity to atone for their sins during the year. We do not eat or drink from sunset the day before until sunset on the day itself. Apart from the obvious sins, the most important ones are about how you behave to other people. Unkindness, expressed in various ways, is the greatest sin of all. I agree with that. Not eating or drinking for twenty-four hours is surprisingly easy. I go to whichever synagogue is nearby and sit quietly, and remember the people I love who aren't with me, and enjoy talking to the ladies who sit in my row; we always chat, even when we're not supposed to. It's akin to being a member of a club. The end of the fast is marked by the rabbi blowing ceremonial notes from a ram's horn – the sounding of the *shofar* (which is *not* a euphemism). It's an annual moment to reset. And then we go and have a lovely meal.

Crime Does Pay

Looking back at my school magazine, my predicted career was never Actress but Probation Officer. I think that was because once having been made a prefect, I switched from being the second naughtiest girl of OHS (the worst-behaved was Tatty Katkov, who was just impossible) into the strictest of disciplinarians in the blink of an eye. I'm not denying that being able to dole out detentions rather than receive them was a heady pleasure. But the key thing for me was being given a new plum role to play – the poacher was suddenly playing the gamekeeper. I relished the opportunity and redirected all my energies and enthusiasms into it with more than a little success.

Once I became an actress, I never planned my career. You can't. If a job came along, and my agent approved, I took it . . . Theatre was my goal and my dream; film was a medium I never expected to work in. To act in a movie felt glamorous and beyond my reach. So, whenever a film was offered, the money, and even the part, felt almost immaterial – there was always the possibility of an exciting location. I was forty-one, behaving badly, but happily settled with Heather in the new house I still live in, in Clapham.

When in 1982 I was finally offered a film job that combined acting with law and order, I agreed straight away. The world of all-female detention beckoned and I was delighted to play my part. It was a role I didn't really have to dig deep to find – playing a bossy, aggressive lesbian prison warder. *Scrubbers* had been envisaged as the female companion piece to *Scum*, which had tackled the brutal world of the all-male borstal to great and shocking effect. Unfortunately, this film did not take the 'female-of-the-species-is-deadlier-than-the-male' approach.

Every shooting day began at 5 a.m., when a motley collection of actresses would gather in King's Cross to meet the large van sent to take us to our location in woody Surrey – Holloway Sanatorium, a Victorian psychiatric asylum in Virginia Water opened in 1885, reputedly where Nijinsky had been kept when his mind collapsed. On the side of the van was the legend: HANDMADE SCRUBBERS – not a strange insult to us but because the production company was Handmade Films, founded by George Harrison to fund *Life of Brian* when no one else would. At that time, King's Cross was a notorious pick-up area for prostitutes, and there were plenty of tarts in those days wandering about the station. We girls were noisy and excited as we gathered for the van. I wonder if they thought of us as competition. We certainly weren't dressed for the part.

The van was like a hop-picking charabanc – a gaggle of girls all jumbled in together, chattering and joking. I have always loved all-girl gatherings and truthfully I don't remember any blokes in the van, except the driver. We sang pop songs; well, I listened because I couldn't sing and some of the girls had great voices. Eva Mottley, in particular, seemed like a rebel, and fierce. She had recently come out of prison for a drug offence, she had spunk and fire, and wouldn't do what she was told. Eva later landed a good part in *Widows*, a brilliant TV series made after our film, but when she was dropped from the sequel, she went back onto drugs and committed suicide.

I played Jones, a highly unpleasant, 'butch' prison officer. There was no change of costume and my lines consisted of barked orders like 'BACK IN YOUR CELLS, GIRLS'. I'm afraid I relished her nastiness; there was no subtlety at all. I should have been ashamed of myself. It was also the first time I shared a bill with Robbie Coltrane, who played Puff Guts. The rest of the cast was full of talent, including my old Cambridge friend Carol Gillies, along with future stars Pauline Melville, Pam St Clement and seventeen-year-old Kathy Burke.

Scrubbers was Kathy's first paid job and she was too terrified to ask any questions. Each morning after disembarking from the charabanc, there was breakfast awaiting our arrival in the hall of the grand Gothic building and then during the day all our food was laid on by the catering crew. No one had thought to explain to Kathy that it was free – and so for the first two days she ate nothing, only daring to snatch a cup of tea. At lunch on the second day, I noticed that she still wasn't eating anything. I went up and asked, 'What's the matter? Why aren't you eating? Aren't you feeling OK?'

'No. I haven't got any money so I just can't. It's all right.'

'For fuck's sake – it's all free,' I said. 'The film company provides everything. Go and have something to eat. Go on – eat your heart out! They give us fuck all else, so you might as well have this.' And I took Kathy under my wing after that. She loved the fact that I seemed so clear about who I was, that I wore a badge announcing 'I'm a Dyke on my Bike' – and my 'don't care' attitude, the way I told people to fuck off if I felt like it, helped give her the confidence to reveal the outgoing person that was always there. Apparently at the first read-through, as we went round and introduced ourselves, I got up and announced, 'My name is Miriam Margolyes and I'm a lesbian.' I still do that at every read-through, but now I add my age to give it even more of a ring.

The joy of *Scrubbers* for me was the other actors. We got on, we liked each other and we laughed together; there was no competition, only shared fun. I felt I was back at school, hanging around with a group of funny, intelligent friends, laughing and joking and having adventures. Kathy Burke was always my favourite but I also enjoyed Pauline Melville, my fellow prison warder (whose performance was coloured by her experience as a former drama teacher at Holloway women's prison), and Pam St Clement. They were marvellous company, irreverent and witty. Pauline went on to become a bestselling writer, and Pam to *EastEnders* as Pat Wicks, the heavily ear-ringed obstreperous former prostitute who became the landlady of the Queen Vic and the darling of the nation. You would have never guessed that in real life, Pam's ringing tones are as highfaluting and cut-crystal as mine. That's acting for you.

When we weren't needed on set, we used to wander through the vast, decrepit building, exploring those areas that weren't being used as a location. The sanatorium had closed in 1980 and as we ambled about the empty corridors and offices, we found piles of abandoned psychiatric notes of the former inmates strewn on the floor and spilling out of the old filing cabinets. It felt a haunted place, full of miseries, and the security guards enjoyed alarming us even more, telling us spooky stories about strange goings-on. They were nasty and enjoyed seeing our fear. I've noticed how some men do take pleasure in frightening women – small-penis problem, I expect.

Our director, Mai Zetterling, had long been my hero. About twenty years older than me, she had been acting since she was a kid. I saw her in *Knock on Wood* with Danny Kaye when I was thirteen and had loved her ever since. Mai had become a scriptwriter, a director and a novelist. She exuded an enormous, palpable sexual energy; sex cascaded from her. Once she gave me a hug, and suddenly I could feel her in my body. And I wasn't expecting that at all. Nothing ever happened between us, alas, although I undeniably detected an openness to sapphic potential.

Mai had had to fight very hard to be a director in a male-dominated industry. And because she had been an actress before she'd been a director, Mai knew what problems we faced. She made each one of us feel involved in the project and involved with her, making great efforts to get everyone a provisional Equity card, at that time essential for continuing in the profession. She encouraged and chivvied us, and used her own experience in the film world to stimulate our energies. Mai was immensely focused, and when she talked to you, you knew she was talking to you and nobody else – but *Scrubbers* wasn't a proper, serious film and it should have been. It didn't tackle things that it should have done; it wasn't a meaningful investigation into the experiences of women in prison. Maybe if it hadn't been such a social film set, if we'd all been more adversarial, if we'd felt more uncomfortable, the film might have been a greater artistic success.

But while we, her cast, loved her, the male crew didn't treat Mai with the same respect. She had to fight every step of the way. So much so that the first assistant director, who was a real jerk, baked a loaf of bread in the shape of a cock and balls and ceremoniously presented it to her at the wrap party in front of us all. When she battered him on the head with it, I only hope she heard my cheers.

When George Harrison came to visit the set, Mai insisted that the whole cast should meet him, because she wanted everyone to be able to say in later life, 'I met a Beatle.' A handsome, hirsute, much-moustachioed figure, George Harrison didn't smile a lot. He was quiet and rather mournful. I think he was shy. So, when a long brassy line of *Scrubbers* enthusiastically queued up to greet him, he clearly felt overwhelmed.

'Hello,' he said lugubriously. 'I feel like Prince Charles.'

Harrison had had his own run-ins with the law of course – a police raid (carefully timed for the morning of Paul McCartney's wedding) found no less than 120 joints in his Esher home, as well as a generous portion of hashish tucked inside one of Harrison's shoes. The officer in charge of the raid, Sergeant Norman Pilcher, was later charged with planting drugs, but Harrison and his wife Patti were found guilty and very heavily fined. Some speculate that Pilcher focused so heavily on arresting all the Beatles because he was gunning for the papers to rename them *Sergeant Pilcher's Lonely Hearts Club Band*.

Of course, I'd never experienced a real prison then. I have since not only been in a remand cell after an altercation over a parking ticket with a motorcycle policeman (see *This Much is True*) but also had a very intense experience in a women's prison in Butler County, Ohio while filming a BBC TV documentary, *Miriam's Big American Adventure*. The women inmates I met were remarkable; I would have been glad to have had them as friends. I got to know several in particular and when I told them how beautiful and intelligent they were, they wept. 'No one ever told us before that we were worth anything,' one of them said when she contacted me a while after. She thought perhaps I would give her money for drugs. Her old life had reclaimed her. But in the prison, they were clean. And themselves again. When you learn a person's whole story, you allow them the humanity they deserve. Years later, I discovered my own family's dark secret – that my great-grand-father had spent seven years in Parkhurst Prison on the Isle of Wight for fraud – and it put a different complexion on everything. I suddenly saw how easy it could be to slip between the cracks and how hard it is to come back. I doubt I'll get to play a prison guard again now. But if I do, she would be very different.

Know Thyself

May I introduce you to my body? Oh, all right then. I can imagine the screams of 'NOoooooooooooo!!' with which such an invitation would be greeted. Tough shit. You're coming with me on a small, guided tour from top to toe, up and down and round and round. ('Once round me, twice round the gasworks,' as friends would cruelly chortle.)

I am a woman, identifying as a Fattie carrying an excess of avoirdupois weighing approximately 94 kilos. Preferred pronoun is 'she', but whatever floats your boat is acceptable. The tour won't take long but nothing will be spared. The whole, the holes – the story – of what it feels like to inhabit this particular woman's body.

I have always liked to look at people, and at their bodies. I am fascinated by shapes – where they differ from mine and where they're the same. I'm not a nudist like Mummy. These days I take care not to shock or disgust by letting a tit fall out. It's perfectly possible to go through life decorously, despite the fact that I am conscious of displays of the most overt sexuality all around me. I confess I am shocked by the insubstantial clothing young girls wear now, especially in the winter. Groups of scantily clad, giggling females, on their way home from a party, decorate the streets, sometimes the gutters, with bare shoulders, pussy-pelmet skirts or sparkly, flimsy dresses leaving little to the imagination. Maybe there's more of my disapproving Glaswegian grandma in me than I thought.

I believe in layers and in removing them throughout the day as the heat increases. In winter, as I write this, I have two layers of everything except socks. But I've come to terms with the fact that my body is not a pretty sight. It's my own fault – I've eaten too much all my life and now the fat intends to stay, settled in for the duration. I hope people concentrate on my face, which is warm, friendly and, although lined, has a girlish aspect which can be quite charming.

The problem for wardrobe mistresses is that I always need adjustment. They can't just put me into a dress and say, 'Perfect. That looks good, now off you go.' There's always a sigh, and then: 'Ah, yes, we'll just have to let that bit out a little and maybe put in a couple of darts.' In every role I ever played, I was *always* being darted. But in our business, you have to make your handicap into an advantage. Once they saw the scale of the problem, the wardrobe mistresses and costume designers (who are high on my list of glorious individuals) rose to the occasion and allowed and indeed coaxed my majestic bosoms into magnificent costumes and actually said they were grateful for the breasts, which brought an unmistakeable aplomb to the characters I portrayed.

Period costumes have always been my friends. The gifted director Christine Edzard, who had been Franco Zeffirelli's set designer, personally fitted me into my costume for Flora Finching in *Little Dorrit*.

I was embarrassed that my director was kneeling on the floor measuring my vital statistics, her mouth full of pins, but Christine was perfectly happy. Flora was based upon Dickens's first love, whom he met again after a twenty-five-year gap. Here he describes her with the chilly eye of a spurned lover:

> Flora, always tall, had grown to be very broad too, and short of breath; but that was not much. Flora, whom he had left a lily, had become a peony; but that was not much. Flora, who had seemed enchanting in all she said and thought, was diffuse and silly. That was much. Flora, who had been spoiled and artless long ago, was determined to be spoiled and artless now. That was a fatal blow.

Christine didn't ignore my belly, she needed it for Flora. She wanted to make films, to tell a story, she wanted to invest Flora's costume with the absurdity and pathos inherent in the character. This inspired me to forget about my body and think about how to serve Flora, using the tightness of the corset and the opulence of the decoration to do so.

One great advantage of excess flesh is that it encourages mirth; the attempt to contain it, to cover it, to *squeeze* it into a garment, can be laughter-inducing. All my costumes reflect this cruel truth, and those of Madame Morrible and Elephant Ethel, Mrs Mingott, and the Spanish Infanta, have over the years celebrated my girth, deliberately accentuated the bosoms, propelled upwards just below my chin(s) and fastened with inexorable powerful hooks and eyes: continental shelves of mammary excess, straining for release from the highly decorative fabrics which were shopped for so lovingly by wardrobe mistresses across the world.

It's easy to concentrate on the body's successes, but it's the failures that take up all the time. Where it works you can just forget about them. But when I got to my late seventies, I just couldn't forget any more. And now at eighty-two, I can't forget about it for a second time because my body's various malfunctions are what I'm having to deal with, most of the time.

I've always had legs obviously, but now they're a bit of a trial to me because I've had a knee replacement, and I get pains down both my legs because of my spinal stenosis. I remember Grandma Margolyes's bowlegs. Daddy had them too, but Grandma's gait and her look were faintly comic, although she herself was not – she was dignified. But her poor, bent legs evoke sympathy in me and now when I see myself walking – not walking, but tottering, stooped and stumbling – I just can't believe that this is what I've become. My body is letting me down. It's taking its revenge because it hasn't been treated well. I have let my body down – that's the truth of it.

My accelerating disintegration coincided with my giving up swimming. I used to swim daily but had to stop because of a problem with my ears and my doctors said, 'When you give that up, things will fall apart.' And they were right. But 'exercise' is a word that fills me with dread. I thought 'core' was a word about apples, but according to my Pilates teacher, mine needs a lot of work.

Joan Collins told me that she does an hour's exercise every day – automatically. I don't know what she does exactly – stretching and bending and that kind of thing, I expect – but she just does it almost unconsciously.

'Miriam, I've done it all my life. I don't even have to think about it any more,' she said.

The truth is that I just can't bear exercise, I dread it. My Pilates instructor used to come to my house in London and we'd do it in my kitchen, but now I make excuses and say that I don't have time. It's feeble; I know I must or I'll die. And of course, it would help with my mobility, indeed with everything. How pathetic I am.

I'm ashamed of my body now. I'm not ashamed of my face, but I am ashamed of my body. I've let it happen. I damaged it. I ate too much so it swelled and billowed. But it's no good railing against the cards you've been dealt. Mummy always said, 'Make the best of it.' She was practical. I think I am too. I've made the best of it. After all, look at me. I may be old. I may be walking with sticks. I may rattle with pills. (Why are there so many pills to take when you get old?) But I'm still here and I'm still earning. What more do you want?

Swearing is Good for You

When I hear Kenneth Tynan credited as being the first person to swear on television in 1965, I am irritated, because actually it was me – in the first series of *University Challenge* two years earlier. I have spent the last sixty years blocking out the expressions of frozen horror on the faces of my beloved Newnham College team of Susan Lee, Liz Hodgkin and Jinty Muir (the unspoken 'Oh Miriam!' far too clearly forming in all their minds) as a 'FUCK' burst out of my mouth.

The whole studio took in such a shocked deep breath that the willowy form of our bespectacled quizmaster, a very young Bamber Gascoigne, shook in the backdraught. He told me many years later that he had never forgotten the moment and he certainly rattled out the next question at double speed. I was duly bleeped out of the broadcast and thankfully the recordings are now lost. If only all my many other excursions into the profane had suffered a similar fate.

I've been reading quite a lot about swearing lately and about the power and psychological purpose of a four-letter word. The words we all use normally are quite, well, ordinary, uncharged. They're dulled by that banality. A swear word, on the other hand, still possesses this sort of dangerousness to it. Suddenly you're going to the heart of a very raw form of language. It pulses with a kind of electricity. It makes your skin prickle. Uttering a profanity, can serve as a very handy escape valve for anger and frustration. Scientists at Keele University have proved that swearing can actually increase your body's ability to withstand pain: volunteers could keep their hand in a bucket of ice water for about forty seconds longer if they repeatedly cursed.

I love swearing – I always have. Of course, it gets me into trouble. Mummy and Daddy hated it when I swore and I always had to apologise to them. 'It's not clever,' Mummy would say; 'I suppose you learned that at Cambridge.' I suppose I did. But there is an undeniable pleasure in seeing the shock, sometimes disgust, on faces when I shout foul language at strangers, often in the car. 'CUNT-FACE!' I shriek through the open window at the offending driver, usually male, who tries to cut me up, beats me to the get-away or threatens me from behind. And I gleefully represent their tiny appendage with thumb and forefinger, to reinforce my rage and contempt. 'Cunt-face' is my rude word of choice; it's unisexually employed, but I haven't found a gesture to indicate an enormous vagina, which would be the equivalent insult for a woman. Odd that size matters so much – women must be small in that area; men, big.

I've always been outspoken. I tend to say the things other people think and don't say. And I'm not going to stop now – that's just who I am and the way I live my life. But bad language is obviously something that is now associated with me. And I who love language, who cherish grammar, who studied literature at a great university with a great teacher, I find it a little bit bruising and painful to think that I'm seen only as a foul mouth. I use words with care, precision, with pleasure. Words to me are a source of huge delight. I'm not just a foul mouth. I can be a foul mouth, though, and I enjoy the moments when I am. But that's not all I am. And, anyway, language is language. And to me the idea of just having one way of speaking is very limiting. In my book, daring in one's use of language is a plus. So, here are my top tips on swearing.

Firstly, you must choose your curses wisely. My top picks would always be 'fuck', 'cunt', 'shit' and 'arse', which are words I'm sure everybody uses – although probably not as much as I do. I also quite like 'knickers', because it makes people giggle like schoolchildren. Ken Dodd and I used to say 'knickers' to each other when we needed cheering up. Only the British would count that as a naughty word, though.

Secondly, swearing is useful to make yourself heard. I swear because I enjoy shocking people, which I confess is one of my great pleasures. Coming from a conventional middle-class background, brought up strictly by parents who were well-spoken, and thanks to having elocution lessons while a student at Oxford High School, I am beautifully spoken. People think it's funny when somebody who sounds like me, swears like me – they react with laughter because it's surprising. But then, you see, I have their attention, and before you know it, they're eating out of my hand. And here I'm treading on dangerous ground, because I'm exposing a part of myself that perhaps I shouldn't: that I'm somewhat calculating . . . It's something my mother taught me because she was a great manipulator. When I swear, I observe the reaction minutely, because if I can control the reaction, I have some sort of power, and I think that's perhaps what I'm looking for. However, my swearing is not purely manipulative. I long for honest and open communion with my fellow human beings and I think that my using rough language slices through some of the bullshit of usual social interactions, avoiding wishy-washy euphemism and cutting straight to the chase. Life's too short to pussyfoot.

Thirdly, you've got to use your discretion. As I have learned to my cost, there's a time and a place for dropping a juicy expletive. It's no secret that I'm shat off with the Conservative Party – well, who isn't? And if you're not, you should be! Practise on those who merit it. Some people find my vocabulary vile. They ask, 'Why do you use such foul language?' But sometimes you just have to say 'cunt-face'. Nothing else fits. I learned that at Cambridge. I'd say my swearing is directed at the most deserving: politicians, and drivers that I happen to meet on the road. I'm not a bad driver, in fact I'm very good, but there are many who are appalling. I'm afraid I do exhibit road rage quite frequently. I wind the window down and let fly. I find a good bellow clears the air.

I've always had a foul mouth, and I'm sure I've been an outspoken old lady since I was a little girl, but I'm a firm believer that the truth is not always helpful. Sometimes speaking your mind can be destructive and pointless, but often these days people invoke 'honesty' or 'freedom of speech' in the most unnecessary situations.

Sweary as I am, the thing I value most is kindness, and I hope people can see that. I worry that we're in danger of becoming a nation of unkind people. When I swear or come out with something shocking, it's usually because I'm trying to bring others some joy. I don't want to upset anyone. Except politicians – they can fuck right off.

———

Of all the swear words, the ubiquitous 'fuck' is the most commonly used. 'Fuck' has been going for a long time and is not showing any signs of weakening or falling out of favour. Listening to young people on public transport, their conversations are so liberally spattered with 'fucks' that the penetration of the word is slightly blunted. 'Fuck me,' they now say as a relatively mild expression of surprise.

Here are a few more joys. 'Cocksucker', for example; this calls up many busy memories for me; I relish the word 'bugger' - it trips off the tongue. 'Arsehole' as an insult really makes me happy. I enjoy the visual specificity. In my mind's eye, the small, puckered circle that is unmistakeably the anal opening is superimposed on the face of the offender, and my rage is reduced by the resultant image. You can't hate an arsehole; you can laugh at it, feel faintly disgusted, but the fury is assuaged. Actually, I'd say most men are arseholes - not all, and the young ones are better than the old ones: as I have made plain, the worst old person I know is Boris Johnson's father, Stanley. He's a complete arsehole.

In the old days, the strongest swear words had a religious derivation and often more than a whiff of brimstone - 'Damnation', 'Zounds' ('God's wounds'), 'The Devil' - but as our belief has waned, they don't pack the same punch as before. I remember fondly my father's Yiddish insults: 'He was a *momzer benenedder*' (that's how he said it; how it's properly expressed in Yiddish I wish I knew); '*shayguts*', '*schnorrer*', '*bayt zemir*' (exclusively for Gentiles), '*curever*' ('whore'; exclusively for women). He never used the word '*schmuck*' - Mummy said it was too 'common'.

One of the recent events in my life has been the popularisation of social media. It's not *really* social, because it involves long solitary hours spent staring at screens, either large or small, rather than real social intercourse - chatting, gossiping, exchanging ideas and look-ing into real people's eyes. It's the tool for some people to become billionaires and then they control our thoughts, our very means of expressing ourselves. And from that has developed the 'celebrity message': people paying for people they see only on screens to send quite intimate messages on more screens to their friends and people they know and love but prefer to reach through others. I make a lot of money working with one such firm – Cameo, an internet business founded in Chicago in 2016 by Steve Galanis. I charge £100 for my messages, and if the recipient doesn't like it, I'll re-do it – no extra charge! I think that's reasonable. I aim to please. But I've noticed the most common demand from my 'clients' is that I swear – using specifically 'fuck' and 'cunt' as their desired words. 'Please swear, Miriam. Please use the word "cunt" and say "fuck" as much as you like. Please don't hold back,' they'll say.

Truthfully, I have to grind the words out, almost through gritted teeth. Swearing needs the impetus of rage rather than the lure of money to evoke its full colour. And it certainly destroys the *fun* – more than anything else in my life, I crave fun. I relish going to town on the sexual aspects of a loving greeting, hoping I'm describing the union of lovers, the sweat, the sperm, the moment of entry (whichever sex), the joy of 'coming together', rather than incorrectly assigning such erotic joys to sisters or family members whom I have wrongly identified.

They seem to think that I'm some kind of swearing machine. Someone once described me as 'a walking swear-jar'. And, of course, that isn't true. I use rough words quite thoughtfully. I know when I'm going to say 'cunt' and when I'm not. Or when I talk about 'cock-sucking', it's a serious business, you know, and some people are very offended by those words. But I don't know what else to call it. I guess you could call it fellatio, but I think that sounds like a flower, not the actual business.

I try hard not to swear in inappropriate places. One of those inappropriate places remains the BBC. I particularly love the *Today* programme. When I'm away from the UK, it's my means of knowing what's really going on. And after over sixty years of listening to it, I was thrilled when the BBC *Today* programme finally rang up. They asked me to record a tribute to Robbie Coltrane who had just died.

'May I come into the studio, because I've never met Justin Webb and Martha Kearney, and I'd like to?' I said. Truthfully, that was my entirely selfish reason. I've always liked them tremendously and thought we would get on.

I got up at six, and their car collected me in time to go on air at half-past seven. I had returned from America the day before and I had jet-lag. I arrived at the Beeb in Portland Place, where a nice young researcher lady met me in reception and took me up to the long waiting room just outside the studio. I don't know who else I was expecting to see, but it wasn't the smirking figure of Jeremy Hunt, surrounded by a small entourage. It reminded me of lagging around a boiler.

'Oh jeez,' I thought. I didn't know quite what to do, so I just said, 'You've got a hell of a job, best of luck.'

He smiled and said, 'Thank you very much.'

I sat as far away from him as I could and, eventually, he went into the studio for his interview. I was thinking about Robbie and what I was going to say. Then Jeremy Hunt came out and it was my turn.

I talked about Robbie and answered their questions and I was very glad to have the chance to express what I felt about him, because I think he was a considerable person and performer. Justin Webb thanked me for coming into the studio that morning, and I said thank you very much, and that was the end of the interview. As I got up, thinking that the mikes were off, I started to say, 'I never thought I'd be sitting in the seat . . .' Then it struck me that I might be still on air. So I stopped, but Justin laughed and said, '. . . that Jeremy Hunt has just sat in, is what you were about to say.' And when he said that, I thought, well, the mikes must be off. And I had never imagined a world in which Jeremy Hunt's and my bottom would be in indirect contact, so to speak.

'The thing is,' I went on, 'when I saw him there I just said, "You've got a hell of a job. Best of luck." But what I really wanted to say was, "Fuck you, you bastard . . ."'

As I said the word 'fuck', Justin rather frantically apologised, saying, 'Oh, no, no, no, you mustn't say that. No, you can't say that! . . . We'll have to have you out of the studio now.'

'We will, with many apologies,' Martha Kearney added, continuing briskly. 'The time now is half-past eight, and time for the sports news . . .'

Overcome with horror, ushered by the young lady researcher, I tottered out. I said rather desperately, 'I thought the mikes were off. You've got to tell them that I thought the mikes were off.'

'No, it's all right. It doesn't matter,' she said, trying to calm me down.

'But it does matter,' I said. 'It's terrible!' I was imagining the listeners choking on their cornflakes.

In the taxi, I was still shaking, because it's an unforgivable blunder to utter such words on the nation's main morning programme – and I felt I'd let myself and Radio 4 down.

I was still shaking when I got home, and then somebody phoned and said, 'You're trending on Twitter!' I felt ashamed about it until the producers sent me flowers to comfort me. Which was very nice of them, because I thought they would be furious. That was reassuring, but the whole thing was a reminder that sometimes you do need to button yourself up. At least I didn't call him Jeremy Cunt, as many others have, including the wonderful Jim Naughtie. With a name like Hunt, it's a *sine qua non*.

'What the fuck's that?' I hear you say.

Look it up, cunt-face!

Never Steal Thunder

Peter Hall once said to me, 'Murder your darlings' – which means, when you think you're being brilliant, that's when you should stop. It's the best piece of acting advice I've ever been given. If you find yourself thinking: 'Oh, I'm doing this bit really well, this is a good bit,' you've actually gone too far. You're overacting, and being a smug actor – there are an awful lot of them.

⸻

When acting on stage, good manners are paramount, for there is an almost unspoken etiquette to theatre craft. When you stand on stage in front of a paying audience, you must be conscious of the effect that you have on your fellow actor and vice versa, so that your performance is fundamentally affected by this crucial interplay. A disregard for this subtle etiquette can potentially derail the entire show.

I've come across actors who make a habit of upstaging their fellow cast members. Some are not aware they're doing it. It's a compulsion to connect; they want the audience to be focused on *them* and they don't quite understand that it's not actually *their* moment. Tony Sher, for instance, who is now dead, bless his soul, when he played Richard III at Stratford in 1984, had huge crutches attached to his wrists, that made it look as if he'd grown an extra pair of legs, an unbottled spider. He took over the entire stage because he would wave them about when he was talking. He was a gifted and remarkable actor, but in this instance I think his need to dominate had gone too far, so far that there was no room (literally and metaphorically) for anyone else on stage. And I've seen other actors, who shall remain nameless, deliberately upstage people in the middle of speeches by waving a handkerchief, sighing very heavily, or even starting to knit. Whenever it has been done to me, my intense concentration on not letting it distract me has often raised the standard of my performance, hopefully also infuriating the perpetrator. It should come as no surprise that the expression 'stealing someone's thunder' comes from the theatre. But it was an unsuccessful playwright's anguished cry, not an actor's: John Dennis's complaint: 'Damn them! . . . They will not let my play run, but they steal my thunder,' on hearing that the method he had devised for making the noise of a storm for his own play of *Appius and Virginia* had been snaffled to intensify a performance of *Macbeth*.

Sometimes the theatre is excessively hierarchical. There's that description: 'A star is someone who lights up the stage.' When Lawrence Olivier walked on, you *felt* that the lights had gone up two points. But the fact is that they actually *had*. Carol Macready remembered that in one scene, she had to follow Vanessa Redgrave onto the stage. One evening, however, she came out first, and suddenly found herself in a blaze of light. But it was *Vanessa's* light, not hers.

'Aha!' Carol thought. '*That's* how stars are made.'

In film acting the director is supreme; she or he decides what the shots are, they point the camera. You could be waving your arms about and knitting all you want, but if they choose not to have you in the shot, you're not there. It is the director and the film editor who make the choice. On stage, however, once the play has opened and the director has gone home, it belongs to the actors.

Theatre performance is something you do as a team. We must all be there together as equals, looking up to our stars and giving them what they need in the scenes, but also preserving our own space when it's our turn. When it's *your* moment, when you are literally in the limelight, you feel it instantaneously, on your skin and in your body. But what *really* fires you and warms you, is the heat that comes from the other actors. You're picking up the baton and passing it on. You adapt to that moment and then you move out of the light. You must be unselfish; you *must* pass the baton. It may be hard, but be sensitive to the moment. Without that sensitivity, you will never be as great as you could be. Be prepared to relinquish the spotlight: you shouldn't always demand to be the focus of attention. That's a psychological need. It's not a dramatic imperative.

I'm quite beady about my moment under the light. We all are. We all like to be the centre of attention. However, jostling for position on stage is both unworthy and undignified. That isn't what actors should be doing. It's *anti*-art because the individual performer should never be more important than the work. I believe in the pre-eminence of the text. The play is the thing.

Always Expect the Unexpected

I love surprising people but I hate to be taken unawares. I want to seem confident, on top of any situation. But a lot of the time I'm scared; scared of *failing*, most particularly. And that's why I seldom watch my own work back. I find it unnerving to see how bad I can be, how ugly I look, how many mistakes I make. It took me forty-three years before I watched my episode of *Tales of the Unexpected*.

Tales of the Unexpected was a popular Saturday-night television series throughout the 1980s. It was the low-budget British version of *Alfred Hitchcock Presents*, adapted from the dark, short tales of Roald Dahl. These were sour stories for grown-ups – no chocolate factories or giant peaches here. Sometimes comic, always nasty, each tale told a sinister story of everyday folk, and always with an unexpected twist in the tail. The first series had been a triumph and it was a highly sought-after job.

Roald Dahl introduced our story, 'Fat Chance', sitting unsmiling in an armchair by the fire. His sepulchral tones invoked memories of Edgar Lustgarten. The cockles of one's heart were immediately chilled as he began to speak:

In the bad old days, when India was full of millionaire maharajahs, these fellows used to bump off their wives with astonishing frequency ... Not for them a coarse bash on the head, or a bloody running through with a sword, or a slashing of the throat . . . A maharajah intent upon disposing of his wife would first go out and shoot a tiger. He would then cut off its whiskers. These whiskers, which were as sharp and spiky as slivers of glass, would be chopped up into small pieces and sprinkled on the maharani's curry at dinner. When eaten, they would perforate the lining of her intestine and kill her off within two days. In other countries, tiger's whiskers are rather hard to come by. So we husbands have to use other, less refined methods, as you will see in a moment . . .

And guess who was playing the wife in this production . . .

It was in 1980, I played Mary, a 'fat pig' of a housewife, married to a pharmacist called Johnnie (John Castle) who was having an affair with Frances, a fellow am-dram player (Sheila Gish). I had to be got rid of. From the first moment of meeting, I and my future murderers were friends for life. That sometimes happens (but much more rarely in TV) and it's precious. John Castle describes it as 'a riotous meeting of iconoclastic people who just didn't care'. We had such a good time – we never stopped laughing and joking together; it was intoxicating and delightful. Our aim was to make sure the whole cast and crew were perpetually quivering on the brink of hysteria. We behaved appallingly the whole time.

John reminded me of the 'full moon' in our first scene in bed together (well, we *were* playing husband and wife). There have been many 'moons' in my long career. It's hard to keep a straight face when you're waiting naked under a sheet for your cue. We're not sure who mooned first; I think it was John: first a lovely presentation of his bum, then it was my turn – hopefully similarly pink and gracious – until, in a shocking flash, he spun round, and then there was no escaping his flying tackle. We didn't need an 'intimacy co-ordinator' – we were well away! Poor John Gorrie, our elegant director, didn't know where to look, but the cameramen laughed so much, they nearly knocked their equipment over.

The rehearsals and filming were in Anglia TV's Norwich studios, so fellow South Londoners John, Sheila and I travelled there and back together. The trains were slow and often delayed, and we spun each other outrageous true stories to while away the long journeys. My tales generally veered into the sexual as I have always been inflamed by trains. I think it's the rhythm that gets me going, it's the going-over-the-cobbles business.

One day I took them through a particularly memorable encounter with a handsome stranger on a German train: where no words were exchanged but once our eyes met compellingly, he and I both knew what we wanted. Still in silence, we stood up and walked to the next section of the train, shut ourselves into the lavatory and got to work. It was odd because neither of us spoke. Not a word was uttered, it was just fumble fumble, suck suck suck ... The speedy sucking and rubbing excitedly echoed the rattling motion of the train until suddenly the stereo turned into mono and I realised with a jolt of pure horror that the carriage was separating from the moving train and we were about to be left behind in the middle of Bavaria. It was as if a bucket of icy water had been flung over me. In that moment of clarity, I realised that keeping hold of my luggage was far more important than Hans, or his hands, so I leapt out of the loo and back onto the moving part of the train, pulling my dress together as I went. My lasting memory was his look of frozen surprise as I tore myself away, hurtling backwards across the carriage, leaving him semi-tumescent with his trousers (or were they lederhosen?) round his ankles. There was no chance to shout 'Auf Wiedersehen', but then again, we'd never even said hello. Anyway, I was never very good at German . . .

I was so engrossed in telling the story to John and Sheila, taking them through it with lots of energetic miming and auditory effects, that I had no idea my story was gathering a much larger audience than I had ever intended. Behind me, the whole carriage was agog, my shocked fellow passengers transfixed at the filth coming out of my mouth. John and Sheila, who could see their disgusted faces, were helpless with laughter.

I knew I'd been cast in 'Fat Chance' because I was fat, John and Sheila because they were damn good actors and pleasing to look at. But you always need to expect the unexpected. Tired of his obese wife and planning a new life with Sheila's character, Johnnie decides to bump me off with the one thing he is sure I can't resist. He buys me a box of chocolates he's injected with some lethal drug, and gives it to me, imagining I'll slowly poison myself as I gobble them up, sprawled in front of the TV, as usual. But he fatally underestimates me. He thinks he's the hero but, actually, *I* am. Here's a taste of the closing dialogue:

Johnnie: So that box of chocolates I brought you was a waste of
   money?
Mary: It was not a waste! I gave it to Frances.
Johnnie: Frances? But she's gone.
Mary: There was a strike at London Airport. Her flight's been
   delayed till this afternoon, so I gave her the chocs to take on

the trip. I bet she's guzzling those soft centres now over the Atlantic and I don't feel a trace of envy. Not a trace. Now I'll make you a wonderful supper. We'll have grated carrot and lettuce and cottage cheese. I'll be as thin as a rake, Johnnie, and you'll love me. And you'll tell me you love me . . .

Watching it for the first time, I looked at my thirty-nine-year-old self very closely. I seldom take the opportunity to confront my younger self. Beautiful as Sheila was, blonde and slender with a mischievous smile, I realised I was attractive too. I only wish I'd known at the time that I looked so *zaftig* – the Yiddish word for 'plump but sexy'. Would that I could achieve that look again!

When I reflect, I acknowledge how lucky we were to have a job that made us laugh. We goaded each other on to further revelations and naughtiness and stories and memories. I thought we'd be friends for ever. It was the cruellest twist that Sheila should be struck down by cancer. First it destroyed her right eye, but she refused to stop working. She played Madame Arkadina in *The Seagull* at Chichester Festival, a black eye-patch covering the tumour with a flamboyance so typical of her. But then the cancer spread and took hold, ravaging her face. I remember that when I went to visit her – John and I went separately – her second husband, the actor Denis Lawson, hadn't warned either of us what to expect. Perhaps there wasn't time and I don't think he could *bring* himself to, somehow.

I arrived at their house and Denis opened the door and ushered me straight in. The difference in Sheila was so shocking, so total, that I had to steel myself not to show it. I felt a wave of pity and sorrow, but thought, 'I mustn't let my face reflect the horror that I see.' It was one of the most difficult pieces of dissembling I've ever done. But Sheila was still there inside it all, and though she was rather weary, we talked and I was able to make her laugh and forget, and I'm glad of that. Being able to gossip and joke about our friends, to tell silly stories, was hard. We both knew this was the last time we would ever see each other; she died about six weeks later, in early March 2005. Her daughter Lou's death, from the same cancer a year later, was a double tragedy I find hard to absorb even now. Sometimes when you think you've come to terms with the sheer unfairness of things, you have an extra shock like that where the rug is whisked from under your feet and you are smacked in the face at the same time. If this was an episode of *Tales of the Unexpected*, the credits would be rolling and the ethereal music would be playing, but seeing as it's life, you just have to pick yourself up, brush yourself off and get on with it.

The Joy of Bottoms

Images of curvaceous fruit and veg – a red apple, a peach, pear, tomato, a butternut squash, a beetroot, finally a majestic aubergine pass across the screen.

> Bums. We don't tend to talk about them but one in two of them may get piles. Itchy, sore pains in the posterior [*This bit accompanied by images of a lemon beside a grater, or a prickly buttock-shaped cactus*]. Sound familiar? Use Anusol, the UK's number one piles treatment. Developed by experts to soothe itching, relieve discomfort, and calm inflammation. For fast, long-lasting relief from piles, trust Anusol.

I'm still doing voice-overs for commercials, but now, rather than the sultry tones that encouraged people to buy 'Special' Manikin Cigars in the seventies, or to 'Take It Easy' with Cadbury's Caramel in the eighties and nineties, I am the soothing voice of Anusol . . .

—

I feel enormous affection for buttocks. They're not overtly sexual, they're universal – and tidy. I'm always happy to see a nice pair of buttocks. Some are definitely better than others; you don't want 'spreaders', but firm buttocks are joyous things. I'm content with mine. They perform the function I need.

I recently discovered a delightful word: 'callipygian'. It means 'possessed of a pleasing bottom', 'having well-shaped buttocks'; from the Ancient Greek, *kallos* = beauty + *puge* = buttocks. The synonyms are 'bootylicious', 'bumtastic', 'callipygous' and 'rumpalicious'. (For breasts, the equivalent of 'callipygian', though not a direct equivalent, is 'bathycolpian', from the Greek adjective which means 'bosoms', 'with deep full breasts', used in the Homeric epics for the pretty Trojan ladies in lyric poetry.) 'Callipygian' is a useful word, I should imagine, when admiring a classical statue of some kind, like Michelangelo's *David* – his bottom is pleasant. But the front botty is somewhat disappointing: the world's tiniest penis.

My dear friend Charles Gardner, was callipygian. On holiday in Gozo together, one morning at the beach, I remember seeing Charles changing out of his swimming trunks and I saw his bottom. 'Oh, you *have* got a lovely bottom, Charles,' I said. And he quickly put a towel round it because he was a gentleman and he was probably rather embarrassed at my sizing him up with his trousers down. It was an extremely nice bottom though; I've never forgotten it.

I've not mooned for many decades and I rather miss it. It's a ploy I have used to dispel tension, to cheer people up, occasionally to show irritation. I've mentioned mooning at Warren Beatty but I forget in how many other film studios I've aired my nethers. A perfectly acceptable ice-breaker, it invariably causes hilarity. Would I do anything for a laugh? You know, I think I would.

Be True to Yourself

Immediately inside my front door are two vast billboards fixed to the wall. The billboards are black, the words on the one nearest the door, white: 'MIRIAM MARGOLYES ... THE INNATE WIT, THE PERFECT TIMING, THE SHINING CLARITY WITH WHICH SHE DELIVERS A COMIC LINE ... ONE OF THE MOST RESPECTED COMEDY ACTORS IN THE LAND.' (Well, everyone needs a pick-me-up from time to time.) If only this glorious praise hadn't come from the newspaper now notorious for its support for Hitler in the run-up to the Second World War. Opposite, taking up the whole wall space from floor to ceiling, is a black-and-white photograph of a beautiful young blonde woman and me, dressed as Laurel and Hardy in bowler hats, striped suits and moustaches: we are dancing joyously, our faces wreathed in broad smiles. I defy anyone to look at it without grinning. I retrieved them from the rubbish bins outside the Ambassadors Theatre in Covent Garden, after the last night of *The Killing of Sister George* in 1995. 'I'm keeping those!' I said to myself as I fished them out of the bin, hailed a taxi and took them home. They have pride of place in my hall: no one can enter the house without noticing them.

There are *not* a lot of parts for people like me. But when there are, they fit perfectly. Because lesbianism was never a criminal offence like homosexuality, we didn't have to hide, but our invisibility was corrosive. Because we couldn't show our love, we were maiden ladies who shared a flat, went to concerts together, often visiting in the evening. But there was an agreed mode of dress, of make-up, of conversation, a covert signal to the interested other of potential adventure. Even in today's more open climate, we are not on display in the same way as our male counterparts. It seems as if there are far fewer 'out' lesbians than gay men. And perhaps because of this, there are few plays that present us to the general audience – and every representation of gay women matters hugely to me. Many people say my lesbianism is strident: it should be. No woman should hide her light under a bush. (Unless, of course, it's mine.)

It was Gay Sweatshop, a short-lived crusading touring group, who were the pioneers in UK gay and lesbian theatre, and, to be honest, it was with some trepidation that I was persuaded to act in the premiere of Jill Posener's play, *Any Woman Can* at Leicester's Women's Theatre Festival in autumn 1975. I didn't want to be a lesbian to the wider world at that time. The most powerful modern sapphic union was that of Gertrude Stein and Alice B. Toklas, who were passionately together from 1904 to 1945, so when the opportunity to be Gertrude Stein was offered, I grasped it to my bosom. Both my sexual and dramatic instincts were aroused. Between 1984 and 1987, I toured America and Australia with my and Sonia Fraser's production of *Gertrude Stein and a Companion*, which Sonia re-wrote, based on an original script by Win Wells. We had premiered the play in 1984 at the Edinburgh Fringe, with Natasha Morgan playing Alice B. Toklas to my Gertrude. She was brilliant, but we didn't get on. It's fascinating how you can act the lover of someone you dislike and yet show undying passion on stage.

Frank Marcus's *The Killing of Sister George* was the first

English-language play in the West End to deal with lesbianism. June Buckridge (Beryl Reid) plays Sister George, a district nurse, in a popular BBC radio serial. She is a tweedy (read: butch) old-fashioned lesbian on the verge of alcoholism. After a drunken fracas in the studio, Mercy Croft, a BBC executive, comes to her flat to sack her. She meets June's girlfriend Childie, fancies her and eventually Childie deserts June. It's the story of a betrayal and a seduction. Beryl Reid's performance made the play famous. She took the title role not only in the original production in 1965, but also in Robert Aldrich's film, three years later. When I saw the production in 1965. I thought it was wonderful, because it succeeded in showing the pain, as well as the comedy. The process of love, whatever the sex, is many-layered; you can be gloriously happy one minute and in despair the next.

Everyone at the BBC Drama Repertory Company knew the story of Ellis Powell, the original actress playing Mrs Dale in *Mrs Dale's Diary*, the long-running radio soap opera, which had begun in 1948 and ended in 1969. I was actually in it quite often during my year with the Rep, as Miss Harvey, Dr Dale's receptionist. It was a part given to many different members of the Rep; not a scintillating role, it must be said. My most frequent line was: 'Oh, the doctor will see you now', which didn't allow for the display of a great range, but it was a successful and long-running radio serial, just like *The Archers* is today. In fact, *Mrs Dale's Diary* was its inspiration. In 1951 the BBC brought in *The Archers* to fill the gap and it's still delighting its devotees, who include Judi Dench. But what made Frank Marcus's play resonate with me was that what happened to Sister George had really happened to the original Mrs Dale, in 1963, two years before I joined the BBC Rep.

Ellis Powell, who been playing Mrs Dale since 1948, was sacked by the BBC without warning. Possibly the fact that she was a lesbian and a heavy drinker were factors. Her seven million fans who tuned in twice a day were not enough to keep her safe. She was often drunk and difficult, and one day the producers had just had enough. They sacked her with the minimum of kindness. She rapidly drank away her savings (her pitiful salary was less than £30 a week) and three months after her dismissal, she died. Her descent was shockingly rapid. In the last weeks of her life, she had worked as a demonstrator at the Ideal Home Exhibition and as a cleaner in a hotel. The world of light entertainment can be very dark.

When my chance came to act in *The Killing of Sister George*, thirty years later in 1995, I leapt at it. The role of June Buckridge had many parallels with my own life – not least that now I was a short, fat woman of a certain age, not to mention a radio actress – and a lesbian.

From the outset, I had an uneasy relationship with Mark Rayment (the director). He was a young, extremely handsome, gay man in his early thirties – and he was the boyfriend of the producer Sir Michael Codron. (Michael still owned the rights to *Sister George* and I think he wanted to give his lover a present of the production.) *Sister George* is a complicated play and I worried that he wasn't quite up to it. According to Mark, as soon as we met, I was immediately putting him through his paces. I opened with one of my favourite lines, 'Are you Jewish?' (still a favourite question today) and when Mark said, 'I'm half Jewish,' I flashed back, 'Ah, so you're only Jewish by insertion.'

We agonised over the casting of the other women in the play. Karl Sydow, the theatrical producer, had entrusted Mark to look after the American actress Bea Arthur (famous for playing Dorothy Zbornak in *The Golden Girls*) when he brought her one-woman show to London. Karl was clear: 'She's here for two weeks. She's gonna be a nightmare. You can babysit her.' Mark thought she'd be perfect for Mercy Croft, Sister George's caustic adversary at the BBC, so Codron wrote to her agent who didn't pass the letter on. When Bea found out, she wrote an apologetic postcard: 'Dear Michael Codron, In my career I have been bitchy, difficult, obnoxious and sometimes a cunt, but never rude, so please forgive me for not replying to your letter.'

Celia Imrie was the next suggestion for Mercy Croft; Michael and Mark had a lunch with her but really it was Mark's audition for Celia – not the other way round. They sat in the cavernous basement of Joe Allen's; Mark says she grilled him relentlessly. But she didn't bite. Eventually, Michael came up with Josephine Tewson, a hugely popular television star; she played Patricia Routledge/Hyacinth Bucket's neighbour in the long-running BBC TV comedy series *Keeping Up Appearances*. Jo was a pleasant, smiley person, an accomplished and experienced actress. She was quite tall and slim, with blonde, bobbed hair and an English face – rather conventional and unremarkable. But she was not right for Mercy Croft and sometimes I wondered if she'd actually *read* the play. She categorically refused to play her as a lesbian and when asked to cut her hair, said, 'I can't do that, my public wouldn't like it.' She was adamant that it remained the way it was, because she said 'her public' wouldn't recognise her as Liz, her role in the sit-com.

Now we needed to cast the romantic lead: Alice 'Childie' McNaught. I suggested Twiggy. When Michael and Mark met with her, she was sweet and lovely but said, 'No, I can't do it. Miriam frightens me. No. Miriam? No! She'll be all over me!' Eventually Michael came up with the perfect Childie: Serena Evans. Serena came from a theatrical family and I had worked with her father, Tenniel Evans, in radio. But we had never met. She was nearly twenty years younger than me, very pretty in a fresh, unsophisticated way, with long, blonde hair, big eyes and a huge smile. Our rapport was immediate, and we were set.

However, I thought it was important to get Beryl Reid's blessing. Some roles you just feel belong to a particular actress. Lady Bracknell belongs to Edith Evans, for example, and always will, even if people don't even know who Edith Evans was or have never seen her. She was a fine actress on film, the Maggie Smith and Judi Dench of her day, but it was her rendering of 'A handbag?' that made her famous. That part is still hers and anybody who plays Lady Bracknell will be compared to her just as anybody who plays Sister George will be compared to Beryl Reid. I knew that it was hers and I wanted her to know that I knew. She infused Sister George with complete reality – you believed in her absolutely.

Beryl invited me to tea at her funny little house, Honeypot Cottage, on the Thames at Wraysbury in Berkshire. It was built in 1933 right on the riverbank and has three thatched roofs each ending in a point, so they look like honey pots – painted white and very quaint, with a beautiful, English garden, full of trees and flowers and moss and pathways. We sat in her living room – chintz and couches and windows onto the garden. I was very nervous to start with and I could tell she wasn't sure about me. But we chatted and I explained I was really seeking her blessing, and came as a suppliant not as a supplanter of her success. In the end, I think she liked me and I think she understood.

There was a famous lesbian club in London called the Gateways, down some stairs in a former strip joint on the corner of King's Road and Bramerton Street in Chelsea, which features in the film. I never went there (probably too scared), but it had opened in the thirties and was the longest-running club in the world for lesbians and women bisexuals.

'I thought I'd better go and have a look, and I thought I'd better take my mother with me,' Beryl told me. 'It was quite an eye-opener because it was just girls there, and they were all snogging and holding hands. When Mummy saw one of these butch girl lesbians go by, she said, "Ooh, look, Beryl, that's a proper collar-and-tie job!" '

In those days it was stereotyped: you were either a butch lesbian, i.e., a 'collar-and-tie job', or you were the feminine one, what was called a 'femme'. Obviously, Sister George was butch; she would've been a collar-and-tie job, no question. And Childie was the femme. Whilst the famous nightclub scene in the film was shot there and some of the Gateways members were featured, it was clear from our conversation that Beryl found the whole business of lesbianism rather distasteful. She said, 'Well I didn't know anything about lesbians. It wasn't some-thing anybody talked about.' Beryl was not a lesbian, and wasn't an advocate of lesbianism in any way. I think she felt people must do what they wanted and let them get on with it, but personally she wasn't interested.

She was pleased that I had come to talk to her though. I think in her old age she felt a little overlooked. Beryl had come up through music hall and came to prominence as a comedienne playing Monica the Awful Child, a Birmingham schoolgirl, in the BBC Light programme *Educating Archie* with the ventriloquist Peter Brough. (In his day he was as famous as Michael McIntyre!) More recently, she had been outstanding as Connie Sachs, one of the old spies in the BBC adaptation of John le Carré's *Tinker, Tailor, Soldier, Spy*. But acting is an occupation with built-in insecurity. She appreciated somebody recognising her achievement; she was quite beady about it. She clearly felt that it was still her part.

With Beryl's blessing and the cast in place, we started rehearsals in early February 1995 with only three weeks before our opening night. That was a major mistake: there was not enough time. I don't think three weeks is sufficient to rehearse any play. And for one that was as complex as ours, we needed *much* more time to explore the themes, the relationships. And besides, it was a huge part. There were a hell of a lot of lines to learn.

More importantly, I wasn't happy with Mark as a director. We've talked it through since and he (such a lovely man!) admits that he really wasn't good enough. One of the issues between us was that I wanted it to be ... 'radical' is perhaps the wrong word, but *The Killing of Sister George* is a famous lesbian play. This was the 1990s and we had important choices to make about bringing a lesbian relationship to the stage. I wanted to stress the sexuality and the lesbian content a lot more, and Mark and Josephine Tewson, in particular, resisted. The word 'lesbian' is never spoken in the play: it's a period piece, it's of its era, and therefore hinted at rather than explicitly stated. There was a lot of discussion, but in the end, the decision was taken not to show any overt physical expression of affection between George and Childie. I recently watched the 1968 film, and the lesbian scene between Childie and Mercy Croft (Coral Browne) was surprisingly explicit, with naked tits, lickings and Susannah York's noisy orgasm. (I told you she was good.) In a review for the *New York Times*, Renata Adler remarked: 'Miss Browne approaches the breast with a kind of scholarly interest, like an ichthyologist finding something ambivalent that has drifted up on the beach.' I don't agree with her assessment: I think the seduction scene is quite arousing!

Thirty years later, our neutered production still generated enormous debate. I did regular 'in conversations' with the audience after the show on a Friday night, and certainly the bulk of the discussion was taken up with how the sexuality was portrayed.

And of course, *The Killing of Sister George* is the story of a love triangle: it's not just the sexual connection between Sister George and Childie, but also that between Mrs Croft and Childie. But Josephine Tewson completely resisted the idea of any lesbian activity, blatantly and stubbornly refusing to see what was as plain as the nose on her face. She said, 'Miriam, why are you going on about all this lesbian nonsense? I don't think they are lesbian at all! And anyway, I'm absolutely not going to have a lesbian kiss. My public wouldn't like that.' Josephine wanted to be a different kind of person: a BBC lady but not a lesbian predator. And Mark agreed with her, or at least he was not strong enough then to force Josephine to acknowledge what the play and her character was actually about.

It was not an easy play to perform and Josephine's obduracy made it more difficult because the slow appropriation of Childie – how, gradually, Mrs Croft cheats Sister George of both her BBC radio job and of her lover – was not properly mapped out. I was not able with Josephine to build the tense relationship that you get when you know that someone is trying to steal your girlfriend. At the end, when she suddenly 'becomes' a lesbian, as it were, it was therefore unbelievable. Serena and I didn't agree with that. And indeed, in the original 1965 production, and in the film, you knew very well that Mrs Croft was a sexual predator.

Mark reminded me of a fabulous moment when I was talking about the S&M content (when Sister George orders Childie: 'Go and eat my cigar', 'Drink my bathwater', etc.), and Jo Tewson didn't have a clue what S&M was. She thought I was talking about Marks and Spencer! 'No, Jo, S&M is when people tie each other up and they beat each other and they enjoy being horrible to each other,' I explained.

'Oh . . . really?' Jo said, disbelievingly.

And I said, 'Well you should know, you were married to Leonard Rossiter!' I had been on the Equity Council with him and had first-hand experience of what a horrible man he was.

It wasn't all struggle and strife, though. I got to do a dance in the middle of the play with Serena Evans, dressed as Laurel and Hardy; Serena as Stan, and me with a false moustache, of course, as Oliver Hardy. That was tremendous fun. Every time we rehearsed it, we collapsed with laughter. And our fourth cast member, Stella Tanner, was delightful. The fortune-teller wasn't a big role (it's not even in the film) but Stella wanted to give it her all. In the first scene when she comes in to read the cards or the crystal ball, she wanted to channel her inner medium, but Mark said, 'Stella, it's not that. It's a punchline: deliver the line, and get out. You'll have much more impact than coming in and doing Stanislavsky, darling, I promise you.'

'Oh, so I can't do anything real? OK then,' she said. There are certain things you just can't overlay too much. She was disappointed but she delivered.

Mark's memory was that a lot of the time in rehearsals was wasted. It could've been nerves, but we would sit around and I would regale everyone with stories and jokes and impressions – of the Greek fisherman asking me to suck him off and another story about a cucumber and all that – and he was constantly having to say, 'Shall we do some work now?' On top of that, during the first week of rehearsals, on 10 February 1995, my father died. He was ninety-six but I thought he would go on for ever. Daddy lived in the basement flat of my house – where I live now. He had lived with me for ten years. He never lost his Glasgow South Side accent and was a quiet, gentle soul – a truly good man. Once he came to live with me, I got nurses to look after him. I was determined he would stay at home with me and not go to a care home. The sweet nurses I found came in every eight hours. He knew them and was happy; that means a great deal to me. But strangely I have no memory of his dying during rehearsals. I do remember the nurse telephoning me in the middle of the night and explaining that he'd had a massive haemorrhage: 'I'm afraid he won't survive the night.' I went downstairs and held him. Mark remembers our chat. 'But you're Daddy's girl, you are,' he told me. I insisted that I wanted to continue rehearsing. I think I might have taken an afternoon off or a day off, but I certainly did not disappear. I said, 'No, let me just sort out the funeral arrangements,' and then I was back at work.

———

By the last Friday of rehearsals, I was still struggling to find Sister George and I kept asking Mark for direction – 'I don't know this woman, and I'm not in her shoes yet.' I remembered how Beryl Reid always started to find a character – with the shoes. When I came back on the Saturday morning, I'd somehow found her. I was wearing a tight skirt suit and I had scraped my hair back and glued it down. I got out of my car and slammed the door and I said, 'Now she's fucking ready! Come on!' I had found this ballistic energy I needed and then I went into the theatre and did the final run-through.

Our opening night was 28 February at the Yvonne Arnaud Theatre, Guildford, a proper West End launching pad. I was still so worried that I asked Michael Codron to my dressing room and I said, 'I really don't think that Mark is up to this. I would like you to get another director or to get someone in to back him up.' He looked at me and said, 'I love Mark and my relationship is more important than your play.'

Unfortunately, Mark walked in on us in the middle of that conversation. As he opened the door, he heard Michael's final words: 'And that's dangerous talk, Miriam, and I won't have any more of it.'

I don't remember anything about the performance in Guildford except the very last word. The light focuses tightly on Sister George's face. She looks out into the audience and says 'Moo', like a cow. It embodies the loss that she'd experienced of her love, her job, and all her pleasure in life. The traditional theatre superstition is that you never say the tag line (the last line) till the opening night. In rehearsal I said, 'I'm not going to say it. It's unlucky in the run-throughs. I'm not going to say the last word.' Michael snorted in derision, 'It's such a fucking stupid superstition.' And it is a superstition. I can't remember how I did it that first night, but I got it right. People were sobbing and laughing at the same time.

When, after Guildford, we went to Richmond, I grumpily said, 'We're just doing a tour of fucking Surrey!' but then we went on to Bath, Norwich, Canterbury and Brighton. When we discussed it recently, Mark told me that his issue was always trying to get a consistency of performance out of me. I never liked saying a line the same way twice and that made him jumpy. Josephine Tewson had done a lot of TV, and so she came with the lines learned down pat. And I wasn't like that at all. Because, for me, it was more than just delivering the lines, because then there's no room to play, is there? There's no room to create and find things. Every audience is different, each night you should be aware of the difference, while keeping rigidly to the text. I think I was searching constantly, improvising and trying to find ways of doing it. But for my colleagues, it must have been rather like work-ing with an alternative comedian – very disconcerting. In terms of performance, each night was good, but it was because a particular scene worked, but then the next night it was another – unpredictable. I wasn't consistent. And I suppose I drove them fucking nuts because Josephine and the other ladies would come to him and complain, 'We had it last night but tonight it's different.'

By the time we got to Norwich, I was truly fed up. Mark was going to do a notes session and I tore into him an hour before curtain-up. 'This isn't working,' I said, and, 'That's not good enough,' and, 'You should've done this,' and, 'I don't like that.' It was like lancing the boil. I got it all out, and we agreed that this would happen or that would change, and so forth. I think we both said things we wanted to say: we cleared the air and then we were friends again. The others were wait-ing nervously for us on stage, and as we got to the wings, I said, 'Now I'm going to scream at you and you're going to scream back so when we walk on, they'll think we're having a fight.' So, I walked on, yelling backwards over my shoulder 'And you're a fucking cunt!' but when mild-mannered Mark shrieked back, 'So are you!' they all fell about laughing because they knew it wasn't real.

After this short tour of the regions, Codron had planned a transfer to the Ambassadors Theatre, London. I didn't think it was good enough. I thought we would get crucified and I was terribly worried about it. Really terrified. The last stop on our short tour before transferring to the West End, was five nights at the Theatre Royal Brighton, so I asked Simon Callow to critique our performance for me. I didn't tell Mark. I don't think I told anybody because one really shouldn't do that. It's not etiquette to get another actor or director to critique a production. Simon was horribly busy, but he came incognito to a matinee. He said, 'You must show the love that is between you and Childie. It's crucial that that is clear to the audience.' That gave me the confidence to feel that there was a performance there, that it existed. And when Simon saw it again in London, he said, 'I know that that's what you had done.'

We opened at the Ambassadors Theatre on 26 April 1995. On the first night, Mark said, 'Let's all get together at five o'clock and we'll just have a little cup of tea and a chat.' We'd had this big build-up, because there'd been considerable press interest, and we knew many big stars in the business were coming; I think he thought it would alleviate our first-night nerves. We gathered on the set giving each other first-night presents and Mark was behaving like Father Christmas, and I exploded, 'I fucking hate this. I loathe Christmas. I just want to go to my dressing room.' But then Mark gave us Peter Hall's note: 'You know the play. You know the lines. Now just go out and be arrogant with it.'

Joan Collins came that first night and the next day there was a picture of us together on the front page of the *Evening Standard*. And we got amazing reviews. You'd walk up to the theatre and see the billboards outside the entrance: '5-STAR PRODUCTION' and 'MIRIAM MARGOLYES TRANSCENDS' and 'WHAT A GEM'. Despite our good reviews, I think Michael lost money. Eight weeks later, the run ended. We did our last performance on 24 June 1995, and, as I told you, when they tore the billboards down and all the rubbish was put out in the dustbins I fished those two billboards out and had them framed.

The truth is, I wanted those billboards not for the review, but because of Serena. A good play is like a spell and the words are the incantation. I loved Heather, and Serena loved her husband, but every night on that stage we fell in love with each other and were torn apart afresh. We had a deep, close relationship. Often, we would eat together after the show and just talk about everything and nothing – and we really did laugh a lot. But when the show ended, she said, 'I don't think we can continue in the same sort of way.' She was right, of course, but I still had to take a deep breath before I replied. Even now it remains one of those friendships where as soon as we talk, however long it's been, it's as if no time has passed at all. And there up on my wall, we are caught in one bright, perpetual moment of happiness, kicking up our heels and dancing together.

Always Be a Cunt

The clitoris is pure in purpose. The only organ in the body designed purely for pleasure, the clitoris is simply a bundle of nerves: 8,000 nerve fibres, to be precise. That's a higher concentration of nerve fibres than anywhere else in the male or female body, including the fingertips, lips, and tongue, and it is twice, twice, twice the number as found in the penis. Who needs a handgun when you've got a semi-automatic?[*]

Forty years after I dressed as an enormous vulva at Edinburgh, I finally got to voice one. *The Vagina Monologues* is an American play by Eve Ensler where various women talk about their vaginas and various orgasms and, speech by speech and story by story, it all builds up to a huge overwhelming climax. I was in a production in 2001 with Siân Phillips and Sophie Dahl at the Arts Theatre. They both towered over me. Sophie was still buxom at that time and truly beautiful, with creamy skin, long blonde hair and huge blue eyes. We had long honest conversations about our lives. Sophie talked wryly about her tough childhood, moving seventeen times by the time she was nineteen. 'All I wanted was a stable life but whenever I told Mum that she used to say, "All right then, we'll get you a stable." It became a sort of family joke.' Every evening, Mick Jagger would pick her up at the stage door,

---

[*] Natalie Anglier, *Woman: An Intimate Geography.*

looking like a debauched fifty-eight-year-old angel in tight jeans, his face perpetually grumpy. Clearly far from his only entanglement, Sophie was a former friend of his daughters Elizabeth and Jade, who were furious about the relationship. I'd never had much time for Mick Jagger but Sophie loved him so desperately that Siân and I worried about her. She may have been voicing a vagina in the production but if anything, he was the cunt. He was always so smug and a smug cunt is such a turn-off.

I love words and the word 'cunt' is the linguistic equivalent of opening a bottle of smelling salts. A cunt is a powerful and beautiful thing. And of course, they're all different. The world is full of representations of the vagina, from the large open lilies in the paintings of Georgia O'Keeffe, to my favourite morning feast of a vulva-shaped smoked salmon roll from Gail's – a tempting moist pink. (Moistness is always so important.)

I've seen a few cunts in my lesbian life; less so now, of course, but I remember them well. One girl had labia which hung down a good two inches below her clitoris – and then another had a clitoris which hung down a good two inches below her labia. Memories, memories! But I digress . . .!

While for Grandma Margolyes in Glasgow, nothing below the waist was acknowledged, that wasn't true for Mummy. In our family, sex education may not have been broached, but there was no body shame nor secrecy. Mummy acknowledged that there *was* somewhere below the waist. She didn't visit it often, but it was there. And, of course, I was in touch with what Mummy looked like naked because she did her housework in the nude. She was too fat to stand on a chair to dust the lampshades; I'm grateful for that. But her ballet training stood her in good stead for our upright Hoover. Our various au pairs were initially shocked but soon took her in their stride.

I remember that one day when I was about fifteen or sixteen, she said to me, 'Last night Daddy and I made love.' She said it with pleasure, just the fact of something nice. It was one of our usual morning chats, nestling in her bed after Daddy had gone to surgery. And then she told me that his penis was small. She really did tell me *everything*. I got the distinct impression she was glad it was small. And I never questioned it. I didn't think, 'I shouldn't know that,' or 'Why are you telling me this?' I never questioned anything that Mummy said or did, ever. She was just the Authority. And I wasn't embarrassed by her telling me. I hope you're not.

The details of sex were not explained, but its dangers were made clear right from the start. Mummy shared with me the pain she had to go through to give birth. She had to have an episiotomy: a surgical incision made necessary because my head was too big to emerge unaided. Although I never wanted to have children, the thought of this sent tremors of horror through my own tender young vagina. It's quite unfair that a penis is meant to be large for maximum effect and a vagina must be tiny. 'She has a cunt like a cathedral' was a common term of abuse when I was at Cambridge. You will never hear that from me. For me, a cunt *is* a cathedral.

While open about her body, Mummy was quite prudish in certain areas. Her only mention of 'down there' was, 'Keep it clean.' As I said, we never had that talk about the birds and the bees in our house. And it was actually our maid, Mrs Baker, who gave me clear instructions when I was about ten years old as to how to wipe my bottom. She felt I wasn't giving enough attention to that essential task.

The only people who go up your cunt are lovers and doctors; it's not a free-for-all amusement park. The techniques they employ are very different, mostly in the area of speed. Lovers tend to be slow and foreplay is important. But we don't want foreplay from our doctors – quite the reverse! Mr Studd, my aptly named first gynaecologist, was both matter-of-fact and friendly. He liked women and treated us with skill and humour. I never asked him about his attitude to clitorises (is that the correct plural?). But my word, he must have seen a few. The problem was, if I had a discharge, I didn't want him to see it, just to treat it. So, we talked more than he looked. But he always lubed with care and went in slowly. It's a habit I would recommend to all.

My first orgasm was when I was eight years old. I was passionately in love with Miss Chase, our form teacher in the Lower Second. One day, walking past her house in Banbury Road with my mother, it happened. I felt a hugely pleasurable heat slowly building in my loins until it was overpowering, leaving me drained, spent. My cunt flooded with juice, just at the thought of her. Just being near her was enough. Afterwards, I was always fascinated by sex. It seemed strange to have such a powerful feeling that went all through your body. When I saw Heather for the first time, I knew. I don't know how I knew. You look at someone, your groin shifts a bit and you think, 'I FANCY YOU.' Heather didn't go home that first night – in fact we didn't get out of bed for a week. Our cunts intertwingled continuously, and it was wonderful. Then after a while, I listened to what she had to say and I loved her mind too – and I still do.

I've always enjoyed talking about sex. Jay Rayner told me how as a young child, he had listened to me holding forth, agog.

'You see the thing is, Claire, we lesbians use our hands a lot in bed,' I explained to his agony aunt mother, who knew anyway – she was a trained nurse. 'You can't just grind cunt on cunt for ever.' (I trust Jay appreciated the insight.)

I don't really want that kind of sex any more. I'm thrilled when people find love and joy in each other's cunts. But hell! I'm eighty-two, I need to be a little bit quieter in that department. Many would agree.

Be Kind

Orpheus Descending in 1988 was the second time I worked with Vanessa Redgrave; her tall rangy figure, her bright eyes all just the same. As before, her politics, shared endlessly with the cast, drove some of them crazy. A convinced socialist and Trotskyite, Vanessa could and did bore the knickers off you talking about it. (And I say this as a believer, a former paid-up member of the Workers' Revolutionary Party.) But though politically humourless, Vanessa loves to laugh, even at herself, and is a fantastic cook. And there is a side to her which is magical. One day in our Chelsea rehearsal room, there was a fire burning inside her. It was the single most extraordinary piece of acting I've ever seen. It happens occasionally, and you hope that it will happen in front of an audience, but in fact, this was just in front of the company in Chelsea Old Church that afternoon. 'I'm seeing a unique artist at the very top of her powers, and I'm so lucky to be working with her,' I thought.

Orpheus Descending, by Tennessee Williams, is set in the Deep South. A charismatic young singer, Val (the Orpheus of the title), comes to town, bristling with sexuality. All the women (including me, the near-blind wife of the town sheriff, who spends her days having intense Christian visions) fall for him. It gave me plenty of dramatic possibilities which I seized delightedly: 'I saw the eyes of my Saviour! – They struck me blind. (*Leans forward, clasping her eyes in anguish.*) Ohhhh, they burned out my eyes! [. . .] And there in the split open sky.

I saw, I tell you, I *saw* the TWO HUGE BLAZING EYES OF JESUS CHRIST RISEN!' Mummy would have loved it.

Vanessa played the lead and was so spectacular that I fell more and more for her as the production went on. I didn't lust after her. It wasn't like that. It was a schoolgirl crush – I was 'cracked' on her just like being back at Oxford High School. By the last night, I *had* to say something. I couldn't let the production end without letting her know. Just after the final curtain call, as we were all going off stage together, I blurted it out: 'You know I've fallen in love with you, Vanessa?'

She stopped dead, looked intently into my eyes and smiled sweetly and very tenderly at me. And then she said, 'But why did you wait till the last night to tell me?'

I've recently learned a new word – 'ghosting'. It means refusing to confront or even acknowledge a person and the uncomfortable situation that accompanies them. I've never done it and to me it seems utter cruelty. The opposite of kindness. Vanessa's full acknowledgement of what I'd said turned what could have been a moment of mortification into almost a benediction. I loved her all the more for her immense kindness, her softness and tact. That's the way to do it.

Then Be Kinder

It was the light that I remember most. The light and the space, the brightness of the sky, the real heat of the sun. Bondi was where I wanted to go first and it was just as I imagined: this stretch of pleasure, with the sea and the people surfing. Australia's a very active place. It's a place where people are physical. They are running, jumping, triathlon-ing and every activity that you can name. I do *nothing*. I am the most physically inactive person I know. I regret it because there is joy in physical movement. But there is also joy in simply watching other people's physical movement.

There was also the weather, the laid-back people, the sense that everybody's on holiday. I know that, of course, they do work hard as well, but there is just a general sense that the Australian world wears shorts. There are lots of tables outside restaurants. It's a lifestyle. In the Britain I knew we didn't have lifestyles. We were too busy just making a living and existing. When I first came to Australia in 1980, I thought, 'I've got to have a piece of this.'

It's a wonderful country and it has a laid-back, amused air about it. The people are different from the English. They seem less weighed down somehow, more light-hearted generally. They're not *un*serious. It's almost as if the wide skies and the weather make everybody a bit more relaxed. But there is a shadow. The treatment of the First Nation people (at the time referred to as Aboriginal) has been appalling. When I first went there, it was not talked about. I can remember once in Alice Springs, there were these drunken, burnt-out figures, lying in the street, and my friends just stepped over them – physically and mentally. They simply didn't *see* them. I challenged the people I was staying with and they said, 'Ah, now look, you don't understand, Miriam, because you don't live here, but they're just unemployable. It's awfully sad, I know, but you can't do anything with them. They drink and you know you just have to let them get on as best they can and leave 'em alone. They're filling up the prisons and they're not educated. It's really an awful thing, but there's nothing we can do.'

I became an Australian citizen on 26 January 2013 – Australia Day. Now I really was an immigrant, just like my great-grandparents had been two hundred years ago in Britain. But *everybody* in Australia had come from somewhere else, except the First Nation people. They alone had always been Australian; for 50,000 years they have peopled the continent, enjoyed their own rich culture and adhered to their beliefs and practices. When the First Fleet led by Captain Arthur Phillip landed in Botany Bay in 1788, there were 250 distinct languages and 800 dialects. Since then, over 100 have been lost.

The relationship of the First Nation to subsequent Australians has been unhappy. Between 1788 and 1900, genocide, the introduction of European diseases, dispossession, subjugation and segregation reduced the Indigenous population by 90 per cent. From 1901 until 1972, White Australia was the official policy for immigration. Between 1910 and 1969, over 100,000 Aboriginal children were forcibly removed from their families. It's a miserable record and the damage it's done to the country is far-reaching and desperately sad. But now there is a really powerful shift and Australians are realising you cannot treat others like that. It can't be allowed. The fate of the First Nation people is the big stain on Australia. It is where suddenly all the sweetness and friendliness and mate-ship is turned off and what is left is a poverty-stricken, miserable rabble that nobody takes any notice of or has respect for. They have a culture far older than ours; we need to learn more about it and remember that they *were* the First Nation *long* before we all turned up. A healthy society is an inclusive society. I remember the farmer in the Outback who said to me, 'Australia is the most racist country in the world.' I said, 'Would you say that on camera?' He said, 'Ah, yeah. You bet I will.' And he did.

I wanted to see the parts of Australia that I didn't know and so I set out to travel 10,000 kilometres across Australia in a camper van with a camera crew. They chanced on the idea for my mode of transport because just before we filmed the programmes, I'd performed Alan Bennett's *The Lady in the Van* in Australia, so I was getting in and out of a van on stage every night. Since then, various documentary producers have stuck me in vans of all shapes and sizes . . . However, when I was actually on the road in that first documentary, getting in and out of a *real* van was an entirely different matter.

I was passing through vast and empty landscapes. No people. Just miles and endless miles of road. It was a different kind of driving than I'd ever known. You didn't have to think about other cars because there weren't any. Australia in the Outback is another continent. I was humbled by it. That desert. My idea of beauty had always been the

Renaissance one, I suppose, which is why I love Italy so much, but on this journey across Australia, I was having to appreciate a new kind of beauty. You know that you have crossed the world. There is no doubt about that.

I hadn't realised what a gap there was between rich and poor. That really surprised me. And I hadn't realised how aggressively the property developers were proceeding. It's a country where robber bandits have been allowed to flourish. I was also shocked by the illiteracy. Fifty per cent of Tasmanians are illiterate because no money has been spent on the education system. So large numbers of people leave school not able to read and write properly. What else surprised me? The rise of the right wing and the power of the Catholic Church and the religious right, for example. It is mirroring America now very much and, cushioned in my liberal bubble, I hadn't been aware of that before. Australia's treatment of immigrants and asylum seekers is brutal. Britain got the idea of Rwanda from Australia's similar use of Nauru Island. It uncomfortably reminds me of the Jews in Israel: finding a wonderful new place on the other side of the world and then stopping anyone else from coming.

A young man called Moj Rezai appeared in my first Australian documentary. His parents and five brothers died in the Afghan war and in 2010, when he was a young boy, he came to Australia. It was a long and traumatic journey by boat. He very nearly drowned and still suffers from PTSD. He doesn't know exactly how old he is but he was probably only eleven or twelve when he arrived in Australia and was granted a Temporary Protection Visa. Somehow the St Vincent de Paul Society took him on and when I met him he was working as a volunteer in one of their charity shops in Melbourne. We went into the back room of the shop and we talked, surrounded by smelly old clothes and tchotchkes and discarded furniture and the detritus of people's lives. And here was this piece of human flotsam and jetsam that had been washed up on the beach in Australia telling me about his life. His story was one of such courage and determination that as it unfolded, I wept.

Moj is somebody that Australia should be proud of. But he's been in limbo now for twelve years, waiting for a decision. He so desperately wants to be Australian. It is, for him, the culmination of a real dream of safety. But because of their barbaric law which says that nobody who's come on a boat to Australia will ever be granted citizenship, he will never have that security of being considered a national. After all this time and uncertainty, he suffers from intense depression; his life hangs on a thread. There are probably about 10,000 people in Australia who are in the same situation.

The word 'migrant' has a pejorative taint about it. It shouldn't. When I was young, migrants were refugees, they were fleeing from terrible things. That's why people want to come to Australia, to the United States and the UK and to other countries in Europe. They're fleeing terrible things. I want just a bit more kindness. If you see the humanity in the other person, then you can open your heart to them. And it isn't done enough.

My family came from another place to this country, and I don't think you ever forget that. My own life experience has shown me how uncomfortable it is to be the Other – the fat, old, disabled, lesbian Jew is the picture I have of myself, because I think it's the picture I'm shown by the wider world. But I've tried to step outside the box that was made for me. I've tried always to be the 'me' that I liked and enjoyed being. I see myself as friendly, unthreatening, chatty, naturally intelligent but not brainy, loving a laugh, wanting company. And my travelling has taught me that if you present yourself the way you are, and don't pretend to be something else, people of all sorts accept you and behave in a similar way. I may look different, I may sound different, but if you prick me, do I not bleed?

Bring Me Sunshine

Sometimes people say, 'You ought to be a Dame.' My response is, 'Darling, I don't think I'm good enough.' Of course, I would have loved to be Damed – and I must confess to a squidge of rage when I see that this, that or the other person has been made one – and I haven't. It's obvious who the Great Dames are – they most definitely deserve their honour. Others, however, while undoubtedly talented actresses, less so. But if you think I'm going to name them, you're wrong! *You* name them – leave me out of it.

I take comfort in the thought that I've done some good work. I have the pleasure of knowing that I've enlarged people's imaginations and entertained them. And that, most importantly, I've made them laugh. I may build big, but I want always to build true.

I like to think of myself as a proper actress but I am perhaps most recognised for my more anarchic roles. Take *Blackadder*, in which I played the libidinous Spanish Infanta, the munificent Queen Victoria, and the deranged Puritan Lady Whiteadder. (To the *Blackadder* writers I was always more than a Dame, bless them.) It was delightful to work with a willowy Tim McInnerny, rubber-faced Rowan Atkinson and sardonic Stephen Fry. They were so much nicer than the Footlights boys I knew. I never minded this lot squeezing my tits, and they seemed to enjoy my bashing them with a turnip. I was so immersed in my part booming away, that the good slaps I gave Rowan while barking 'Wicked child!' nearly knocked him over. Later I found out that my wallops had actually made his eyes water, while a corpsing Tony Robinson looked seconds away from hysteria. But he held it together (just): no wonder he ended up as President of Equity.

Me: Edmund, I trust you have invited no other guests.
Rowan: Certainly not.
Me: Good. For where there are other guests, there are people to fornicate with.

They made me realise that comedy wasn't necessarily competitive, it could just be fun. Overacting becomes a positive pleasure when everyone else is doing it.

We filmed in the BBC television rehearsal rooms in Acton; a seven-storey brutalist concrete block known ironically as the 'Acton Hilton', but much loved. On any given day, the building contained the gamut of British light entertainment. It was showbusiness cheek-by-jowl in all its glory. There was an air of palpable excitement. You never knew who you were going to meet. You would be in the canteen on the top floor having a croissant next to John Gielgud on one side and Norman Wisdom on the other. I was gobsmacked with excitement at meeting Morecambe and Wise in the lift. They were just as twinkly and kind in the flesh. They seemed to know who I was, which was more than I did at the time. They deserved their place as the kings of Light Ent. Everyone queued up to be a guest on their show. Who will ever forget the legs of Angela Rippon as she high-kicked up from her news desk and danced with them? Even forty years later, whenever I run into Angela on *Loose Women* or somewhere, I'm longing for her to give me a twirl.

Around the same time as *Blackadder*, I worked on *A Kick Up the Eighties*, a lesser-known but clever BBC comedy sketch show. It was the brainchild of a young producer, Colin Gilbert. The cast was me, Tracey Ullman, Rik Mayall (I knew he was brilliant; I just couldn't work out why!), Richard Stilgoe, Ron Bain, Roger Sloman and, in the second series, Robbie Coltrane. Robbie was complicated but brilliant. He had quite a sour, angry take on the world in many ways. I think that's what gave his acting a remarkable depth and power. Of course, he was funny, but he made you laugh on both sides of your face, so to speak, because he saw the pain of life as well.*

We were all away from home and spent a lot of time together. I remember laughing a lot. Robbie was as good at accents as I am. He wasn't working-class. He came from quite a middle-class background in Rutherglen outside Glasgow. His father was a doctor, as was mine. He had a rollicking, expansive spirit, which made you want to be with him and bask in his warmth and in his appreciation of life and food and drink and sex. He relished other people's talent. He was roguish and daring, lusty and occasionally belligerent and very greedy. He laughed a lot and enjoyed laughing. He was the sort of person I would have liked to have been had I been a man.

I shared a flat with Tracey Ullman, who was lovely then, but had rather less time for me years later when she was the eponymous star of *The Tracey Ullman Show* and I came out to try my luck in Hollywood. She was probably very busy but I feared that she saw me as a hanger-on, angling to get into her very successful show.

----

* As do I. How can one not? The world is in a parlous state.

But in Glasgow, in the beginning, it was tremendous fun; I remember being cast as a down-and-out tramp in one sketch and our wardrobe mistress, who had a dry sense of humour, quietly remarking, 'Oh that'll be your own clothes then, Miriam.' (Cheek!)

Working with Tracey was a lesson in professionalism. Even then, at the beginning of her career, she knew how to present a song and had a powerful voice and the gift of mimicry. Our Toyah Willcox Masterclass (check it out on YouTube) has both of us in bobbed blonde wigs and short studded dresses made out of bin bags, as she tries to teach me how to dance robotically. We are both jumping up and down, lisping out the lines of the song. Her impression is spot-on, mine ridiculously terrible. Mind you, I had no idea who Toyah Willcox was at the time, and I end up wailing: 'Oh, it's no good. I'll never be as bad as you.'

In 2006 I was a guest at the *Evening Standard* Theatre Awards. We were in a vast ballroom, at the Savoy I think, Joan Collins, Maggie Smith and Sir Peter Hall – all of us seated at our various crisp-white-linen-tablecloth-bedecked tables – and then in the middle of the award ceremony, a power cut suddenly plunged the room into complete darkness. The microphones stuttered and failed; Ned Sherrin, the awards presenter, was left floundering on the podium and there was a long universal groan and then a miserable silence. After a couple of moments, a few people started fishing out cigarette lighters and others turned on their mobile-phone torches, which provided a certain amount of flickering light. It was clear that the award ceremony itself had ground to a desperate halt. After five or ten minutes of general chaos, I noticed people getting up, clearly thinking, 'Oh, sod that! This is going take hours to fix.' And they started to drift out.

I felt such a pang for the people who were waiting there to find out if they had won an award. Being shortlisted is the culmination of a year's hard work. It's an important moment in any actor's or producer's or director's or writer's life. It was unfair that a faulty fuse box should deprive them of the joy.

'What can be done?' I thought. And then the answer struck me: 'Well, the only thing *I* can do is get up on that stage and tell a few jokes and hope that they last long enough.' No one else was doing anything. I was the self-elected cavalry and with incredible chutzpah, I climbed onto the stage and boomed, 'BE QUIET.' And as I know how to project my voice, even though the microphones weren't working, I was able to get people's attention.

'Look, you can see there's been a malfunction of the electricity system. Everything is going to be working again soon. In the meantime, would it be all right if I told a few Jewish jokes?' When everybody clapped and shouted 'Yes!', I felt that I'd been given permission to go ahead. I said, 'Well, I only know two that I really like.' And changing my accent to New York Jewish – that's essential – off I went.

The first one was about two old Jewish men: Morrie and Abie. Every week, they would meet at one or the other's house and find out what had been going on in each other's lives. So, this week, Abie totters into Morrie's house, sits down, Morrie's wife brings him a lemon tea with two lumps of sugar, the same for Abie. And Morrie says, 'Abie, have I got something to tell *you.*'

'So tell me!' said Abie.

Morrie says, 'Well, you know how me and the wife always like to go to a nice restaurant? Something a little different, you know, not every night, but from time to time? And this week, oy! Did we strike lucky.'

'So tell me,' Abie said.

'Well, we go into this beautiful restaurant. Pleasant lighting, lovely ambience, not too noisy, comfy seats. The waiter comes up, he gives me the menu. Oy! Such a menu! It was delicious. A bit of chopped liver on the side with rye. Then a little chicken soup with matzah balls, of course. Then something a little different: I had spinach. I never have spinach, but they say spinach is good for you, so I had spinach. Then there was the beef brisket, and then we had the carrots, roast potatoes, peas, a little side of baked aubergine . . .' And he goes through the whole meal with Abie, listing every side dish and the entire contents of the dessert trolley.

Abie says, 'Nice, nice, very nice.'

And Morrie said, 'I was so happy, I was satisfied and you know what, it was reasonable – not too expensive. The price was right, the food was good. Amazing! Where do you find such a thing?'

Abie says, 'Exactly, Morrie. Where *do* you find such a thing? What's the name of the restaurant? You sit here telling me all about the food you ate. What's the name of the restaurant? Don't keep it to yourself like that? Tell me.'

Morrie says, 'Of course I'll tell you! What do you think? We're friends for fifty years and I'm not gonna tell you the name of the restaurant?' There was a pause and he said, 'The name of the restaurant is . . . Oh my God. *What is it?* What's the name? Wait a second. Aha! I got it. There's a flower, comes in all colours, beautiful perfume, but you gotta be careful, it's got thorns on it. What d'ye call it, that flower?'

'Oh,' says Abie. 'You mean, like a rose?'

'That's it,' says Morrie. 'Rose. ROSE! *What's the name of the restaurant?*'

The second joke is about a Jewish grandmother.

Grandma Ruthie is a typical New York Jewish grandmother. Every week, she takes her grandson Sheldon to the beach at Coney Island. It is the high point of their week. They sit on the beach, have a picnic and talk to each other – a precious moment in both of their lives. So, this day, they're at the beach. It's a wonderful spot, a glorious clear sunny day, not a cloud in the brilliant blue sky: no rocks, beautiful golden sand and sparkling green sea. She's sitting on a blanket with the picnic she's lovingly prepared. And little Sheldon is playing close to the waves. She's always looking to make sure he's safe, to see the chubby little figure toddling across the sands and paddling in the shallow sea. And when she looks up, she sees that whereas it *had* been a lovely sunny day, now it was turning blustery. And ominous dark clouds were forming rather quickly. The sea was getting a little wild and the wind was coming up. A storm was building. And then in the distance, and suddenly not in the distance, but frighteningly close, a huge wave comes rolling and rumbling towards the shore . . . and snatches the little boy, her precious darling Sheldon, and hurls him out to sea.

Grandma Ruthie was desperate. She ran from one end of the beach to the other, crying, 'My grandson! My grandson! Sheldon! Sheldon! Help me, help me! Help me, please! He's drowning in the sea!' But Sheldon had vanished into the violent churning depths. And then she fell on her knees and called out to God. She raised her hands to the Almighty and she beseeched, 'Please, Lord. Don't take him away from me. All my life I keep all the Commandments. I keep a kosher house,

I light the candles every Shabbos, I fast Yom Kippur. I do everything you ask of me, God. Now, down on my knees I am begging you, PLEASE, bring back Sheldon to me!'

And amazingly, the sea calmed, the wind died down, the clouds seemed to disappear. The sun came out and in the distance, another wave came forward, gentler, gentler. And slowly but surely, she sees little Sheldon, her beloved grandson, being borne on the crest of a wave in towards the shore. And finally, he was gently dumped at her feet. Grandma Ruthie fell on her knees again, raised her hands to the skies, and called out to the Almighty, 'HE HAD A HAT!!!'

It brought down the house. As Dickens said, 'There is nothing in the world so irresistibly contagious as laughter and good humour.' It was like being a stand-up comedian and I loved it – *and*, most importantly, I had rescued the *Evening Standard* Awards from the brink of disaster.

The woman who was overseeing the event was eternally grateful. Ever afterwards she made sure that I was invited. Until in 2009, that is, when the newspaper was sold to the Russian businessman Alexander Lebedev. Since then, I've never been invited again. But I think I had the best of it – in fact, I think my generation did in every way. We had comedy geniuses like Kenneth Williams: 'Infamy, infamy, they've all got it in for me . . .' Ken and I had a lovely time doing jokes on the radio together, falling about whilst our voices stayed serenely RP, without a quiver. Comedy felt simpler in those days.

I loved watching *Dad's Army*, which was, to my mind, the greatest television comedy series ever made. It showed a sweeter England, though one strangely empty of women. I'm going against my feminist instincts by loving it, but it still makes me laugh. In Captain

Mainwaring, Arthur Lowe gave eternal life to a unique, archetypal comic character. But like many great comedians, he was an odd fellow – I didn't know Arthur Lowe, but I share this story. He lovingly restored a steam yacht called *Amazon*, an elegant vessel built in 1885, and used it as his floating hotel when on location. One day he invited an actress in the cast (who told me this story) to stay on *Amazon* with him and his wife: 'It's very comfortable, you'll enjoy it,' he said. Delightedly, she accepted his invitation. She did indeed have a lovely time, but on her last morning at breakfast she found the bill under her saucer! Perhaps Mr Lowe was simply erring on the side of caution; every gravy-train dries up eventually, particularly in comedy, and he may have been saving for that inevitable rainy day.

Comedy is nerve-racking; I believe most comedians would agree. However famous or realised their life and career, we can't help feeling insecure. It goes with the territory; we think, 'I haven't got that right yet, I've got a long way to go.' It's a statement of colossal impudence to expect people to pay money to watch you. I have a horror of short-changing people. And of course, if you're a failure – if people don't laugh, and if your jokes fall flat – you know RIGHT AWAY. Past success means nothing. So, I have always tried to take a deep breath, gird my loins (whatever that may mean), and step up to the plate (whatever *that* may mean). And then, I just do my best and try to be kind, generous *and* entertaining. To quote Mark Twain: 'The human race has only one really effective weapon and that is laughter.' Admittedly I never found him very funny.

These days I don't follow comedy scripts any more, I extemporise, mainly due to the aforementioned phenomenon known as Cameo. The video requests are often for birthday messages, or for Christmas or wedding anniversaries. They can be a get-well message or something the Americans brought in called 'roasting', which means being deliberately rude to the person selected. Occasionally, I am requested to give someone a pep talk or wish a cancer sufferer better. That is very tough, but I take it seriously and try to offer comfort, give good advice and be real – it seems we are all desperate for authenticity, probably because we are constantly being lied to and made fools of by a corrupt, incompetent government. I only hope my genuine desire to make people happy, to comfort them in distress and always tell the truth, comes across. Making people laugh is a Good Thing. If I swear, curse or expose my bottom or breasts, what harm am I doing? It's a grim enough world, let's be kind to one another, and to hell with the cunts who try to deceive and mislead us.

I Won't Have It!

I took part recently in a *Guardian* Q&A. I particularly liked this question: Who are the top five biggest bellends in the world?

I had to look up 'bellend' – what a happy discovery: I like the word – it has a visual element I appreciate. The people I loathe most in the world are Vladimir Putin, Nigel Farage, Boris Johnson, David Cameron and Benjamin Netanyahu.

———

From the earliest time, I have said what I think. It is imperative to make clear where I stand, to affirm what I believe in, what I support and what I reject. Age has not altered that. I doubt I shall stop now – it's who I am and how I live my life. I only regret my outspokenness on discovering I've upset or offended someone: I hate being unkind. When I see something or someone doing wrong, I *have* to speak up. When I need a loud voice, I use it. As Richard E. Grant once remarked about me (I hope, fondly), 'I think her volume button fell off at birth.' Even aged eight I argued keenly against all perceived injustice, whether it was having to finish a full serving of tapioca, my most detested pudding; shake hands with the playground adversary who had plainly cheated; or the preposterous notion that 'children should be seen and not heard'.

When I was about twelve, I went for a walk after school with my friend Barbara Geach. Her mother was Elizabeth Anscombe, a renowned follower of Wittgenstein and a brilliant philosopher, but a hopeless housekeeper and mother. She couldn't look after her seven children, so Barbara had to do it. Despite her valiant efforts, their home in St John's Street, Oxford, was a twentieth-century version of Mrs Jellaby's in *Bleak House*. Mind you, I never said that to her. And I kept all thoughts about 'telescopic philanthropy' to myself. But that day, as we walked near Oxford station, deep in conversation about the object of my latest 'crack', I noticed ahead a factory chimney stack, from which was billowing dense clouds of black smoke. Only the year before, the Great Smog had claimed 4,000 lives in London alone, due to similar inner-city pollution. Had they learned nothing?

Appalled, I marched across a yard and right into the factory, dragging poor Barbara in tow.

Once in the office, I said crisply to the receptionist, 'I would like to speak to the managing director please.'

The receptionist asked why.

'I need to speak to him about the smoke belching out of the chimney and I need to speak to him NOW!' Thanks to elocution lessons, my voice carried and someone speedily came to fetch the pair of us, standing there in our school uniforms, Barbara now looking rather worried. She hadn't expected things to go this far.

The secretary led us into the managing director's office and I began.

'I'VE COME TO COMPLAIN ABOUT THE DIRTY SMOKE POURING OUT OF YOUR CHIMNEY. This is disgraceful. You are poisoning the atmosphere. It's all very well having a factory, but there are responsibilities. You've got to be aware of your duties and not contaminate the town and the people around you.'

He clearly didn't have a clue what to say to this bumptious, self-confident teenager and looked at me blankly. I didn't know it at the time but I was part of an army, and this was my first assault against capitalism's careless destruction. Later that year, Sir Anthony Eden's government passed the Clean Air Act and it became illegal to pollute the air of cities in that way. That's the way change happens. You have to lead the charge.

Although I couldn't *force* the managing director to stop the smoke, I had to tell him off. I relished being a protester but, sadly, am not always suited to the rough and ready nature of revolution. Years later I much admired the Aldermaston Marches – but I didn't join them because that would have involved camping, and Mummy's line about Jewish girls not sleeping on the ground was deeply instilled in me.

Some enjoy and approve of my outspokenness and some *really* don't. Most of the Jewish people I know plead, 'Miriam, *sei schtum*, just keep quiet. It's not much to ask.' On the contrary, it's *everything* to ask. Because who are you if you don't have opinions and feel able to express them? What is the point of living and not taking a moral stand when you see the need?

I believe strongly in unions, the weak and less powerful need protection against the ruling classes. For example, I always take up the cudgels and represent my fellow cast members in any dispute with the management or the director – I quite naturally assume the role of 'the mother of the company'. In fact, I have often put that into a formal role when I became Equity Deputy – a trade union shop steward. Now, after three stints on the Council lasting six years, I remain an Honorary Equity Member.

There can often be bullying in the theatre and on set. My audition for *Reds* in 1980 would have set anyone's alarm bells ringing. For one thing, it was in the unusual surroundings of Warren Beatty's trailer. He was sitting at his desk and I was standing in the open doorway. He looked me up and down and his opening line was 'Do you fuck?' I wasn't having any of that, so I shot back, 'Yes, but not you.' It did shock people when I told them about it, but I knew he was just trying it on. Warren might be a world-famous film star, but he was still a chancer.

But fair play to him – he did cast me as the Secretary of the Communist Party and I was always ready to speak up after that if there were any problems on set. One thing that really upset the cast was Warren's irritating habit of filming them without warning – I challenged him on it. He said, 'I'm sorry, I don't have time to prepare people. If I want to take a quick shot, I say their name, and they must be able to act straight away.' I found that rude and inconsiderate and I told him so. He stopped doing it, so I think he understood, but he was definitely irked. He's not somebody I would call the mother of the company. The motherfucker of the company maybe . . .

Recently I was in Palm Springs for Yom Kippur, our Day of Atonement. I was fasting as usual and the rabbi very kindly assigned a pleasant lady to look after me. It turned out she was a Trumpy.

I asked her, 'You don't really like Trump, do you?'

'Oh, he's wonderful. He's the person who's going to get us out of the shit that we're in. He's just marvellous.'

'I can't believe I'm hearing this,' I said.

'You don't like him?' she replied, incredulous.

'Like him? I think he's as bad as Hitler.'*

---

* He's number six on my list.

'Oh, that's absurd,' she said. 'That's just absurd. I can't believe you think that. You're wrong. He's *wonderful*.' This was awkward but I was a guest in this synagogue, albeit a paying one, and I didn't want to have a row.

'Well, Melanie,' I said. 'I don't know how we're going to get on today, because I disagree with you most vehemently on this matter.'

We did in the end get on very well because she was a nice lady and we both tried hard; amazingly, we're now friends on Facebook. But I find it both ridiculous and scary that a Jew could think well of Trump. To me, his behaviour goes against every tenet of our faith – and I had to let this lady know how I felt.

And as I have got older, my moral imperative has increased. We know it's easier to be evil, but more distressingly, it's also more *fun* to be evil than good. And this has really bitten into England. I say England, specifically, because I don't believe this is the case in Ireland, Scotland or Wales. England has become an evil country. I believe the rot set in under Margaret Thatcher but it's even more dispiriting to look back over the last long decade of Tory rule. My mood has darkened since I wrote my first book. My outlook is dourer, more contemplative and pessimistic than it was before. I didn't know whether to disguise it or to dig deeper. But I must acknowledge it. We are living through horrible, desperate times. The situation is dire and people are suffering.

I can't remember ever feeling more adversely affected by public events than I do now. It's like a constant dark cloud. For me, these last twelve years have seen a collapse of all the nation's hopes. We are in an economic and social shambles and, in my opinion, everything stems from Brexit. Even Nigel Farage admits that it's been damaging to the country – and what a thoroughly unpleasant individual he is. For me personally, it has been a disaster. My country has been taken away from me and the people I thought I knew and trusted, I now no longer know or trust. My plans to retire to Italy have been stamped on. Brexit is like a cancer at the heart of everything that's wrong.

At the time of writing, there have been five Tory leaders in the last decade (three in the last eight months!). I was delighted when my bête noire, the ghastly Boris Johnson, was finally ousted, but surprised Liz Truss was picked as his replacement. I thought, 'How interesting. The Tory heartland have plumped for the most unglamorous and the least impressive candidate.' First Ms Truss finished off Her Majesty – the combination of having to spend forty minutes with the departing PM Boris and his wife Carrie and *then* immediately have an audience with la Truss would have done for anybody, never mind a frail ninety-six-year-old. Then she stabbed the economy with her financial plan to shaft poor people while patting rich people on the back and giving them lots more sweeties. The markets went crazy and the pound tanked. According to one source the Truss/Kwarteng 'Growth Plan' cost the UK £30 billion in a single day.[*] When her Chancellor resigned, Truss blamed him, most ungenerously, for what she had herself insti-gated. And just a few days later, looking like a rabbit in the headlights, she was forced by her horrified party to resign. You can always depend on Tories to stab their leader in the back.

At first, I took pleasure in her downfall. But suddenly I felt a twinge of sympathy. And I thought, 'What's happening to me? I'm feeling sorry for a Tory? Have I gone soft in the head?' But the glee with which

---

[*] The Resolution Foundation.

she was annihilated didn't feel right. After all, the whole Cabinet had agreed her budget policy. They all should have carried the can. Undoubtedly there was misogyny in her humiliation. They knew they could bully her and it was the worst sort of bullying. You could say she was stupid and deserved it. And in her case, I do see a failure of intelligence, rather than a failure of morals. She wasn't intellectually equipped to fulfil her role. She shouldn't have taken it on in the first place. It was sheer hubris. Would I set myself up to be Prime Minister? Absolutely not. But I don't feel too sorry for her – her generous severance payment (£140 grand a year for life!) will salve her wounded ego.

Ultimately this is all the fault of Boris Johnson, that bluff, blond buffoon, a malign creature. He is a disgrace; an inveterate liar and a cheat. He is also abominably lazy. He doesn't know what he's talking about half the time. Somebody who has worked in the parliament offices told me that he never read through a briefing properly. He just came in, scruffled up his hair and winged it. Certain weasel MPs would still be happy to have him as their leader because they are so desperate to keep their jobs. For them it's not about the country; their only concern is staying in power.

Tory MPs now blur into this bunch of bland, white, puny, middle-class males. But the Conservative party was at one time honourable; it had principles (even if I didn't agree with them) and included remarkable people. These Tories are like a class of naughty children: it terrifies me that they have such power to affect all our lives. And these are the people whom when I was little my mother used to call 'the best people'. She voted Tory all her life. I don't think even she would now.

They are running our country into the ground. I can't bear it. Why isn't everybody outraged? On my last book tour, when I visited Jeremy

Hunt's constituency I turned to the audience and asked, 'Who amongst you voted for Hunt?' There was a pause and about a hundred sheepish hands were raised. 'I hope you've learned your lesson,' I roared. 'Don't do it again!'

I was seven years old when the NHS was created. Our health service is the flagpole of Britain, one of the most compassionate pieces of legislation ever passed. My father had a small list of patients, he never earned a great deal, but he wasn't a doctor for the money. He loved medicine and he strongly approved of the NHS. The Tories, however, are running it down: that's why we think, 'Oh, the NHS is hopeless. We can't get an appointment.' They are undermining it by consistent underfunding, privatising it by stealth. My father would hate what medicine has become; doctors don't look at you now, they look at their computer and it feels as if their goal is to get you out of their surgery as quickly as possible.

Compassion has disappeared from the Conservative tote bag. They are truly now the Nasty Party. We need to find our consciences again and act upon them. At all costs, these Tories must be trounced at the next election.

The moral high ground is a slippery place, however. Full disclosure: I have to admit that I'm as easily bought as the next person. The only thing that made me write a book in the first place was because my publisher offered me a lot of money. And for all my morality and my talk of being honest and having integrity, you only have to find the right price and I'm anyone's. I have this vision of myself as a person shining with honour and I certainly act like it: I only wish it were true. I'm not *dishonourable*, but it's salutary for me not to give myself moral airs and to remember that I've taken the money too.

We must not close our minds to the truth, otherwise we're as guilty as Boris Johnson and his henchmen. I keep thinking, 'What would their mothers say?' When I do something naughty, I always think, 'What would Mummy say?' I know she would be horrified, because she was always, despite her lack of education, a lady. I never made it to being a lady, just an old dyke I'm afraid. And now this dyke is overflowing!

I've been seriously considering specifying that no Tory can rent my house. Then I thought, 'But that's silly. You cannot proof your life against Tories. Would prospective tenants have to fill out questionnaires to prove they've voted Labour? We are all human beings and, in the end, I need to fall back on my humanity to show me the right path. Be kind to your fellow human being. That's where these Tories will always fail. They're simply not kind enough. And be FAIR: treat others as you would have them treat you. Fairness is all. So now I'm going to amend my advert to read 'Brexiteers not welcome' and leave it at that.

The Importance of Being a Character

I've been a working actress for almost sixty years now and I'm often asked about the ones that got away, the roles I wanted, should have played, but never was considered for. The closest I've got to playing Cleopatra, eyes all kohl-circled, firmly clasping a writhing asp to my bosom – 'Give me my robe, put on my crown; I have immortal longings in me' – was in a reading in a Dallas fundraiser. Please note, however, I *have* played Queen Victoria (three times now and counting). I was never a member of the National Theatre or the RSC; I don't know the reasons, but I refuse to believe it was because I wasn't good enough. A lot of it is to do with luck, being in the right place and free at the right time. But I've lasted well, I've improved as I've aged and I'm not bitter, only grateful for the career I've enjoyed and the fun I've had.

I remain unashamedly, a character actress. And I've always tried to bring to my roles the same energy, fire, commitment and skill that a leading lady fires across the footlights: Stanislavsky said 'there are no small parts, only small actors', and I've always thought of *my* character as the centre of any play or film in which I act.

It's why I am so passionate about Dickens. He knew all about small parts. His books may often be named after their conventional leads (*David Copperfield*, *Nicholas Nickleby* or *Barnaby Rudge*) but his particular joy lay in creating the vast and vivid sea of supporting actors; it is undeniable that Betsey Trotwood, Mr Dick and Miss

Mowcher pack as much punch and stay in your mind longer than the eponymous hero. He invented over 2,000 characters and the energy with which they people his books is unforgettable. Take Mr F's Aunt in *Little Dorrit*, introduced as:

> an amazing little old woman, with a face like a staring wooden doll, and a stiff yellow wig perched unevenly on the top of her head, as if the child who owned the doll had driven a tack through it anywhere . . . [her] propensity to offer remarks in a deep warning voice, confounded and terrified the mind.

She silenced one dinner table with the following fearful remark: 'When we lived at Henley, Barnes's gander was stole by tinkers.' Another magnificent one-liner coming out of nowhere is: 'There's mile-stones on the Dover road!' Her stentorian pronouncements carry as much doom as any of Lady Macbeth's (another role I have, incidentally, not been asked to play).

I've never felt that any of the parts I've acted were small roles, however few lines they might have had. Often, you see, without these seemingly more minor characters, the play or film would fall apart. And, when I make the role mine, the audience follows my lead. In *Romeo and Juliet*, for example, the play may be named after the lovers, but the voice of reason is the Nurse, a role I played twice, firstly in the 1996 film directed by Baz Luhrmann, and then in Peter Hall's Los Angeles theatre production in 2001. The Nurse holds the strings that bring Romeo and Juliet together. But I remember Baz saying: 'The Nurse can't be allowed to be present at the end of the play because she's betrayed Juliet.' She doesn't recognise the love that Juliet feels and instead admonishes her, effectively saying, 'What are you talking about? Romeo belongs to a family that is not acceptable. You must marry Paris. Paris is the one for you. Not Romeo.' The Nurse's opinion is sensible but Juliet is not interested in reason, she only wants Romeo. And so I disappear from the play, but my monologue recounting nursing Juliet as a baby, remains one of its tenderest moments.

Working again with Peter Hall in 2006, I was delighted to be cast as Miss Prism, in *The Importance of Being Earnest*. It is a part I was born to play – a rotund, respectable English governess, barely containing her violent, boiling sexuality. She has wit ('The good ended happily, and the bad unhappily. That is what Fiction means') and a guileless, single-minded determination to snaffle her man. This production offered the added bonus of playing alongside Lynn Redgrave's Lady Bracknell. I loved her huge sense of fun and her honesty. She was open from the start: 'You know, I've had a bad time. I'm in remission at the moment, but I've been told it's an aggressive cancer. I don't know when it will return.' But she didn't let it overshadow her life or hold her back in any way. We became firm friends – thank God, because for reasons that will become clear, for me this production was by no means plain sailing.

You see, there was a problem. The object of my character's passion, as conceived by Oscar Wilde, was a mild, sexually repressed country vicar, the Reverend Chasuble. But Terence Rigby, the actor cast as Chasuble, said, 'No, no, no. Chasuble is not interested in Prism. I mean, there's nothing going on between them.' But it's crystal-clear from the text that there is. This play specifically is about setting up couples. They may not be the sort of couples that one would have in mind – elderly and not particularly attractive, in our case – but the work is supposed to be a celebration of unbridled love. So, there I was acting my part, but with an actor who was not prepared to act *his*.

Our director, Peter Hall, was never tremendously organised, and some time before, he had been casting another play and had cast two people in the same role. Owing to this oversight, two actors had turned up to a first rehearsal both expecting to play the same part, and Terence had been the one Peter 'let go'. Understandably, he felt he owed him and said to me, 'Miriam, I can't compel Terry to do what he doesn't want to do and most particularly I can't because I had to sack him before and I don't want to do that again. He doesn't deserve it.'

I stuck to my guns and refused to change my performance – Peter loved it. My Miss Prism positively throbbed with sexual longing. I didn't allow Terence to deflect me from the passage of my lust. That's the point. She may be a governess, she may be tightly laced, but that doesn't mean that her cunt isn't flowing with desire. So, there was I, boiling with love and lust and not able to pass it on to my recalcitrant Dr Chasuble. He spent every night running away from me across the stage whilst I remained a pressure cooker, steaming towards him – and the more repressed Terry wanted to be, the more I seethed out at him. And it worked.

My performance was lustful and sexy, but I made sure I kept my behaviour within the strictures of a Victorian governess. The phrase 'prunes and prisms' is meant to encapsulate a repressed, pent-up kind of person. Well, that's Miss Prism to a T, and that's why Oscar Wilde called her that. She was all heart, all love, all longing, but as a Victorian governess was not free to express her hunger – she poured it into her sentimental three-volume tome which Lady Bracknell described as having 'more than usually revolting sentimentality'. That was my Prism.

It was gruelling night after night to be chasing and to have to be madly in love with this Chasuble; but that's what you must do. You must believe with such fervent integrity that you *do* love this man and that he loves you, so that the lust and longing informs every cell of your body. And because such powerful emotions were so trammelled in this short, fat, tightly corseted, black-laced woman it was hysterically funny – which is what it should be.

Audiences relished Chasuble clearly saying in all his gestures and expression, 'I *don't* love you, Miss Prism, and I really don't like this situation,' while I was brushing aside all his evasions, refusing to acknowledge his froideur, rubbing my thighs and basically saying, 'Oh yes you do, Dr Chasuble. You *do!*' That was what I was determined to show. No matter Terry Rigby's objections – I did it anyway because I knew it was right.

Looking back, of course, there are roles that I wish I'd played; Mrs Klein in Nicholas Wright's play of that name, or Masha in *The Seagull* ('I'm in mourning for my life. I'm unhappy.') would have been wonderful; and in film, any of Bette Davis's roles, especially the Grand Guignol *Baby Jane* stuff – what fun that would have been. There is an anxiety in being the lead however. *Mother Courage* needs real courage to take the part but then Brecht is a bugger at the best of times.

All we can ever use in creating a character is our own personality, plus what we've learned, plus what we observe, plus what our fellow actors give us. It's thrilling because it happens right then and there, in the moment, a flash of inspiration, a sudden understanding, a rapport that shifts with each development of mood. When the team forges on, inspired by the director and the text and the audience, it's the most magical, satisfying experience in the world. Ego doesn't rule, only the joint egos, the combined skills, the shared excitement – and it is the generous performer, the wise performer, who allows the baton to be passed to a fellow actor who then passes it back. Theatre is the great democracy: but it can be unfair too. But who said life is fair? If you can give your character the weight the author intended, you have honoured your gift. And what more can anyone do?

Don't Let the Bastards Get You Down

I've always been little and fat; that can deceive people into thinking you're a pushover. Well, I'm not. I'm not a Christian; I won't turn the other cheek unless it's a buttock.

I've always stood up to bullies. To make anyone feel small is a nasty thing to do, because one of the things you realise as you go through life is that everybody is scared inside. If someone speaks to me in an aggressive way, I immediately call it out. 'Who the fuck do you think you are . . .?' I bellow. 'Don't speak to me like that! I won't have it.' And if I see somebody mistreating a dog or whipping a horse, I'll shout, 'Stop that right now!'

When I was ten, I saw a man beating up a woman in the street. I was deeply shocked and upset and I ran straight back home. I went to Daddy's surgery and I said, 'Daddy, come quickly. You've got to come out and stop this.'

'What are you talking about?' he said. 'Stop what, Miriam?'

'*Please*, Daddy, this man is hitting his wife. You've *got* to come quickly because she could be hurt!'

'Well, I'll get in the car,' he replied. 'But I'm not going to say anything to them.' We drove round and round the streets of Oxford but I couldn't find the couple again. And Daddy was clearly relieved; it was always like that. Whatever the difficulty– even something as trivial as having to ask for a fork in a restaurant – it was Mummy who always had to step in. And that infuriated me because I felt it was Daddy's place to solve things but invariably he ran from confrontation; I hurl myself towards it.

Nobody bullied me at school; I wouldn't have it. I don't think anybody tried, except Miss Palser in the Upper Third. She was poisonous; a cruel, evil snake of a woman who loved to make people cry. What a cow! My mother would not tolerate it; a doughty fighter on my behalf, she marched into the school and complained. Mummy was always the soldier – the general, actually – in my army. She would never stand for anybody hurting me or subduing my thunder. My secret weapon against bullies has always been comedy. From the earliest days at school, I found out that if you make people laugh, they will let you do almost anything. It proved a useful weapon in many situations. I've scored many a goal in hockey while playing Left Inner, because I flashed my bottom at the goalie.

That said, being funny hasn't always worked in my favour. At Cambridge, the otherwise all-male cast of the Footlights Revue sent me to Coventry in 1962. In revenge for my getting the laughs onstage – I felt that they ensured that, offstage, I would be invisible. They might say they simply didn't like me. As far as those boys were concerned, I was just *too* funny and they wanted to take me down a peg or two. I am talking about it here because it still hurts sixty years on. At the time I took pains to act as though it didn't bother me, but I went home and wept every night. I want to be fair to their comic genius. They are deservedly some of the most famous members of their generation but they were horrid to me. When I found out I hadn't been invited to the end of show party, I went direct to the president of Footlights, an amiable fellow called Chris Stuart-Clark. He was flustered and surprised, suggesting it was 'an oversight'; I politely disagreed. I'd more than earned my invitation – and no jumped-up public schoolboys were going to stop me attending. And I did.

Have I been a bully? Well, I don't like to think it. I don't want to be and I don't *think* I am now. The bully always looks for the weak person, or the weakness in a person, they sniff out some vulnerability and then aim for it; I hope that's not in my nature. I have twisted arms in my time, I can be bossy, edging on dictatorial. But I disapprove of that sort of behaviour too.

In 1982, I was cast in the title role in Pam Gems's *Queen Christina* at the Tricycle Theatre in Kilburn. Our director Pam Brighton wasn't there for the first week of rehearsal; she'd gone off to direct something else. As our time was limited, I said to the company, 'I think we'd better rehearse on our own.' When Pam Brighton came back, she called a meeting and announced, 'Show me what you've got.' When we performed the scene we had been rehearsing, she looked up at us on stage and said, 'That was bloody terrible! I don't know what you were thinking of. It's a disaster!'

I thought, 'Hang on! I'm forty-one years old. I'm not going to be belittled like a schoolchild; I'm not going to stand for this. No director should talk to her cast like that!'

There was a pause. Very slowly, I walked off the stage, gathered my bits and walked out of the building. As I passed Pam Brighton, I said, 'I don't know what this is. But it's not a rehearsal.' The cast on stage didn't move or speak. The exit door of the auditorium swung slowly behind me. I got in my car and drove home.

The phone was ringing as I opened my front door. It was Pam Brighton; she said, 'What the fuck are you doing, Miriam? Get back here and start rehearsing properly!'

'No, Pam,' I said firmly. 'I'm not coming back. *Ever*.'

She tried to scare me: 'We'll report you to Equity. You'll never work again.'

'You know what?' I replied. 'I don't care. You weren't there for the first week of rehearsal and you should've been. And now you're blaming us because we tried to get it right? How dare you! Nothing on earth would make me come back and do this play with you.'

And I didn't. The production went ahead, and they had to find somebody else to come in and play Queen Christina. Pam didn't report me to Equity but I had to shell out for my costumes, and for all the publicity posters and material with my name on them. It cost me about £500; no matter, there was no way I was going to go back and work with bully Brighton. I have no idea how the production turned out – obviously I couldn't go and see it. Many years later, Barry Humphries, an old friend of mine through my Australian connections, married Lizzie Spender who had played the lesbian love interest in *Queen Christina*. She and I became friends and we still are.

Some directors are famous bullies. They invariably tend to have a whipping boy (or girl) in the cast whom they pick on. I would never let myself be put in that position. Christopher Morahan, a brilliant director, was one such bully. The only time I was ever directed by him was over thirty years ago, in 1990, with Simon Callow and Stephen Fry in *Old Flames*, a Simon Gray play for BBC television.

When I entered rehearsals I was mindful of his reputation and decided to protect myself. I would not allow him to call me by my first name.

'Please always call me Miss Margolyes,' I said. 'And I will call you Mr Morahan.'

Consequently, Mr Morahan found someone else in the cast to pick on. I can't remember who it was, but he was simply awful to him; to my shame, I did not speak up for that person. I should have confronted Mr Morahan – and I didn't.

Sadly, long before Trump, there were bullies in America. I remember this chap tailgating me in Santa Monica – that's when somebody drives far too close to your rear bumper. He was hooting me and shoving me so I stopped the car dead, right in front of him. I opened my window and threw the car keys out onto the verge, and then I got out too. The man also got out of his car and walked threateningly towards me.

'What the fuck are you doing?'

'No one bullies me,' I said.

'You're out of your mind,' he said.

'I may well be,' I agreed. 'But I'm not going to be bullied by you pushing me along the street.'

'Get back in your car for Christ sakes,' he said. 'You're wasting my time.'

'I can't, I've thrown away the keys. What are you going to do about that, then?'

He said, 'I'm going to call the police.'

'What a good idea,' I said. 'You do that. Call the police.'

'Lady, you're out of your mind,' he said for the second time, adding, 'You're fucking nuts.'

And he called the police. And a lady officer arrived.

'Ma'am, what is the problem here?' she asked.

'This gentleman was tailgating me. He was pushing me with his car and I won't have it.'

'Ma'am, we got a problem here. There's a great big line right behind you. You're gonna have to move your car.'

I said, 'I will move my car, because *you* have asked me. But I will not be bullied into it.'

She said, 'Cut the crap, ma'am. Just get back in your car and move.'

I said, 'Well, I have to find the keys first.'

She said, 'What do you mean?'

I explained that I'd thrown the keys out of the car window.

'You what? You threw your keys out? Lady, you're crazy. Just find them. Right now!'

I did so quite quickly because I knew where they'd fallen. And I got back in my car and drove off. I had achieved my aim, which was to cause the bully behind me to waste half an hour of his clearly extremely precious time. That was my revenge. I WILL NOT BE BULLIED. In the face of such behaviour, courage is important, and steadfastness. If you believe in something, hold to it. Don't let anybody put you down.

Adventures in Heavy Petting

It was W. C. Fields who said, 'Never work with children or animals.' But as a voice-over actor I've anthropomorphised so many animals in my time – from the glow-worm in *James and the Giant Peach* to the blind snake, Mrs Plithiver, in *Legends of the Guardians*, from Dolly the chimp for PG Tips to Fly the sheepdog in *Babe* – I feel I can dismiss that as rubbish. On the set of *The Age of Innocence*, for instance, surrounded by five tail-wagging Pomeranians, despite the uncomfortable corsets and the fat suit, I serenely held my own. You see, I am assuredly an animal person.

J. Alfred Prufrock measured out his life in coffee spoons; I have measured out mine in pets. Firstly, Bonny – an English springer spaniel of real honesty and nobility. Affectionate, tan and white markings, quite sturdy. My parents always had dogs. Well, Mummy did. She also had a talkative and talented parrot (Polly, of course) who died of heatstroke at their crowded engagement party in 1930, deeply mourned, but I suspect Daddy was quite glad. Then, in their first marital home in Plaistow, East London, they had Bonny Mark I – a wire-haired terrier of amazing intelligence. Famously, he devoured the guests' plates of smoked salmon on the dinner table and left Mummy and Daddy's hors d'oeuvres untouched; he knew where his masters sat.

When I was nine Bonny Mark II was collected from the Oxford pound. Bonny II never lied; that was his great strength. He loved us all equally, he sat at our feet when we ate. He never pestered, he never demanded, he just looked – and we melted. He was untiringly loving, and when we had to put him down because he was thirteen and ill, our hearts broke. A replacement there could never be, but another dog was a possibility.

Back to the dog pound and we found Whisky, a black and white Scottish Border collie, a natural thief of charm, wit and boundless energy who lived till he was seventeen. We all adored him. He came everywhere with us, even to Scotland, where Grandma Margolyes, never an animal-lover, found his proximity quite threatening. 'Don't put him against me,' she begged, meaning, 'Don't make him think that I'm an enemy. Don't encourage him to dislike me.' In the end, she loved him too.

He had no morals whatsoever. He was a bounder who would do anything to get food. He lied incessantly, swearing he hadn't been fed; food could never be left out – he demolished everything. Unscrupulous but affectionate, he went straight for the cunt when ladies visited – and nosed there as long as he was allowed. He laughed all the time, a great pink tongue lolling sideways out of his mouth, black eyes sparking with mischief and affection. He ran like the wind, like collies do, barked loudly and impressively when the doorbell rang, or when birds flew overhead, or when it was time for his walk. He knew he was king – we all knew it. The au pair girls loved him too – and putting him down when the vet advised was one of the most terrible days of my life.

There never has been another dog; I long for one but my peripatetic life prohibits such a thing. I always speak to dogs I meet in the street; I long for their snuffles and tail-wags. Dogs are attached to people, cats to places. And so, in London, when I finally had my own place at 108 Gloucester Terrace, the place cried out for a cat. Jan Adams, Heather's dear friend, found Wooty, all black and sweet. She would go for rides in our shopping trolley when we went to nearby Church Street and Bell Street Markets; it was a real basket on wheels, big and safe.

Every Saturday morning, Jan, Heather and I would wheel Wooty in her basket while we shopped all around the Edgware Road. My kosher butcher was in Boscobel Street and my friend Mervyn Jacobs ran the antiques emporium on the corner of Church Street and Lisson Grove. Gay as the breeze, slender as a whip, shrewd as all get-out, with a permanent orange suntan long before Trump, he nosed out bargains and alerted me to them.

I took up with Heather in 1968 and she's obsessed with cats. Thus, my passion for Heather inflamed my own passion. In 1975, I moved from the Gloucester Terrace flat, crossing the Thames to Clapham, to a house with a long garden. I had no cats to share the house with, and then Fate (more commonly known as the BBC) brought my newest cats to me. While I was playing June Morris, a District Nurse in *Angels*, a BBC TV series centring on a group of student nurses at St Angela's Hospital, I mentioned I was looking for a cat, and the star of the show, Érin Geraghty (playing Maureen Morahan), happened to be looking for a home for her sister's kittens. She went to her house in Bromsgrove and bagged two – a male tabby and a female of all colours, orange and white principally, and brought them to me in her Mini. I named them June and Morris after my character in *Angels*. June was haughty, prim and walked carefully as if on tiptoe. She was affectionate but controlled, she had barriers. Morris was a thief, ruthless, absurdly affectionate and demanding.

The 'Angel' felines were installed first; then Reuben appeared. Well, he didn't actually appear, but one day I caught a glimpse in my back garden, of a little black shape running away to hide under a pile of logs the builders had thrown out while my house was being renovated. He was the one who took my heart for ever, because he needed it more than the others. He had been abandoned and traumatised and it was two months before I could tempt him into the house. There was a little hole under the stairs which the builders had left and he used to crawl in there and only come out at night to eat the food and drink the milk I left in little bowls. He was utterly beautiful. Coal black with green eyes, full of solemnity and sadness and the loudest purr of all. Eventually he grew in courage and allowed me to touch him. I named him Reuben after Jacob's oldest son, always unfortunate. He would purr and then suddenly take fright, and rush into the sanctuary of the under-stairs hole. He was never tamed; I never could control him, and one day after four years, he disappeared. I think he wasn't well and went away to die. I still mourn him – he was a symbol to me of the immigrants who desperately seek a haven and are denied.

In old age, Morris (he stayed with me long after the others died) suffered from the feline equivalent of Alzheimer's or dementia and wailed and howled through the house, saw visions and never knew day from night. It got to the point where he was seriously disturbed and pathetic and I had him put to sleep, admittedly with a sense of relief that both our sufferings were over. But when you take an animal to the vet and know you're not coming back together, there is a pain like no other, an anguish I cannot describe. Thank heavens I don't have children; to lose a child must be an agony I could not endure.

Some cats are appallingly bossy. Heather's cat, Riley, who lived with her in Amsterdam, was just such a cat. She was all black, quite sturdy and possessed of the loudest roar you ever heard. One Christmas, Heather lent her central Amsterdam apartment to my friend, John Tydeman, the adored head of BBC Radio Drama and his lovely Aussie partner, Tony Lynch. On Christmas Day, quite early in the morning, John phoned us in some distress. It seems that Riley, who was an aggressively territorial cat, in his words, had decided she would not allow the two men (both six foot tall) to leave the apartment to attend Christmas Mass, and she was 'on the stairs, growling. We cannot get past her. What should we do?' I couldn't help laughing; Heather said, 'For goodness' sake, you're two grown men. Just get a broom and shove her out of the way.' Tony said she made friends with them afterwards and was really a sweet little cat, but in the beginning was a 'total control freak'. Just like some people, I suppose.

Our current masters, here in Montisi, Italy, are the siblings Abu – huge and heavy (he weighs nearly 7 kilos) – and his tiny, pretty sister Tilly – naughty and spoilt, she kills anything that moves. Heather christened them both. She named the male, tiger-striped cat Abu, which is Indonesian for 'ash', or 'grey'. Mind you, Abu is a vicious killer too. Whenever he's caught a creature, he makes a peculiar kind of wail; a horrible high-pitched yowl, triumphant in its nastiness. And then he comes and deposits the limp, bloodied corpse of the unfortunate small animal (mouse, bird, rat, lizard) inside. Now when we hear that noise, we won't let him in.

But with most humans they're unusually affectionate, jumping on laps without warning, suddenly arriving on our pillows for prolonged cuddles. When I've been away from them, in London or elsewhere, I find that re-entry can be difficult; there's always a space where they don't know me, and then we fill it. With Heather, too, when we've been apart for months, there is a similar adjustment period.

At night, Abu and Tilly stay in the barn at the back of the house. We've made beds for them and they get in and out through a little swinging cat door. But when I went in this morning, they weren't there. They couldn't be bothered to wait for me to get up and feed them. It has been quite warm here this winter, so perhaps they went out to hunt for their breakfast. Usually they're waiting for me expectantly, scuffling around my feet. They don't seem to grasp that if I'm going to feed them, I need a clear way to their plastic cat food box, which we keep tightly locked away with a heavy log on top, because they're adept at opening it and getting at the food. Abu has learned how to open the kitchen door. Anywhere they smell food, they are immediately attentive; potato crisps are a favourite.

We need cats here in Italy because we have mice. And rats. The mice are not wicked, they're just country mice who want to move in for the winter, but we'd rather not have them. We've always had cats at La Casella – all of them arrived looking for a home. We found our previous cat ceremoniously laid out, dead, below my bedroom window. Three days before, I had leaned out of that very window and told one unpleasant neighbour exactly what I thought of him. We found the timing highly suspicious. In our devastation, we vowed never to have cats again. However, Luca, our Sardinian builder and regular saviour, found a litter of kittens for us at the farm up the road. He insisted we took two, Abu and Tilly.

When I'm writing or on a Zoom call, they're normally in the background, posing on the windowsill, languidly draped on top of a table, or Abu lies on the floor and wants to be cuddled. At least they have now grown too big to sit on the computer keyboard. Animals are like that. But when it's warm and sunny, like this morning, they disappear, going about their own feline business. Cats are extremely secretive. They don't tell you where they're going. They just go and then, hopefully, some hours later, I hear a rattle at the door handle which is an indication that they have come back for their supper and they wish to be admitted. There's a pleasing simplicity and honesty about animals.

At this moment, Abu looks serious, as if he really has duties to perform. He nearly lost a leg in a vicious attack. The perpetrators have never been identified. People love their pets and our delightful neighbours reject the notion that their Jack Russells could have been responsible. The cat, frantic with pain, amazingly made it home, and Rosella, our cat-sitter, took wonderful care of him during his six weeks' house arrest while he recovered. Now we worry as to what will happen to them when we die; cats usually live for twelve years and we know we won't. I think we might end up leaving the house to them and hoping future carers will take care of them in familiar surroundings.

But I've been lucky enough to experience large, wilder animals. In South Africa, I filmed *The Place of Lions* and came frighteningly close to a cheetah, which is the fastest animal on the planet and can run towards you at 70 mph. I was with Hugh Laurie and Alfred Molina in a safari park and the cheetah had slipped its keeper's tether and came to stand extremely close to me in the open. The others were further away. The keeper spoke softly to me, in a curiously stilted voice, slow and slightly strangled in his delivery.

'Don't move,' he said.

'Don't worry,' I replied instantly, with an equally strangled delivery. I held my breath; I was quite still. I looked at the cheetah, he looked back at me. I knew he could take my face off with one swipe of a paw. His eyes were expressionless, greenish and wild; they looked across me as if I weren't there. After a scary pause, he moved away.

Once in America, while filming a documentary, I visited a private zoo in Georgia, something I disapprove of. 'Would you like to stroke a tiger?' the owner asked. Not many opportunities had come up in my life to do that. The tiger was uncaged but I was protected by a barred wall. The beautiful animal came towards me: I was told to call to it. The owner said, 'Never turn your back on a tiger.' I never have. But through the bars I stroked its bristly coat; it purred. *It did!!*

Of all the big creatures, my favourites are elephants. Because I'm fat, and was often called an elephant as a child, I feel a kindred spirit to these great creatures. When my parents took me to London Zoo, I always rushed to see the elephants, and in India, my first sight of an elephant walking down the street was unforgettable. I was in a hotel having breakfast and it lumbered past. I ran out, my serviette still tucked into my collar, and begged to be allowed to feed it. The mahout handed me an apple, the elephant's tiny eye clocked it, and the curling trunk moving towards it delighted me.

Filming *The Real Marigold on Tour* in Sichuan province, China, with my fellow oldies Wayne Sleep, Rosemary Shrager and Bobby George – a dancer, a chef and a darts player – we visited the Chengdu panda research base. When I saw my first giant panda, I cried. The extraordinary thing was that the panda was looking back at me. In my whole life I would never have dreamed that I would look at an animal like that and it would return my sympathetic gaze. Tears rolled down my cheeks as I fed it a bamboo shoot. 'So beautiful,' I said, mopping my eyes. 'It's a piece of magic.' But Rosemary Shrager was impassive. 'It's just a panda,' she said with a shrug. But the panda wasn't looking at her.

Are You a Catholic Jew
or a Protestant Jew?

There is an old joke in Northern Ireland about a tourist who gets lost in Belfast. Straying into a no-man's-land between Protestant and Catholic neighbourhoods, a balaclava-clad man grabs him and asks: 'Are you a Protestant or a Catholic?' The tourist stammers: 'I'm a Jew. I'm a Jew.' And the masked man says: 'That's all very well, but are you a Protestant Jew or a Catholic Jew?'

I was born into an observant Jewish family: my parents believed in God, but He was never discussed. They didn't sit at home reading the Torah on a Sabbath – my home life was much the same as that of my English school friends – but we always had Friday night dinner at home, when Mummy sometimes lit candles, but not always; we went to synagogue (which we call *shul*) three times a year; celebrated Passover; fasted from sunset the night before to sunset on Yom Kippur (the Day of Atonement); and as a child I attended *cheder* (Sunday School) and didn't take it seriously.

The Oxford synagogue had been a disused lecture hall on Richmond Road, Jericho; rather cold and shabby, not at all like the comfortable building which replaced it, long after I left Oxford. Our rabbi in those days was a learned, warm-hearted, distinguished academic, Professor Chaim Rabin, with curly black hair all around his head. He was one of my father's patients and before coming to Oxford had been briefly interned as an enemy alien on the Isle of Man, because he had been born in Germany. He was unpretentious, short, fat and cheerful, and his wife, Batya, was our *cheder* teacher. She was slender, shy and beautiful, and we children treated her disgracefully. I remember running about, being noisy and objectionable, and because poor Mrs Rabin had no discipline at all, we learned very little. I learned far more about the Old Testament in Miss Plummer's Scripture class at Oxford High School. The Rabins went to Israel after the war and I stayed with Batya in Jerusalem on my first visit there. She was utterly loveable and had clearly forgiven me for being a disruptive pupil and remembered only my father and how good a doctor he was.

We were observant but not Orthodox Jews. We adapted the dietary laws to suit us; did you know it's Mosaic law not to eat rabbits, that fish must have fins and gills, that meat has to have cloven hooves *and* chew the cud? I still follow our rules – but not because I believe; I do it to honour the memory of my beloved parents, whose unquestioning acceptance of their religion never wavered. I knew I'd have to marry a Jew eventually, and I knew Jews were 'better' than Christians. We always felt a bit sorry for Christians; their food was awful, they lacked 'style', and they just weren't as clever as we were.

And then, in my twenties, I realised that every time I was in synagogue – instead of praying and contemplating God and sins and all that – I thought about nothing but sex. I wasn't getting much but I thought about it all the time. God rather dwindled as a focus of attention, but I never felt less 'Jewish': I was always delighted when Jews won the Nobel Prize, which they often did. Wikipedia states that 'the percentage of Jewish Nobel laureates is at least 112.5 times or 11,250 per cent above average'. Like my mother, I always noted when there was someone Jewish on television. Even after the stroke which took away her speech and mobility, she would point at the television whenever a Jew appeared and smile.

I have *always* felt Jewish, would describe myself as a Jew, and am delighted to be one. This is the first time in my life that I haven't been a member of at least two *shuls*. Both my synagogues in South London have closed: first, Bolingbroke Road Clapham Synagogue in 1997 and then Streatham Shul in 2022.

North Londoners in the Stoke Newington area will be familiar with the old-fashioned traditional garb of the Orthodox Jew (the 'Jewish gaberdine' Shakespeare described), as there has been a Lubavitch community there, the largest in Europe, since the 1920s.

My hard-working young American Chabad rabbi in Battersea, Moshe Adler, wants to teach people about Judaism, and he and his family are hospitable and kind. They have often welcomed me to their home and services, and I relish their attempts to keep me within the fold, but I am a lamb who has strayed.

Rabbi Adler is a man who lives his faith, but many do not. And the hypocrisy of it all disgusts me. The naked materialism of many Jews disappoints me; the money spent on weddings and bar and bat mitzvahs, the flaunting of cars and houses and clothes, depress me.

There are, of course, things to criticise in every religion. Don't overlook the Catholic priests and their all-too-frequent paedophilia. And the absurd arrogance shared by the Church of England and the Muslims. Everyone is sure they're right. Of course, I have friends within all these groups. I'm still in touch with Jennifer Flanders and her family of twelve children, whom I met filming my series on America. She still prays that I will see the light of God and return to the fold (bless her), but I cannot believe in God, I just can't. The problem of pain and wickedness explodes the whole God concept. And it saddens me that horror is allowed to flourish in the name of religion.

I see God as a giant fraud and the pathetic corruption of the American Southern Baptist televangelists provokes my rage and pity for those who believe. I hope in time my prejudices will lessen and my anger will abate and I will 'allow' religion in other people, but at the moment I can only see the harm it does: the deaths caused in Ireland, in Palestine, in Israel, in Iran, in India – everywhere where rabbis and priests and mullahs and imams and Scientologists spread lies and cause havoc in families and nations.

But when the roll call of Jews is again made – and it will be – I shall stand up and be counted. For Jews of my age, the Holocaust is not merely history, it is a daily reminder of what humanity – educated, intelligent, hard-working God-fearing, 'cultivated' people – can do to one another. I can never forget that, in my lifetime, a few hundred miles east of where I was born in Oxford, people were herded into cattle trucks by their neighbours and friends and gassed because they were Jews. My parents were sure Hitler would occupy the British Isles, and he nearly did.

—

Antisemitism is on the increase, possibly exacerbated by Jews themselves, who can often show a contempt towards non-Jews. We feel sorry for Christians. Groucho Marx talked about not wanting to be a member of any club that would accept him – that certainly sums up how we feel about the Christian world.

After the war, people everywhere felt they couldn't say anything against Jews because what had happened in the Holocaust was so awful. When I was seven, the state of Israel came into existence. But far from solving 'the Jewish problem, it re-started it. Today, antisemitism flourishes in England (and elsewhere) as a result of the appalling Israeli policy towards the Palestinians.

My family was never Zionist, but I did go to Israel as a young woman. I worked on a kibbutz in the Negev as a seventeen-year-old, and while I hated it, mainly because it involved washing up for five hundred people, I thought the idea of a kibbutz was rather a wonderful socialist notion. I didn't know very much about Palestine: I felt that Israel had won a war and the Jews would survive. And that was good. But little by little, as I became more political, I educated myself. The more I read books and articles about the situation, the more I became critical of Israel.

When I went to Palestine in 2012, I saw for myself the contempt and cruelty with which Israelis treated Palestinians. I met Palestinian people and listened to their personal stories. I saw the devastation of the hospitals that the Israelis had bombed. I saw incredible overcrowding. I saw the filth and stench in the streets of Hebron; I saw the nets that the Arabs have to put up to protect themselves from the settlers who shower them with muck and rubbish. It was a searing experience that really shook me.

The Palestinian people were not being treated in a humane way; they told me how their lives have been disrupted, made miserable; how they had been humiliated, arrested and most poignant of all, how they had been torn from their homes, and their lands taken away. Their daily lives are being squeezed and destroyed and since they never see Israelis to talk to, they feel a hatred of them. I'm not surprised. I would if I were treated in the same way. I, as a Jew, have the full right of return – no Palestinian does. It's just not fair. The Israelis feel they can carry through things without reference to international law; what they are doing is illegal. Yet nobody seems to be taking any notice.

I have always been outspoken in my criticism of Israel and it has cost me dearly. Recently, I talked with David Baddiel about this. David indignantly refutes any lumping together of Jews and Israel. I think he's wrong. I don't have an allegiance to Israel, but what happens in Israel *does* concern me. Because now antisemites have an excuse to support their vile bigotry. Too many people, including Labour voters, are muddled about this. It's lazy thinking. But to hate and attack Jews because of your feelings about Palestine is *not* acceptable. It's the Israeli government's persecution of Palestinians that's the evil – not being Jewish. It's possible to be proudly Jewish and vehemently anti-Zionist. As I am.

Those Jews, like me, who speak out against the wickedness of the Israeli government, are tarred with the epithet of 'self-hating Jew' – but I will continue to speak out. I am sure if my North London Jewish critics, who lambast me as a 'fascist' and a liar would visit the Occupied Territories, cross over into East Jerusalem and experience for themselves the trials of being Palestinian, they might modify their views and perhaps encourage a change of behaviour in Israel. The climate in Israel is hardening against the Palestinians: more illegal settlements in the Occupied Territories are planned, and the Israeli Minister of National Security recently announced the government's intention to ban any showing of the Palestinian flag in public spaces. I am not optimistic for the future.

I can't answer the question, 'What is a Jew?' I just know I am one: a non-believing Jew. But how do I spot the others of my kind? What is 'Jewdar'? Often, it's someone's name that gives it away. Before 1787, Jews didn't have last names, but Emperor Joseph II decreed that all Jews in the Habsburg Empire must adopt fixed hereditary surnames. And the names were assigned by administrative clerks, often using the names of materials (gold, silver, diamond, cotton); or trees (Birnbaum: pear tree; Kirschbaum: cherry tree); or, as in my family, physical characteristics of the man (Gelbard: yellow beard; Grosskopf: big head). People took their names from rivers or towns near their home (Posner: from Posen; Danziger: from Danzig). But sometimes you just have to look at someone and you can tell their Jewish origin.

I look typically Jewish – I'm short and fat, with large, dark, expressive eyes and frizzy wild hair. A hooked nose is often called a Jewish nose; a flamboyant personality is thought to be Jewish; olive skin, frequent gesturing . . . I think vocal characteristics play a part too. I've studied voices all my life and there is a thickness, a nasality, to London Jewish voices. I have much enjoyed copying this voice for various characters I've played. But I must be careful because I am dealing in stereotypes – well-worn descriptions which border on the racist. Some people are obvious Jews, others are not. My mother had fair hair and blue eyes; Goldie Hawn is not an obvious Jew, nor was Lauren Bacall. But we are on dangerous ground here; it's safer to keep my Jewdar to myself.

I acknowledge there is a contradiction at the heart of my attitude. I reject any religion which teaches discrimination and divides people; I deplore the contempt that so often Jews have for non-Jews. And yet, I LOVE being Jewish. It's one of the first things I say when I introduce myself. I declaim it from the rooftops. When *Spamalot* was in preview, I remember I went along with the rest of the *Wicked* cast. There's a bit in the show where King Arthur (Tim Curry) asks, 'Are there any Jews here?' – naturally, I bellowed back at the top of my lungs, 'YEEEEESSSSSS!' and, after a slightly surprised pause, Tim replied, 'Jolly good!'

The history of my people and my family are the roots which nourish me. When I was invited to be on *Desert Island Discs*, one of the pieces of music I chose was the Kol Nidrei, because the fine ethics of the Jewish religion inform my life. I relish the chopped liver, the matzah balls, I am defiantly proud of my Jewishness and its rich traditions. I may not observe them but I insist on their being recognised. Each year, on 27 January, I remember the six million, including my own relatives who were murdered in the Holocaust. Its lesson is never to forget.

I never can. I never will.

Beauty is in the Eye of the Beholder

If you're fat, people tell you, 'Oh, you've got lovely eyes,' as if that more than makes up for it. Which it doesn't, but it doesn't mean I'm not proud of my dark brown eyes. Mummy used to say, 'Eyes are the window of the soul.' And they are.

You can usually tell from people's eyes if they're lying. It's the eyes that give it away, the little darting, oblique glances, the frequent blinking. But conversely, if they don't turn away, if they stare unrelentingly, if they try to fix and hold your gaze to theirs, that can also be a sign of a lie. And if they fancy you, it's the eyes that say so. I think of Princess Diana's downward gaze. Oh, she was a flirt, that one.

Heather has blue eyes. Daddy's were dark brown. He was handsome when he was young. But I don't think he ever knew that he was handsome. He never thought about things like that. And Mummy's were a brilliant bright blue. Icy. When she got angry, her eyes fixed you and were like points of fire. Grandpa Walters's eyes were blue too. He was the seductive one, the conjuror.

Family Matters

I've always been fascinated by families because I didn't have one; there was only Mummy, Daddy and me. Mummy's family became inaccessible through a long and bitter legal battle over a will, and Daddy's weren't interested. I never met my father's father, Grandpa Margolyes, and Grandpa Walters (Mummy's father) died when I was six. I knew Grandma Walters well because she came to live with us, but she died when I was just eleven. By the time I left school, everybody was dead. The last of my grandparents was Grandma Margolyes. She was eighty-nine years old. It was 1959 when my Auntie Eva telephoned Daddy to say that she was dying. My parents left immediately for Glasgow by car, leaving me alone at home. They thought that it wasn't appropriate for a seventeen-year-old girl to see someone die, but I wanted to be there, because I loved her.

I didn't have the money for the train fare so I went to my father's assistant, who was looking after the practice while Daddy was away. Dr David Smith was a charming man and a skilled doctor. He was also a drug addict (quite common in medical men, apparently). Many years later I knew another doctor, a Harley Street specialist, who injected himself with testosterone during a consultation with me. I didn't know whether to be insulted or pleased.

But David had also injected himself in front of me during a conversation. I'm assuming it was with morphine. He suddenly said, 'I've just got to give myself an injection. Do you mind?' When I said, 'No,' he rolled up his trouser leg and plunged the needle into his calf. I was interested but not shocked, I knew he was wrong to ask me not to tell my parents and I felt uncomfortable, but as I didn't want him to get struck off, I didn't.

David gave me the money and I caught the train to Glasgow. When I arrived at Aytoun Road, Pollokshields, my parents were amazed but ultimately pleased: they thought I was safely at home in Oxford. Grandma was still alive and I went immediately upstairs to her dark bedroom. I remember I felt sad as I held her hand. The curtains were drawn, the room was dark, and I could barely see her little face. I remember she had whiskers on her chin, her eyes were closed and no one spoke. I stayed only a few moments. She died a day or two later with all her children – Daddy, Uncle Jack and their sisters, Aunties Doris and Evelyn – by her bedside. I wasn't in the room but I'm glad I made the journey to say my goodbyes.

I have always felt that one should mark the end of life in whatever way seems appropriate at the time. I always cry at funerals, even if I didn't know the person. I remember attending the funeral in Singapore of my friend Vivienne's grandfather. I walked in the procession to the graveyard, weeping uncontrollably. We had never met, but the knowledge that he was dead, and his family was honouring him, made me inexpressibly sad.

White is the Chinese colour of death but a Jewish funeral is all black. Grandma was buried the day after she died. As Jewish women traditionally do not go to the graveyard, we stayed in the house, preparing the food for those who had gone. All the mirrors were covered and little tears were made in the clothes of the mourners. Mummy tore my dress just a little; she made sure it was reparable – which was rather against the rules.

We did sit *shiva*, the Jewish word for a period of mourning, traditionally sitting on low chairs, receiving the condolences of visitors. Food is always involved, so I helped Auntie Eva to make tasty smoked salmon sandwiches. She was a good hostess and we talked as we buttered and spread. I think Grandma's four children sat on low chairs, but the rest of the guests just mingled in the usual way. People don't stay long and, just as at a 'wake', you talk about the one who has died. Grandma was a quiet soul, kind and sweet, but not the stuff of rip-roaring anecdotes. One I do remember, however, is that when my Cousin Gloria's son Henry was born in 1957, Grandma promised she would knit him a pair of socks. She cast on the wool with good intentions I am sure, but found she only had enough for one sock. Rather than waste the wool in her basket, she finished the other sock in an entirely different colour. It made sense to her, but it was talked about for many years after as an example of Margolyes 'frugality'.

Daddy hadn't lived at home for thirty years but he had loved his mother and was sad. He didn't cry: I think I was the only one who did. All my Scottish relatives were there; I'd never been aware of them before. They were vibrant and characterful, especially the Pasevitch sisters, Essie and Ada, my first cousins once removed, children of my Great-Aunt Sarah, sister of Grandpa Margolyes, who phoned each other every day and were devoted gossips of flair and fun. One of their favourite stories was about Essie's husband, Dave Adams. He had been a naval tailor and lived in Greenock, where he had once made a suit for Prince Philip. They met again some years later. The Prince recognised Dave and smiled affably. 'Ah yes, Adams,' he said. 'I remember you made a suit for me in Greenock.'

'And I've never been paid for it, Your Highness,' said Dave with some courage.

The Prince moved away but the bill was paid a few days later. If you don't ask, you don't get!

I had always loved the stories of my parents' childhoods, hearing about Mummy's sisters and South London theatres and music halls, and about Daddy's poverty-stricken early days in the Margolyeses' cramped apartment in the Gorbals, a family of six in two rooms. Mummy was an accomplished raconteur and enjoyed painting a picture of the days gone by, particularly of the large Michaels family, (her cousins) though they were dismissed as 'rather common' according to her highly class-based hierarchy. Grandma Walters's sister, Fanny, married Max Michaels, a huge, unpleasant, bully who worked in the rag trade, making dresses. Fanny and Max had fourteen children. They were a noisy, high-spirited lot; Jessie (married to Henry) had a dress shop and lived above it in Stratford East; she always kept a fiver in her suspender belt. Mummy used to imitate her Cockney accent. 'Ooh, I just love that fried fish you bring, the plaice is delicious'; Cissie (my first cousin once removed) was flamboyant, famed in the family for her sexual activity. Mummy would not have described her as a 'goer' but I would. She emigrated to America after her daughter married a GI. When she came to see me in Oxford when I was little, she brought me a red tractor, with a moveable crane. It was my favourite toy.

Daddy, however, was less well-versed in his wider family tree. I remember asking, 'Do you remember anything, Daddy?' He said, 'Well, I recall the name of the place we came from, where my father was born. It was called Amdur. I do remember that.' Amdur, a small *shtetl* in Belarus, then part of the Russian Empire, is now called Indura and I later went there in search of my past.

———

In my admittedly limited experience, the three most prominent areas on the internet seem to be: pornography, cats, and genealogy. I've dabbled in all three. I provided the darkly sultry voice of the temptress in the Manikin Cigar advert. 'I come to show you why Manikin flavour plenty enjoyable. I need water. See? Water make leaf stretch. Wrap cigar well. Mouth enjoy flavour. Yes? Manikin flavour special.' I have also spent much of my life being owned by various cats. But genealogy is my passion.

The person who first got me really interested was my beloved cousin Selwyn Torrance. He was an actuary, born in Edinburgh, who grew up in New Zealand and ended up living in Philadelphia. About forty years ago, he drew up the family tree on my father's side as far as he knew it, and he sent everybody a copy. Before then, I didn't really know anything about Grandma Margolyes's family, the Turianskys – or the Goldstones or the Sherwinters or the Pasevitches – but my imagination was immediately and permanently kindled.

Selwyn fired me up – and I've been passionate about investigating my lineage ever since. Genealogy has become my most important hobby. I suppose being an only child and not having a family of my own – no parents, no brothers and sisters, no husband and no children – genealogy has offered me the family I never had. I'm not a lonely person, but I have a need to delve into the past and find out about lost cousins. And I can't stop; once I've got one member of a family, I try to find out everything. It becomes obsessional. I've got 15,000 relatives in my family tree, most of whom are dead, because I 'widened out' beyond the immediate family.

I went miles further than my direct birth family. I wanted more so I followed relatives by marriage, too, and then I got interested in names. There were some people called Silverstone, for example. Was I related to a racetrack? It would originally have been Silberstein, so I followed all the different families, digging deep into their past. I have always described it as being a detective in history – and it gives me the right to ask personal questions of complete strangers; at least, I think it does.

I am now a member of the Jewish Genealogical Society of Great Britain and, pre-Covid, I tried to attend their conference every year. These conventions aren't at all like 'Comic Con' (see 'Be a Fan') – they're much more serious, and the people are much more obsessed. You attend lectures and afterwards you can talk to experts and other attendees. We sit about and discuss fascinating developments in the genealogical sphere. We call it *schmoozing*.

The field is always changing; for example, genealogy has been revitalised by the possibility of registering your DNA on websites. This has caused the number of my family associations to hurtle upwards. Just a few years ago, I discovered that I had two first cousins I hadn't even known existed. A man in Swindon wrote to me to say that we were first cousins once removed. Derek Austin and his brother, it turned out, were irrefutable living proof that my Grandpa Siggi (Walters) had fathered at least one illegitimate child. We worked out that Derek's grandmother Edith had lived just round the corner from my grandparents in South-East London. Siggi had an affair with Edith and she had a child. That child was Derek and his brother's father. Neither had any inkling of their Jewish blood, nor of their roguish grandfather. You can't hide from DNA; the double helix strangles the adulterer long after The Lie is told.

I now get messages every day from people saying 'We share some centimorgans' – a centimorgan is what they call the particle of a DNA chain. Don't ask me why or what that is. But I find it fascinating to know how I'm connected to people.

Now I have become my extended family's expert and my cousins often come to me to make sense of the missing parts of our shared history. Not everyone was happy to discover that we had a criminal in the family – another result of my genealogical digging – but I was thrilled. Every family is full of secrets and lost relatives, but today, thanks to genealogy, no one need remain lost.

In 2009, I reconnected with a whole branch of my mother's family of which I'd previously been unaware. According to Mummy, Max Michaels, the brutish paterfamilias, was not a nice man and two of his sons emigrated to America in 1910. They were not only running away from him, but I believe one of the boys had got a girl pregnant and they were fleeing the scene.

I decided to find them and enlisted the help of my genealogical guru Paul Cheifitz. He discovered from the ship's manifest that they'd changed their name to Mitchell when they went to America. Paul gathered all the obituaries and birth and death certificates and tracked down the family. The brothers had settled just outside Boston, both married Irish Catholic women, and brought their children up as Catholics – assimilating so successfully that one of their daughters even became a nun. The two brothers had a lot of children. There are many of them there, outside Boston, and we found a phone number, so I rang it.

'Is that Mr Mitchell?'

And he said rather warily, 'Yeah.'

'Now, you don't know me. My name is Miriam Margolyes. I'm a British actress and I'm Jewish.'

There was a pause, then he slowly said, 'OK . . . So why call me?'

'I think that we are cousins,' I said.

'No, I don't think so. I don't think so because we are definitely *not* Jewish. We don't have any Jewish members of the family.'

'Well, may I suggest this? If you would be kind enough to give me your email address, can I send you the proof that I think confirms our relationship? And I will phone you in about four days, after you've had time to have a look at it and see what you think. And if that closes the matter and you think it's nonsense, then I'll just let it go.'

'OK,' he said. 'That's fine.'

I sent him an email with photographs and the various scanned documents; then five days later, I rang. When he answered, I said, 'Oh hello, it's Miriam Margolyes again.'

There was a brief pause and then he said, 'Shalom.' It makes me cry even now. 'Shalom.'

'So, you had a good look at it?'

'You know what, Miriam?' he replied. 'You know why there is no doubt? You sent me the photograph you had, and we have the *exact same photograph*.'

'Gosh,' I said, overwhelmed. 'I think I'm going to have to sit down.'

'We couldn't believe it, Miriam. Because you know my dad and my uncle, they didn't like Jews. They were quite antisemitic, as a matter of fact.'

'Really?'

'My aunt is a nun,' he said. 'And you know, it's just hard to believe because Dad kept his past life absolutely secret . . . There was no suggestion of any connection with Judaism.'

Elsa, my second cousin, one of Max's granddaughters, told me that in 1948, the Michaels brothers had told her, 'Do not contact us and do not call us by the name Michaels. We are Mitchells now.' I think it was because of their father. He was such a bastard and I suppose they just wanted to recreate themselves in a new country and put all that nasty family history behind them.

I told him that I was due to travel to Boston later that year.

He said, 'We're gonna have a reunion! We'll have such a big lunch party.'

'Just one thing . . .' I said. 'No pork please.'

And they did hold a big party, in the garden with marquees big enough to seat sixty-two members of the Mitchell family, who are not small. There were so many people, mingling and laughing, crying and taking photographs. It was an incredible experience. But I never will forget that first 'Shalom'.

⸺

I would love to do *Who Do You Think You Are?* If they'll have me, that is. I am still in touch with the producers. The first time we talked they said, 'You know everything. There's no point.' And I do already *know* a lot about my ancestors, because I've been on many genealogical quests for forty years. With families there are always new avenues to be explored, especially now DNA doesn't allow hiding places.

When I started genealogy, I had no thought of actually going to the *shtetl*s my family came from – those small Eastern European villages where Jews lived and died, disliked and attacked for hundreds of years before the Holocaust. But in 2008 the BBC took me to Amdur in Belarus, the home of my father's family, and much later, in 2013, I was also able to visit Margonin in Poland (my mother's family town). Although in different countries, they were much as I'd imagined. I went in cautiously, knowing that not a single Jew was left in either place.

In 2005, I was making a film in Lithuania, about Edward and Mrs Simpson – I was playing her kindly Aunt Bessie – and I went first to Mass in the huge cathedral in Vilnius. It was packed with the flat, peasant faces I'd seen in wartime photographs. Immediately, I felt uneasy, I knew these people were my enemy, I felt acutely aware that the history of Lithuanians killing their Jews was little spoken of now, but nonetheless true. Throughout the filming, I visited several mass graves, despite local Lithuanians averring there were none. That is not true; Lithuanians killed their fellow Lithuanians because they were Jews. It is still an edgy subject and one of the reasons I campaign for Holocaust truth, despite my powerful pro-Palestinian stance on Israel. I want to force people to acknowledge what really happened, knowing they prefer to avoid the truth.

It was different in Poland. Margonin is a small, pleasant, sleepy town in their Lake District. Following Mummy's rule of going straight to the top, I found the mayor and once I explained the reason for my visit, we were warmly welcomed. He showed me the archives, the remnants of the old Jewish cemetery, and gave us a good lunch in the Grand Hotel with delicious *pierogi*. You can't escape *pierogi* in Poland

– I just had to check they made them with beef! The old, thatched-roof houses were still there; no signs of Jewish occupation. But the school records of Margonin confirmed my family's existence. We traced my mother's family back to 1790.

Later that year, I met Kamila Klauszińska, who finds Jewish cemeteries and mass graves and gets teams of young Poles to restore the old gravestones. Although not a Jew, she has dedicated her life to righting the wrongs of history. The horror of what happened doesn't change, but her sense of purpose in retelling our story restores my faith in humanity.

⁓

Genealogy must be about the living just as much as the dead. That's why a family tree is such a comforting thing. It's not just a list of names but a plunging into a world that still continues, a group of funny, imperfect, often annoying but also loving and loveable people connected to me. When I look at my tree, I know I am part of an enormous linked chain of 15,000 souls – and growing! With that big a tribe, you can never be lonely. Now go and grow your own.

Believe in Yourself

Acting is a scary profession. You can tell yourself you're an actress all you like, but if nobody asks you to act, then what are you? Rejection becomes the norm and that is damaging. Is it sheer stubbornness repeatedly to risk more doors slamming in your face, or is it a sign of inner confidence honouring the gifts you know you possess? I am often asked where I find my zest for life; how have I kept going. I don't know the answer – it's who I am. But believe me, it is the rejections I remember rather than the triumphs.

I feel strongly that if you have a loving family as a foundation, you can do anything. I was extraordinarily lucky. The unconditional love my parents showered on me has protected me from the dangers of my precarious profession. I knew they adored me and they did all they possibly could to help and encourage me. I always felt confident; even when I was not terribly successful at 'growing up', I knew who I was and, on the whole, I liked what I knew. My mother said, 'Go forward. Don't look at those on each side of you. Think about the road ahead. It's not about what other people are doing. What matters is what *you're* doing.' She believed in me totally. And she told me so repeatedly. Did it make me conceited? Probably, yes. But it meant I could go on through whatever disappointments lay in my path. The words of advice I most often heard from my parents were, 'Do the *best* you can, Miriam.' They would always stress 'the *best*'. My duty was to pursue excellence.

I realised that I was going to find life interesting but difficult. I am naturally profoundly lazy, I fritter time away, I don't focus, I am easily sidetracked, I procrastinate. So, I have not done the best I could. Nevertheless, I keep going.

When I emerged from my mother, I had caused her immense pain and worry from the moment of conception. Not only was she afraid to have a baby (two cousins had died in childbirth) but I was literally cut out of her. Yet from the moment the nurse put me in her arms, Mummy dedicated her whole life to me. I knew immediately that I wanted to connect with people. Mummy told me how I followed everyone with my gaze, even from the pram. And people were always stopping her in the street and asking to look at me, exclaiming, 'Oh, what a beautiful baby!' I was indeed ferociously gorgeous.

Mummy gave me the confidence to be who I am. Being an only child can be lonely, but it also means there is NO COMPETITION! I was therefore the complete focus of my parents' adoration. That's the upside: the downside is that, despite my self-belief, I have always suffered agonies of self-doubt and anxiety. Possibly that's normal – it certainly rescued me from the loathsome smugness and conceit to which I might otherwise have been subject.

Going to school is a great leveller. I longed to meet other children and found no difficulty in making friends. I was never shy. I'm sure my ability to make people laugh helped my self-belief. People like people who make them laugh. I spotted that pretty quickly.

Miss Stack, our imposing OHS headmistress, taught us *A Midsummer Night's Dream* in the Lower Third. It was obvious I was to read the part of Bottom. Even aged nine, I was a good Bottom and I revelled in the moment. I put on a cockney accent for comic effect. (I still do that!) Years later I realised it should have been Warwickshire. 'Methought I was enamoured of an ass,' Titania says waking up – well, I was that ass.

When I left home and went to Cambridge in 1960, I thought I was free, I could do whatever I wanted. Of course, that wasn't the case. My parents often visited, staying in the comfortable guest apartments at Newnham College, and had no intention of 'letting me go'. They never have. It's obvious from the way I write about them that I am still in thrall, almost willingly. My therapist Margaret Branch's efforts to pull me into independent maturity largely failed. The power of their adoration hasn't lessened as the years have gone by. I am a child for ever, wiser, stronger, richer certainly than I was, but a child nevertheless; and it may well be that my stunted emotional growth both helped and hindered my development as an actress.

After I left university in 1963, I dreamed of going on the stage. I didn't envisage any other life despite the difficulties and my lack of formal dramatic education.

In the beginning it was extremely hard. I had no theatre connections. That's an understatement – I knew no one. And when I couldn't get a job, I had a crisis of self-belief. I was weeping and carrying on. Mummy sat me down in my bedroom and we had a long session. She said, 'You've got to go on, you've got talent.' She made it clear that she utterly trusted in my talent and wanted me to continue. I remember the way she said it – with passion and considerable ferocity. Daddy never featured in these discussions. He didn't understand the theatre, faintly distrusted it, and probably thought it was best to let Mummy handle the whole situation. He saw it as an 'expense of spirit in a waste of shame'. Even once I became successful, in his heart of hearts, I don't think he changed his mind. He cheered up considerably when he realised I was making money, but alas he never saw it as a worthwhile occupation.

Rejection is always a bitter pill. I cannot sweeten the moment for you, it hurts like hell. But if you're going into show business – or chasing any dream – you have to be able to swallow hard and continue. Don't allow yourself to be deflected from your goal, don't let puny naysayers win the day. Dig into the deepest part of yourself – the *pupik*, as we say in Yiddish; Gentiles translate it rather weakly as 'the belly-button', but I call it 'the inner you', the part no one can reach or damage – and rise again.

Not long after I became a professional actress, I auditioned for John Harrison at Leeds Playhouse, then one of the leading repertory theatres in the country. Just as at Cambridge when trying to get into the ADC, I was dressed in green trousers tucked into hockey socks (well, it was cold) – and I forgot the lines of the Chorus from *Henry V*, the piece I had absurdly chosen to perform. 'O for a Muse of Fire!' I boomed and then stopped. Mr Harrison was clearly underwhelmed. He joined me on the stage. 'Are you absolutely sure you're set on a stage career?' 'Oh yes,' I said. There was a pause. Then Mr Harrison delivered his verdict on me: 'If I were you, I'd think again.' I remember standing there looking at him thinking, 'You silly man. You can't see my gift. You can't see the talent. What a fool you are.'

That's an unusual reaction for an untried actor. Most people would accept the view of the person taking the audition. They would probably think, 'Oh God, I did badly there; I'm hopeless, maybe I should give it up.' But I never thought that. At least, I certainly didn't on that occasion. On the contrary, the voice inside said, 'You are an actress.

You have a future. You're going to make it. Never mind what he says.' And on I went.

I'm addressing this bit to those of you who are at the beginning, trying to get a job, fighting for work, desperate to prove to yourselves that it is worth the effort, that you have something to offer. I know it's harder now than it ever was. The goal is to *be noticed*. Get parts, even small parts. Write letters but don't make them too long; offer to work for free; call in at film companies; waylay people you admire and ask them for a job; send twenty more letters to cancel out one rejection; pay attention to who's good on TV or in films; note the names of directors you admire and when you write to them mention the work they did that you liked. Go to the National Portrait Gallery, find someone you resemble and write your own show about them. Keep reading, watching, writing; remain artistically alive. Be punctual, smile when you come on stage, look happy to be with them, even if you're scared stiff. Do your homework, so you know something about them you can refer to, KNOW THE LINES, offer more than they ask. I'm specifically referring to show business here, but my advice can relate to any job interview. If you make an effort, you get results.

My determination and confidence eventually won me parts, but I was not an overnight success, by any means. My first few roles were small but I made myself pleasant, so they'd remember I was nice to have around. A grumpy cunt won't work for long. Once I was successful in landing the audition, my confidence didn't necessarily follow me into rehearsals. With me, the process of acting is quite slow. I take time. I have to work extremely hard to learn my lines. I lack discipline. But I concentrate, I welcome direction. I enjoy being part of a team, I relish the camaraderie and working things out together. We're not always there by the first night, but that's the magic of theatre. You can grow, you learn as you go, and you improve together.

Actors are famously superstitious. Sometimes I might put my left shoe on first and not the right, for example. But these little rituals don't help me with my character. They just help with my nerves. Before each performance I concentrate, shut out everything else, and because I get panicky, I continually remind myself to take deep breaths. Then I am an empty vessel ready to be filled by the character that I've built up over the weeks of rehearsal. I know where the pauses should come, where my character is uncertain. I know all those things and I let the character flood into me. The spirit gently crosses the stage towards me, I breathe in and the character enters and is locked in for the night.

The real terror of live performance is forgetting my lines. It has happened to me about three times in fifty years. The most recent was in my last performance at the Park Theatre in 2019 in a difficult play by Eugene O'Hare, *Sydney and the Old Girl*. It was a three-hander, with Mark Hadfield and Vivien Parry – two marvellous artists, who couldn't have been more supportive. The first act was table-tennis fast, Mark and I blasted across at each other, a mother and son exploding with malice and hidden pain. No space for pauses, and I faltered. I went round and round trying to fasten myself back to the text. I got there in the end, but it was a passage of terror I shan't forget. Luckily, I don't think the audience knew. That's the beauty of modern plays. In 1979, I was in Snoo Wilson's *Flaming Bodies* at the ICA with Julie Walters. I had an eight-page monologue and by the first night I still didn't know my lines. I was frightened. So much so that I ran out of the theatre and jumped into a taxi. Julie followed anxiously and then we were driving round and round London. Julie was desperately trying to persuade me to go back to the theatre. I wouldn't.

'Oh, go on, Miriam, we can do it together,' Julie begged. 'PLEASE!'

'I just can't,' I wailed and we drove on.

The bemused taxi driver silently kept his eyes on the ticking meter as the fare kept increasing.

I didn't do the performance that night. I just couldn't. I didn't know my lines. People were told to come back the next night. But I went home, pulled myself together and somehow drilled the monologue into my head overnight; I performed the play on the second night, and all was well.

Luckily, I've nearly always had good reviews. I believe there is a certain uncompromising quality to my acting, an inner confidence, that allows me to grab hold of a role and not be dissuaded. Once I've decided that this is my character, this is how I'm going to behave on stage, then you, the audience, will accept me, you will make room for me, you will enjoy me. Audiences acquiesce because there's nothing else they can do. Even writing about it makes me want to go on stage this minute and experience that joy of feeling my character taking control and demanding to be 'let out' to live.

As an actor there's never a moment when you think, 'It's going to be all right, it's all going to work out.' It isn't like that. After every job finishes, you're straight back to thinking: 'Will I ever work again?' Insecurity goes with the territory.

When I began, fame must have been a consideration – I mean, it's part of being in the acting profession – but I honestly don't think it was my motivating factor. In my childhood, my idols, such as Laurence Olivier, Vivien Leigh and Marlene Dietrich, had a level of celebrity on a scale beyond anything I could ever have dreamed.

I never imagined that *I* would be famous. No – for me the fulfilment came simply from acting. And it still surprises me to be seen as successful. I've always had an outgoing personality which people remember, but I didn't think that would ever translate into a wider sphere. So, it is a delightful discovery that audiences and readers like me. Not all, of course. I am loathed by many. I have been called vile and hideously ugly and foul-mouthed and talentless. The tag that really stung was being called a 'National Trinket'. I've since adopted it. But inside, I know it was really meant to sting – and it did.

Even if I don't continually ask 'Do you like me?' as I did at school, I still worry that people might dislike me. When invited to 'dos' at Buckingham Palace, I felt ill-equipped and unworthy. It's hard to believe there's anything 'posh' in Australia, but in Sydney recently I was taken to the polo ground and I was conscious of feeling under-privileged in that unfamiliar environment of wealth and poise. I don't dress well, I will never be elegant; I felt ill at ease. On the surface I seem confident – indeed, people often think that I'm pushy – but inside I'm quaking with inadequacy.

Somehow, I rise above it. Passionate curiosity about those to whom I speak rescues me from embarrassment. That's what Mummy wanted for me; she gave me the courage and tenacity to believe in myself.

Many people of my age with my disabilities might say, 'Well, I'm done. I've had enough; I'm going to get old and do nothing.' But there's something that prevents me from that. If I have people around me, even if it's only a work meeting or a visit from a telephone engineer to sort out my landline, having an audience gives me new energy. I still thrive on having people to talk to and things to learn and so I am energised. Give me an audience and I'm young again.

That has always been the case. Take my time in America, for example, when my series *Frannie's Turn* wasn't taking off. People said, 'You're going to be so rich you won't know what to do with yourself!' I knew that wasn't going to happen. And when it didn't, I wasn't surprised or disappointed. I just thought, 'Well, I tried it, and a television comedy series wasn't necessarily what I wanted.'

Failure didn't knock me off my course. If I'd been a different kind of actress, it could have been a moment of great tragedy. But it wasn't. I love to think that I might create something unexpected even now. It is a source of delight to me that my work in documentaries has found favour and that I continue to explore the world. Despite being disabled, I remain employable, and I hope this encourages others to try new endeavours. The plain truth is you can't ever know what's in store. Except Death – that unavoidable curtain-fall you cannot cheat. Ever looming nearer, but so far I'm carrying on. I only wish Mummy could know that I've done all right. I'd love to be able to give her that pleasure.

How to Stay Married

Heather and I have been together for fifty-four years, although only civilly partnered since 2013. And we only did that because if one of us were to get ill, doctors won't discuss the loved one's condition with the other, unless formally joined. As we hurtled toward eighty, we felt that that was a risk we couldn't take.

When I was looking for Australian citizenship, I had to prove our relationship, which was hard, because we have always lived apart, me in the UK and Heather in Holland. Using the rather enticingly named legislation called Same Sex Spouse Entry (they explain it thus: 'there is only one category of visa available to the same-sex partner of an Australian permanent resident or citizen: the Interdependency visa category'), I gathered photos and letters and holiday receipts and statements from friends, to prove we really were a couple. It worked and now I am safely spliced in both England and Australia and am a full voting citizen of both nations.

We are often asked for our recipe for a successful relationship. We met in what is now a ridiculously old-fashioned way – no internet pervings whetted our appetites. We were introduced in London by our mutual friend Katerina Clark; she and Heather were both on scholarships at Yale and came on a research trip to London together. My first sight of her was as she sat in the back of a VW Beetle as I was being collected from my Bayswater flat to go and watch *The Charge of the Light Brigade*. I glimpsed a head of startlingly white-blonde hair, blue-grey eyes and a thoughtful expression. She seemed slim, not very tall, and quiet. The minute I saw her I fancied her rotten. Of course, I had the advantage because I knew she was gay, but she didn't know I was. She thought I was too noisy to be gay. I showed off relentlessly, insisted on sitting next to her at the movies and never looked at the film. And the following week, I plotted a lunch date and insisted Katy bring her. The mashed potato I served was the only aphrodisiac – it was enough. We embarked enthusiastically on a full-blooded sexual explosion, which was hugely enjoyable and deeply satisfactory, both standing up and lying down. We fucked vigorously and continuously and merrily. I don't think we talked much then; our mouths were otherwise engaged. But in the brief comings-up for air, I knew I was onto a winner: I knew that she was 'the one'. Heather had no such certainties, poor soul: she thought it was a holiday romance, quite pleasing but with no expectations whatsoever.

When she returned to America, we wrote proper letters to each other on aerogrammes. There was no email then. And we explained in those aerogrammes who we were, what music we liked, what books we were reading, sharing every moment we could in writing. She taught me about Schubert (classical), about Flatt and Scruggs (bluegrass), about the Spice Islands, and shared her research on the colonial Dutch empire and her knowledge of Indonesia. When she came over to stay, she cooked me exotic dishes using sambal, the frighteningly spicy Indonesian chilli sauce which makes the hottest curries taste as mild as custard in contrast. And I learned about the world of academe from the inside. I became familiar with another person, another mind, much more wide-ranging and comprehensive than my own. In

Welcome to my house. This eight-foot-high billboard of Serena Evans and me laughing in *The Killing of Sister George* in my front hall greets all visitors.

My grandfather's cherub statue is made of such solid Carrara marble that it took seven men to drag it down into my basement. Whenever I see it, I know I'm home.

Three noisy vulvas: with Sophie Dahl and Siân Phillips in *The Vagina Monologues*.

At first it was fiction when I played Alan Bennett's *The Lady in the Van*. Then it turned into fact and a series of wonderful jobs all over the world.

With Alan Cumming from *Lost in Scotland and Beyond*.

With female trucker Heather from *Miriam Margolyes: Almost Australian*.

I love being on the road – here I am in *Miriam Margolyes: Australia Unmasked*.

Whether as Miss Prism, boiling with lust for the Reverend Chasuble in *The Importance of Being Earnest* . . .

. . . or as the Nurse in Baz Luhrmann's *Romeo + Juliet* trying to persuade Claire Danes's Juliet to pick a more sensible boyfriend than Leonardo DiCaprio's Romeo: character *is* plot.

I really hope I'm not the reason these three are looking so glum – admittedly they are downwind. Daniel Radcliffe later went on to warn Alan Cumming about my farting on the Harry Potter set.

On *Wicked*, Nigel Planer shared his horror about my flatulence: 'Oh for God's sake, Miriam!'

The multifarious joys of chat shows.

My first, rather restrained, appearance on *Wogan*, trying desperately not to fart or swear.

These days I let it all hang out, here surprising Robert Peston into nearly falling off his chair on *Peston on Sunday*.

And then on *The Graham Norton Show*, my spiritual home, asking poor Matthew Perry questions that he was NOT expecting.

Hanging out with a post-pubescent Daniel Radcliffe and friends.

I've always loved animals, from my adored childhood pet Bonny to the ones I've acted alongside.

Playing Miss Crawley in *Vanity Fair* in 1998.

They say, find your happy place –
for Heather and me, it's Italy, our
beloved cats and our olive groves.

Here is the label for our olive oil,
complete with portraits of the three
owners – guess which one is me?!

Becoming the cover star of *Vogue* at the age of eighty-two was not what I (or the world) expected. I loved every minute of the shoot with Tim Walker.

My amazing adventures continue . . .

return, I taught her about being Jewish, about Dickens, I shared my friends, my hopes for my career.

No one will be surprised to hear that my letters were affectionate, highly sexual in content and shockingly explicit. I felt great sympathy for Prince Charles, as he was then, when his private words to Camilla were leaked. We all say silly, sexy things to people we love. And no one would want their 'sweet nothings' to be emblazoned on newspaper front pages across the world. We also phoned each other (she was based in New Haven, Connecticut), and we made plans. She would visit; I would visit. Then she got a job in Malaysia, I worked in the UK and Europe, and on we went.

The weeks turned into months, then years, then decades. We are both busy, professional women, our jobs matter to us: I have to be in an English-speaking country, she has to be where the archives of the Dutch East India Company are available, so she settled in Amsterdam. We decided to give up nothing, to stay together, have separate establishments in separate countries, meet when we could and have the best of both worlds. We're fiercely independent and very different: we each need our own space. I like to be with people but she prefers solitude; she is reserved, quiet, a historian and a scholar, engrossed in her own intellectual world. She doesn't want to be the centre of attention. It's important to find ways of being together but also separate. For many years, two great English writers and lovers, Margaret Drabble and Michael Holroyd lived at different ends of London from each other – one in Hampstead, one in Ladbroke Grove. I always thought that that was a perfect arrangement. And so far, for us, it has worked.

But everyone (and every relationship) is different. I'd be insane to try to push our way of sorting our lives onto anyone else. We did what was best for us. And I do believe in continuous communication. We phone EVERY DAY at least once, sometimes more. Often quite late at night. Heather has always been more predictable in her timetable; either at the university, working, lecturing or teaching, or at home in her study looking over the Prinsengracht canal in Amsterdam. As I'm often on the road, touring or filming, she doesn't always know where I'll be, so it is always me who phones her.

It's important to have a loving partner. Life is sweeter shared, and there is no one I would rather spend my life with. We have been honest, sometimes painfully so. And once we separated for six months, certainly the bleakest moments of my life. I was unfaithful. I was foolish and stupid and Heather just wasn't having it. She was quite right.

Never stop working on your relationship. I knew I could never survive without Heather. I know there could never be a more perfect person for me. I pleaded to start again. We did. This is not to say that it's easy. It is not, and of course we have fierce disagreements. Heather is very clear-eyed both about me and our relationship. She is loyal in the sense that I know she loves me, but she also sees my faults, with a sometimes pulverising clarity. My friends tend to accept me and love me and allow me to behave badly. She won't.

Heather only met my parents after Mummy had the stroke. Mummy's strong personality was still evident but, alas, the stroke had taken away her speech. She could only say, 'Pouf, I want.' It was a terrifying seven and a half years until she died. Heather could see that it was a family disaster and was immensely supportive. My parents and I formed a tight little unit and would sit together watching television, while Heather scrubbed their kitchen, which had got very grubby, as a self-elected charlady. She was staggered by the way we took it absolutely for granted. And it still is one of the things that she finds most infuriating about me. In fact, she says I expect *everyone* to be subordinate to *my* interests. ('In reply,' she points out, 'Miriam will be charming and generous, but it's clear that's the way it has to be.') Well, everything's a trade-off. I can always rely on Heather to tell me the truth.

In my parents' generation, everyone pretended things were OK, keeping a lid on problems until things got so out of control that it all bubbled over; I think the way Heather and I communicate is so much healthier. Talking openly about everything, it means nothing is off limits and it's very cleansing. I like Heather's perceptions: she sees me clearly and has decided to accept some things about my behaviour and not to accept others. She won't have any nonsense. (Strict disciplinarian!)

Heather has had to manage her debilitating chronic fatigue syndrome for so long that she tends to give short shrift to my health problems. She doesn't think that I should be allowed not to walk – she's not unsympathetic, but quite beady about my not doing things. She thinks I don't try hard enough. Her thesis on me is that I was spoilt as a child. And I'm afraid it's true. There's a certain judgemental hardness about her, which I relish. I wish sometimes that she was a little more understanding, more forgiving of my faults. But Heather is also just as hard on herself. I, on the other hand, am very loving with her *and* with myself. She agrees that I am much kinder than she is.

Small gestures can warm the heart. For example, she switches on my electric blanket every night before I go up to bed. Every morning, I light the fire in the large sitting room in our house in Italy. It's a wood-burning stove, made of iron – just a big square box with a chimney which goes up to her bedroom above. So, when the fire is lit below, she is cosy. And I am happy.

Another area where we agree totally is politics. Heather is on the left – perhaps not as far to the left as I am, but she certainly agrees with me on most major issues. Her venom for the Israeli government is even more pronounced than mine. She grew up with conventional Australian parents, who didn't have much to do with Jews and retained fairly old-fashioned attitudes to them. I tease her from time to time about being an antisemite. My own views on nearly everything have sharpened and become more entrenched. I am less tolerant than I was. The present government shenanigans infuriate and disgust me. I find Heather's views more sensible and more informed than my own. We don't read tabloids and I subscribe to the *Times Literary Supplement* and the *London Review of Books* and post them on to her in Amsterdam.

I always wanted someone cleverer than me, just as my mother did. I can learn from her intellectually, but in worldly matters, I am the superior. Heather is ridiculously gullible and has been cheated many times by unscrupulous door-to-door salesmen; she falls for the most obvious sob story and gives money to clearly criminal types. I never do. My mother taught me how to spot an imposter, a liar, a phoney. Now I'm equally adept – and proud of my quick annihilations of spam merchants. When they phone, always at lunchtime with a scheme to make money and ask for me by name, I simply say: 'Oh, she died about three weeks ago.' They ring off sharpish!

Sex in any marriage is important. Now it's calmer days and sex is a sweet memory – while I don't need it any more, I'm happy to talk about it and it makes me laugh. Sex is not to be sneezed at. But the love must be there; without that, all is pointless. We love each other and I have been sustained, comforted and reassured by our relationship; it's the central spine of my life, and it has been since I met her. I still go off to work, to film, to do documentaries, but the coming back is very sweet. She retains her separate primary residence, as do I. Neither of us ever plans to retire, but I hope that perhaps we might be able to live in one town, in one place together. I've actually bought the flat next door in London and I thought it'd be quite nice if she lived there, where I won't be in her way, and we can come together in the evenings. Because the highest joy I know is to be in the same room, either talking or silent, reading or watching a film, and looking upon her dear face and being grateful she's in my life, that I chose my partner so well and that we made a life together. Here are my ten tips on how to stay married:

1. A ROOM OF ONE'S OWN – Virginia Woolf suggested that every woman needs a room of her own. I heartily agree. But to my mind, *everyone* needs private space, to think, reflect, be oneself. It's creative separation.
2. TALK TO EACH OTHER (and listen to what the other says), ESPECIALLY DURING SEX.
3. SEX DOESN'T LAST, SO ENJOY IT WHILE YOU CAN – remember, as I said on TV: a good radish is better than bad sex.
4. RELISH THE DIFFERENCES BETWEEN YOU – don't try to make the other the same as you.
5. BE KIND. BE RESPECTFUL – words can bite and wound. Don't do it.

6. DON'T GAMBLE WITH YOUR HAPPINESS – just being married doesn't stop your noticing another possibility. But it's seldom worth it. Like giving into your desire for lemon meringue pie, a moment on the lips and forever in the shit.

7. DON'T FUDGE, DON'T BE GLIB – this person knows you and still loves you.

8. IF YOU'RE NOT HAPPY, FACE IT – AND TALK ABOUT IT!

9. NEVER LET THE SUN SET ON A QUARREL – a true cliché.

10. MARRIAGE IS VOLUME ONE – you haven't finished writing. Keep at it. Make Volume Two even more interesting. Like this book!

Face Your Whiskers

I tumbled out of the womb, my head covered with black curly hair. When I started school, I wore it in fat glossy bunches on either side of my head. My hair has always been unruly and has caused comment – some envied it, others, like Grandma Walters, considered it a problem to be solved. Mummy decided that dousing my locks with olive oil would tame them. It undoubtedly gave my hair a glorious shine, but I suspect it also made it rather stinky. One day in the Third Form, when Valerie Scott commented loudly on the odour, I floored her with a right hook and she had to go to hospital. Thankfully, she forgave me, is still my friend and has never mentioned my smelly hair again.

Perhaps because my hair was black, when I was younger, I looked more Jewish. But I've always liked women with white, blonde or grey hair. I find them devastatingly attractive. Always did. On that first encounter with Heather, it was her glorious white-blonde hair that first attracted me.

But I simply hate washing my hair. I'm afraid I don't even go to the hairdresser regularly to get it washed and dried. I just brush it until, every so often, Heather says, 'I think it's time you washed your hair.' And then I do. I never dry my hair. I just scrunch it and leave it.

And I don't use deodorant. I haven't used it for years, actually. I've never sweated much under my arms. But I always beg people to tell me if I stink. I ask them, 'Do I smell?' I wash the areas carefully, it's an important daily chore to keep oneself fragrant, properly washed – and moustache free. Even as a young child at school, hairiness was something that we girls somehow understood *wasn't* good. You want it on your head and your cunt and nowhere else. That's the rule of hair. You knew that you had to get rid of whiskers and if you had hair on your nipples or your legs, they had to go too. I gather that most young women today shave their pubic hair or have it removed completely, by waxing. Well, let's put it like this: just let them grow to my age and they won't need to spend money at any beauty salon.

Luckily, excess hair on my body hasn't been a problem. I never had particularly hirsute legs or underarms, for example, but I used to shave them because everyone else did: I don't need to any more. And I've never had hairs on my nipples or chest. But now, to make up for that, hair pops up on my chin and upper lip – not like a moustache, but I will admit some are long! I've got one that regularly appears on my neck and curls round so that you can't see it at first and then one day – there she blows! The first time I spotted it, not realising its power and length, I pulled and pulled – it was like a rope! If I have any beauty advice for the older woman, it would be to carry tweezers and a magnifying mirror in your handbag, and use them. Now when I go into make-up for a chat show, it's the first thing I ask: 'Tweezers, and do my whiskers please.' They're always happy to do it: in fact, they're delighted to be asked. They probably look at the hairy chins, nostril and ear sproutings on the women and men sitting there in front of these mirrors surrounded by bright lights, and are simply longing to get stuck in. One make-up artist told me that many women won't acknowledge they've got chin hair or a moustache. I haven't got time for that sort of rubbish. If you've got whiskers, face it and deal with them: otherwise, you'll go round looking like Brian Blessed and there is only room for one of them in this world.

Be a Fan

Oxford High School was all female and in that oestrogen-charged haven, I harboured intense crushes on other girls and famous people and I was not alone. We talked obsessively about the various objects of our affection.

For a child of the fifties, I had oddly old-fashioned tastes. My obsession with our young Queen Elizabeth II continued, and the yellow walls of The Den outside our kitchen were plastered with her photographs, clipped from the newspapers. And I dreamed about her very often. I still do. I can't recall any details. I just know that we were inhabiting the same space and sometimes we had quite warm conversations.

But as Britain rattled into the Pop Age, I remained like Victoria (Elizabeth's great-great-grandmother) resolutely unamused. I was never a modern personality. You could describe me both inside and outside school as a 'swot'; popular culture passed me by. I've never liked rock 'n' roll or pop music. I never understood it. Lots of girls my age screamed themselves hoarse for Elvis Presley and Johnnie Ray. I ignored them. I stayed tuned to the BBC's Home Service and *It's That Man Again* or the Third Programme. Later, in the early sixties, the Beatles and the Stones also left me cold. I was NOT their fan.[*]

---

[*] When Heather christened the fling that made me realise I was a lesbian, 'Norwegian Wood', I had no idea it was a Beatles song till I got the edit of my first book back. It took me over fifty years to get the joke.

My passion has always been reserved for the theatre, a different and somehow timeless world. Laurence Olivier, Vivien Leigh, Marlene Dietrich, and Richard Burton were my heroes. I had an autograph book and I was determined to meet them all.

In February 1966, Richard Burton and Elizabeth Taylor came to perform *Dr Faustus* by Christopher Marlowe, at the Oxford Playhouse. At that time, they were the biggest stars in the world and the tickets for the show sold out in minutes. When my unstoppable friend Mahnaz suggested that if we queued all night outside the Playhouse box office, we might be able to snaffle some matinee tickets, I agreed like a shot.

Oxford in February is very cold, but we were young; we wrapped up warmly and we persuaded ourselves that we were having fun. And truly – we were. At about two in the morning, as we sat on our little chairs dozing, we noticed a wonderful Rolls Royce saloon pull up outside the Randolph Hotel. A couple emerged but instead of going straight into the hotel, they walked towards the queue and started to chat to us. It was Burton and Taylor. Stars at close quarters are heady stuff. They were sure of themselves and the welcome they would receive from the waiting queue. They were entirely relaxed, enjoying our delight in them and the absurdity of our waiting for hours in the freezing February weather.

'You must be mad to do this,' Burton said. 'Give your names to my friend here at the stage door and join us tomorrow for a drink.'

Taylor didn't say much but she looked superb; almost the entire time her lilac eyes were smiling.

We felt chosen, uplifted – somehow at the centre of the earth. Proximity to Celebrity kept us warm after they left us to go to bed at the Randolph. I remember little of the show, just being there was the enchantment. Then we gave our names to the stage door, along with the university fans, and clustered in a Dressing Room – an ordinary space made astonishing because *they* were there. Drinks were served. At some point, boldly I said, 'You really must play *Anna Karenina* together.'

Burton looked up, amused. 'You mean, you want her to speak?' In *Dr Faustus*, she was playing the silent role of Helen of Troy, 'the face that launch'd a thousand ships and burnt the topless towers of Ilium'.

Everyone, including Taylor laughed. The show played for six weeks; it was good-ish. He spoke like an angel; and as he had wanted, Faustus's last speech was electric. We parted, but I have never forgotten that joyous moment.

I met Marlene Dietrich later that year when she came to Britain to do her show at the Golders Green Hippodrome – later a television studio but in those days a top variety venue. After the show, I queued outside the stage door with all the others until finally she came out looking impossibly glamorous. Then she climbed onto the roof of the car that had come to fetch her and sat and talked to the throng of fans for over an hour. She was utterly compelling. She clearly enjoyed our adulation and flirted and teased and joked until the years fell away from her and you could have sworn she was a young girl again, making eyes at all of us. I called out, 'Du warst wunderbar.' That got her attention. She smiled delightedly. 'Sprichst du Deutsch?' she exclaimed. She leaned down, cupped my face in her hands and kissed me.

And I remember distinctly when Laurence Olivier walked out of the stage door of the New Theatre in Oxford, wearing a little brown trilby hat, and raised it, I was so starstruck, I came over all funny. So much so I started to cream in my knickers. As Graham Norton commented drily, 'There is, perhaps, no greater compliment.'

———

The point for me was to meet the real person that I admired so much. I've only ever joined two fan clubs, those of Dusty Springfield and Barbra Streisand. Just two years older than me, Dusty was a true lesbian icon. If only it had made her as happy as it has done me – but she turned her pain into Art. I wish we'd had the chance to meet. Barbra and I did; I joined her fan club in the throes of the excitement of working with her on *Yentl*. Unlike Richard E. Grant, who commissioned an enormous sculpture of the left side of Streisand's disembodied face (the side she prefers to be viewed from), which proudly sits amongst the shrubs in his back garden, I let my membership of her fan club lapse. I wasn't quite so enthusiastic about acting with her the second time round. Of course she is talented; she just wasn't as nice as I had remembered – or hoped.

Now that I am finally enjoying a certain level of celebrity, I love it. When I did my first book tour, people waited outside the stage door for hours to say hello. If only I was mobile enough to jump on a car roof to speak to them! Protecting myself from Covid aside, the only time it got frightening was in Lithuania for another film role. I was at a ballet matinee, enjoying the show and, suddenly, I was mobbed by a screaming group of Harry Potter fans. They were surprised that I was so on edge. But usually when Jews are mobbed in Lithuania, it's to kill them. After I got my breath back, I smiled and signed some autographs, so it ended well at least.

I've been a successful actress for over half a century and it is strange to me that it is some of my more minor roles that have inspired the most devotion. Thanks to *Blackadder*, men of a certain age still shout 'Wicked child!' at me in the street, somewhat nervously, as if sheepishly hoping that I will brandish a phallic turnip and start beating them round the head. But the role that has stood me in best stead, was playing Professor Sprout in the Harry Potter films.

I haven't read the books and to be entirely honest I slept through the premieres, so I have never got the point of the films, but so devoted are my followers that I was delighted to find I had an 'in' on the 'fan convention' circuit. It was Sylvester McCoy, Doctor Who Mark VII, who got me going. He told me about travelling around the world, being paid to appear at events called 'Comic Con', 'Awesome Con' and 'Chicago TARDIS', meeting science-fiction buffs and being photographed with them. I rather liked the sound of that. Of course, I wasn't in *Doctor Who* then, BUT I AM NOW! Just you wait till you meet the Meep.

Sylvester went to his first convention thirty years ago, in Greenville, South Carolina. He was cast on the Monday, and on Thursday, off he flew. It was to be the first of many: even though there have now been fourteen or so Doctor Whos, he's still flying off monthly to exciting destinations all over the world. The convention has matured from a few fan-based gatherings in halls around the country to vast aircraft hangars. He put me in touch with Julian Owen, who is one of the most honest and hard-working convention agents in the UK. Julian started off in Virgin Airlines, being a problem solver at Gatwick Airport. In 2007, he was called on to help a tall man on crutches. It turned out to be David Prowse, the genial weightlifter turned actor, who played

Darth Vader in the *Star Wars* trilogy. From that first encounter, whenever David travelled to a convention, he asked for Julian to be his personal helper, and Julian realised there was another career awaiting him and he looked after David until the actor's death in 2020. Now, in 2023, he is the convention agent for 185 clients, and we all get a personal and friendly service. With competing events in all four corners of the globe, there is cut-throat competition between the vying convention organisers, each trying to persuade the biggest stars to attend their event. Julian likened it to the violent Glasgow ice-cream wars of the 1980s; in an attempt to dissuade me from appearing at a rival convention, I remember one producer going so far as to slur the competition by suggesting he had a criminal record for paedophilia. It didn't work; Julian knew the whole story.

A convention is an ideal conduit for fans to meet and speak to the object of their adoration. In the huge venues, tables are set up with photos and memorabilia for sale. The celebrity sits at the table (in Covid times, perspex screens protected us like cashiers in the bank), flanked by a 'helper', who takes the money – nearly always cash – and keeps it safe, takes the 'selfies' requested, sells the photos and other merchandise on display and brings snacks and drinks to their charge.

Conventions are a lucrative hymn to popular culture. From all aspects of entertainment and sport, under one roof with their public, there we are – in the flesh. Small shows are more fun to attend – there is a closer atmosphere, it's easier for fans to chat to celebrities – but those gatherings are not where the big bucks are made. The big events last a whole weekend: there are VIP passes of varying prices, panel discussions and Q&A events which are great fun, and photo sessions, where fans queue up to have their photo taken with the celebrity of their choice.

It's a 'day out' and one delightful aspect is the dressing-up, which is called 'cosplay'. Fans go to enormous trouble to reproduce the costumes of their favourite screen characters. I have been flummoxed by the variety of Professor Sprouts who approach the table, often bearing wands for me to sign, and they have clearly spent a lot of money on the 'merchandise' models of the characters in their favourite movie. Every blockbuster movie for the last sixty years is represented: *Batman*, *Spider-Man*, *Star Trek* and all the other modern ones I don't know.

Young men and women (and many not so young) clank about with swords, capes, fake pistols, intricate wigs, fat suits, astronaut suits, Mr Spock ears, or even ballgowns. They climb inside UFOs made at home. The invention is dazzling. Once I saw a naked Princess Leia, just covered with body paint. She was enjoying displaying herself. There are a lot of bosoms on display; people might snigger as the lady swishes past, but no one is attacked or molested. It's about having fun; families come, many generations.

I am heartened when I see people like me, in wheelchairs, and disabled children with their families, enjoying the experience.

I thrill at meeting fans; I adore meeting new people and finding out about their lives and longings. I try to have a proper conversation with them, discover why they attend such conferences. Memories are shared, political affiliation discussed, criticism accepted.

Gay women are particularly fun to talk to; sometimes they confide in me or ask advice. They might come with a new girlfriend for my approval; I doubt I'd ever say, 'Leave her this minute!' but I do ask them to stop and think if it's just lying down that matters. 'You have to be able to stand up and like it,' I tell them. 'What's between the ears is just as important as what's between the legs.'

People often approach the objects of their admiration trembling with excitement. As we know, the word 'fan' comes from 'fanatic', and excessive fandom can become frightening. There are many cases of deranged devotees following their object of desire home and climbing drainpipes. But my fans don't seem to be scary; they're mostly women, often quite elderly and invariably polite. Beyond the highly regulated realm of the fan convention, it's true sometimes it can be a nuisance if I want to read or I'm having a meal with chums but I simply don't understand actors who are grand and unavailable. Without your fans, where would you be?

I can't always deliver what they want; blokes particularly ask me to quote from my lines in *Blackadder*. 'That was forty years ago – do me a favour!' I say plaintively. But of course, I'm delighted. To be remembered and liked is a huge privilege, and conventions allow actors to repay, in some way, the pleasure the fans give us.

An aspect I shouldn't gloss over – and, indeed, would quite like to examine – is the collision of egos which can occur among the celebrities. We're all aware, of course, of our relative status in the business. One of the perils of our line of work is having to compare ourselves with our colleagues and be forced to accept our pecking order in the seating of the Hall of Fame. Many of the convention attendees are retired actors, or people who would rather be working but don't get asked so much; their fame is in the past, in the reruns, the remakes, the memories of older fans. Convention invitations are an important source of income for such people, but it can be galling to be positioned right next to a current major blockbuster star, whose fans line up hours before the object of their devotion arrives and queue around the block, and then to see your queue is pitifully small in comparison.

There is a joy in meeting old friends, people who may have worked together years before, and the Green Room is full of anecdotes and delighted recognition of a long unseen face at the doughnut queue; it's a mobile Denville Hall, the superb home for aged actors in Northwood, Middlesex. But equally, I sometimes spot former acquaintances and colleagues I don't want to see or talk to, so I always ask Julian to place my table next to Sylvester's, so I have a chum to talk to – and not an old enemy. Julian says, 'The lower the profile, the bigger the ego,' which is probably true everywhere. But as the convention highlights the sharp financial difference between us, it can't be sidestepped.

Counting the money at the end is quite fun, though. All transactions are in cash and let me assure the Inland Revenue that I never cheat or hide money in a mattress. My father repeatedly instilled in me the utter necessity of complete fiscal probity; I and my accountants adhere to his precepts with fidelity.

The cash is kept in a snazzy folder which has to be returned to Julian at the end of the engagement. Periodically, an employee of the management comes to take the folder to the office. The helper must count it very carefully. At £20 a pop, my photo fee, it can mount up quite quickly. The photos, which are my only merchandise, are laid out on the table. There's always several of me as Professor Sprout, some alone, some with the children and the other members of the Faculty of Hogwarts School. I am the Head of Hufflepuff House; many of my fans wear the house uniform. But I also display other photos of roles in my career – as Madame Morrible from *Wicked*, or from *Merlin* or

Call the Midwife, or *Babe* or *Romeo + Juliet*. Julian said I used to be identified only as Professor Sprout, but now it seems my celebrity status also springs from *The Graham Norton Show* and from my Cameos on TikTok. Professor Sprout would not be amused.

I am a dabbler in this world but I have close friends who spend much more time there. Probably the most expert (certainly the nicest) is Barnaby Edwards, who has another life as a Dalek, one of the evil alien species that are Doctor Who's nemesis. Barnaby has been a Dalek for thirty years; he is the longest-serving Dalek of them all and of course, for the fans, he is a catch, because they can see him at last, without the supremely uncomfortable costume in which he spends his Dalek life. He attends all the *Doctor Who* conventions that can be fitted into his other professional obligations as director, actor and painter. Most convention contracts allow us to cancel if we can prove we have been offered work, as the organisers make their money from the brightness of the stars attending, not unlike Wimbledon.

Barnaby has insights into the world of conventions. He quotes a joke: 'What do you call someone who hates *Doctor Who*?' Answer: 'A fan.' You see, everyone feels passionately about their favourite Doctor and is furious when the Doctor is changed. Fans are conservative by nature; they may embrace science fiction (which I detest), but the details must remain the same. Barnaby is generous to his fans, more than I am. He believes autographs – what he calls 'signage' – should be free, but he charges for the photos, as it costs money to produce them. 'Selfies' are free. He regards conventions as 'the icing on the cake of my career'.

We first met in 2008, recording a *Doctor Who* audio-story called *The Beast of Orlok*. Nigel Planer had forewarned Barnaby: 'She will fart, you know.' He must have remembered that from our rehearsals (in glorious odourama) in early 1984 for 'Summer Holiday', my ill-fated episode of *The Young Ones*. Ill-fated because a five-week strike by 700 scene shifters delayed filming till April when I was already booked on another job. So Maggie Steed got to play the pained mother ironing away in Neil's room – and I got to escape from domestic drudgery yet again.

But I digress. Barnaby's favourite story about conventions refers to Sigourney Weaver, one of the nicest women on the planet. A fan had bought a ticket for a 'Meet and Greet'– the culmination of a lifetime's admiration – and finally he was going to meet Sigourney. His excitement mounted by the second. At last, Sigourney arrived and stretched out a hand to greet him. He fainted dead away. A considerable amount of time passed. He awoke, and stared straight into the eyes of his goddess. She had waited by his side until he recovered. She would not leave him until she was satisfied he was all right. That's a star. And long may conventions flourish so that fans can breathe the same air as those they dream about.

Sofa So Good

The sofa has become my favourite piece of furniture, entirely as a result of the larks I've had luxuriating and showing off disgracefully, as a guest on the various talk shows to which I've been invited. At first I was scared, but then I came to realise that I was rather a whizz at them. And now I've grown to really love talk shows. It is such a pleasure not only being considered a celebrity but meeting long-admired eminences and being paid for it (crucial!) into the bargain.

So what is it like for the other guests? Imagine finding a quiet park bench where you expect to bask calmly in unquestioning admiration and then being assaulted by a fat, friendly but nosy octogenarian, who immediately wants to know where you first had anal sex. And I have to confess, the glorious audience reaction often spurs me on to further acts of rudery.

A talk show is an entertainment. It's *supposed* to be extemporised; it's supposed to have the shine of unrehearsed artlessness. In fact, a lot of work is necessary to create that artifice. Most chat shows are carefully crafted and honed, but once your bottom is lowered onto the sofa and the audience ordered to clap by the studio manager, both guests and host are required to maintain the fiction of complete spontaneity. But it's not a fiction to me: my joy comes in reacting to the moment. Something remarkable happens when you let go of what you thought you were going to say. Once we get involved in the conversation, anything can happen and I suck in the glories of the unrehearsed. The unexpected is insanely seductive. There's nothing better than a reckless conversation in which you are encouraging danger and skirting it at the same time. And luckily the hosts agree, but not always the guests.

It can be a scary process when you know millions are watching and your job is to make the audience laugh. But if there were no risk it wouldn't be fun. I refuse to be described as a comedian, I don't stand up and tell jokes and I loathe canned laughter. Unexpected, genuine hilarity can form a blissful connection between those on the set and the audience. The unpredictability, the sharing, the bravery is exciting and when the host is quick, intuitive and responsive, it makes for an exhilarating evening for everyone.

Never forget danger is very useful – that shock of alarm reminds you that you are alive – and anyone who encountered the late, great and completely unique Dame Edna Everage recognised her cruel delight in going too far. Dame Edna violently hurled all her guests out of their comfort zones; petrified, all they could do was cling to their seats, smile weakly and pray for it to be over, while the audience screamed with laughter. I'll never forget her telling Jeffrey Archer: 'If you can't laugh at yourself, you might be missing the joke of the century.' The moment when the guest jumps off the cliff – and we all follow like lemmings – that's the moment when the chat show transcends entertainment and becomes Art.

My first taste of this world came in the mid-eighties on Terry Wogan's show, where my fellow guests were Patrick Macnee, Ben Elton, Nigel Havers and Tony Slattery. But the main attraction was Terry himself. I liked him enormously. Highly intelligent and sharp, he was always an appreciator of people; you could say he was God's first attempt at fashioning a Graham Norton. I mean, you can't say that Jonathan Ross is heart-warming. He's astute and I like him. But he doesn't have the sweetness of Terry and Graham Norton. To be a good host and interviewer you *must* be a wholehearted appreciator of others.

Looking back at the surviving *Wogan* footage, it's undeniable that I cut a more muted and respectable figure than today. (I haven't been considered either muted or respectable for many years, thank fuck.) I was always counselled not to talk about farts or sex; my agents worried that if I were too much of a loose cannon, I just wouldn't get any work. It was all right for guys to let rip, but girls were expected to be niminy-piminy. And so, I held myself in for years.

The turning point came when I unexpectedly won the Los Angeles Critics Circle Award for my depiction of Flora Finching in *Little Dorrit* in 1989. I moved fast, I flew to America, I got a press agent and Johnny Carson asked me onto *The Tonight Show*. I hadn't seen his programme so I didn't know what to expect. I just knew that he was incredibly influential. The usual reason to go on a show is to publicise a book, or a TV programme or play; for this you don't get paid. I was selling myself. I thought, 'Oh, Christ, I hope this works.' And so, one day there I was, sitting beside him, looking into his calculating blue eyes.

I didn't care for Johnny Carson much – he was *not* an appreciator, a celebrator of talent. He was far more interested in himself than in me. I was there to be his foil, so that he could spin a story about himself or tell a joke or be amusing. It became clear that I needed to wrest control of the show away; after all, I was there to showcase myself. I managed it quite cunningly, turning the focus back on him and asked: 'Well, how many times have *you* been married?' His surprise and slight discomfort delighted the audience who roared with laughter. I took it from there and was quite saucy. The truth is that we were using each other. But he could sniff out a success and asked me to return. And from that show, I got an agent, an extremely good job and my life in America began. And when Johnny retired, his successor Jay Leno (a complete darling) happily inherited me. Win, win, win.

From an early age I realised that dirty talk goes down well in most circumstances. But American talk shows were both tense and decorous. The guests can often be uptight on camera, preferring to hide rather than reveal. Back then even saying 'bowel movement' scared the shit out of American talk show hosts. Not me. I was determined to have fun whatever happened. Once invited on a chat show, I say the first thing that pops into my head. The lovely truth is there are no lines to learn, no marks to hit. I can simply relax, enjoy the company of the host(s) and my fellow guests, and that's when the naughty nuggets slip out, to discombobulate or dazzle.

My success on *The Tonight Show* shot me straight into the American Big Time. On the show I met the great Jewish humorist and comedian Carl Reiner, best friend of Mel Brooks. He was a genius and, as it happened, a great friend of Norman Lear's, the television writer and producer who subsequently became my producer. Norman hosted lovely suppers at his house in Beverly Hills where I joined Carl and Walter Matthau, one of the most delightful men I have ever met. I could have gone straight for Walter. His lugubrious delivery, dry humour and baggy face were infinitely seductive.

When I returned to Britain to teach at Hogwarts, chat shows had proliferated and there was a new, more relaxed mood. I particularly enjoyed *The Graham Norton Show*. Graham positively encouraged me to say whatever came into my head, on one occasion sharing with the audience our recent encounter with Dolly Parton. He described, with emotional recall, my enormous echoing fart in the tunnel under Wembley arena when queueing for the meet-and-greet. I think he was quite shaken but it had been building for ages. Thank goodness Graham is not afraid of a bit of smut: immediately following the Fart, he asked me to relate a Shit story. And off I went.

'It was so embarrassing,' I said. 'I hope this isn't going to offend people. Actually, I hope it is. I was invited to a dinner party in Los Angeles. The hosts were my dear friends Martin Jarvis and his wife, Roz. The other guest was Richard Harris's son, Jared, whom I was dying to meet. His father had once told me to fuck off at breakfast, but I hoped Jared would be more charming at dinner.

I know it sounds as if I talk about nothing but shit, but when I got to their house I was desperate to go to the loo. So I flew into their bathroom and had an enormous shit. I flushed firmly and washed my hands. As I was leaving, I saw to my horror that my movement hadn't moved. It wasn't going down; there it remained, inexorable and unbudging, in the bottom of the bowl. I had to join the others and in my rush I made a terrible mistake, I flushed the loo again! And it took its revenge. Not only did the turd not go down – au contraire pubic hair – it actually bubbled up to meet me! I was terrified it would surge up and over the bowl, and continue its faecal progress through the house, in a veritable poo-nami. I backed away and out of the loo, closed the door, rushed into the dining room where Roz was serving the hors d'oeuvres and instead of saying, 'Hello, Jared, I've always wanted to meet you,' I blurted out, 'I've blocked the loo with my shit. And I don't know what to do!' Roz, like the trooper she is, promptly put down the hors d'oeuvres, donned a pair of plastic gloves, picked up the plunger and, on the brink of hysteria, left the room. After quite some poking, she succeeded in dislodging my cloacal bundle, while I made friends with Jared and we all laughed for the rest of the evening.

To this day, the thing that sets me apart on talk shows (over and above the likelihood that something scatological will pop out of my mouth) is that I often haven't a clue who the other guests are nor what they've done. My excuse is I'm not interested in popular culture. I didn't mean to offend handsome Dominic Cooper but if I'd said *Mamma Mia!* was a good film I'd have been lying. His flare of shock at my honesty led into a much more interesting conversation. But, equally, you never know where a true reaction is going to take you. For example, as I've never watched *Friends,* when Matthew Perry was on Graham's show with me, I had no idea who he was. I told him why:

Me: Many years ago, when I lived in Los Angeles, Norman Lear introduced me to Marta Kauffman and David Crane. I really liked David Crane and I couldn't stand Marta Kauffman. I thought she was a monster. And they wrote *Friends.* So, I thought bugger it, I'm not watching *that.*

Matthew Perry: She's actually quite a lovely woman.

Me: Don't say ANYTHING!

Matthew Perry: I won't.

Graham Norton: No need, I'd have thought at this point, it being on telly and all.

Matthew was expecting a bland conversation that stayed on the surface of things, but I was warming to my theme and immediately launched in, burrowing deeper. I asked him if he was an alcoholic. On reflection, I really wish I hadn't. Later in the show, I think I made the poor man nearly faint, when I talked about my physical reaction on meeting Laurence Olivier for the first time. Matthew looked at me, confounded, then said, 'I don't think I've ever been more uncomfortable. I think this is the worst moment of my life.' That was one of the few times I didn't quite 'mesh' with another guest.

On another outing on Graham's red sofa, I met will.i.am (whom I discovered that night was a Black Eyed Pea – and I didn't know who they were either). From the start, I adored him. We were in the same boat as he didn't know me from Adam, but he was wonderfully open to my outspoken grammar lesson on his over-frequent use of the word 'like', a pet aversion of mine. When I explained I didn't know many black people and welcomed the opportunity to know more, everyone else got very twitchy as if I'd made a racist remark. But it was the simple truth: I wish I did know more black people. Anyway, I've loved him ever since and admire his generosity in helping kids to read; he has given away millions to educate young people. What a mensch!

Graham Norton: Miriam, I hear you've entertained people on planes. You had been doing a film in Morocco? And you were travelling back?

Me: Yes, it was *Poor Little Rich Girl*. It had been a difficult shoot and everybody was a bit depressed and tired. And I thought my breasts might cheer people up. In those days they were curvy, they had some life in them. They're more Salvation Army now, raising the fallen. I didn't mean to be offensive at all, I meant to be, you know, caring and loving and I just took off my bra and streaked down the middle of the plane, from first class right through to economy, and it was wonderful.

Graham Norton: Did you get a round of applause?

Me: Actually, no. They were just shocked faces. But I will do anything to cheer people up.

Graham Norton: That's very nice of you.

Despite my love of nocturnal naughtiness with Graham Norton, I am also a regular on daytime shows such as BBC's *The One Show*, ITV's *Loose Women* and *This Morning*, on which, because they are broadcast before the watershed (in other words BEFORE 9 P.M.), you *can't* talk about shits, sex and bottoms. Let me explain, there is a great difference between the morning and evening talk shows. Mornings are about cosiness, companionship, relaxed conversation. At night, there is challenge and rudeness and daring . . . Mornings are uncompetitive and warm-hearted; egos are less in evidence. Of all the morning shows, I particularly enjoyed being on *This Morning*, with Holly and Phil. They were warm, welcoming and ready to join in the frolic. I liked being their Agony Aunt, when I was allowed to say exactly what

I thought about husbands behaving meanly. I feel sad I shan't have the chance to make Phil laugh again; he was a darling then and to me he always will be.

Coming back to the watershed, of course we need to protect the innocent from nasty things; but let's go for something much worse than four-letter words and mild bawdiness – let's forbid politicians from lying before 9 p.m.

How to Be Woke
When You're Eighty-Two

In 1941 my parents expected the Nazis' imminent arrival. They fled Plaistow for Oxford after their house took a direct hit from a German bomb. As they cowered in the cellar, my mother pregnant with me, they thought it was the end of the world. But this Jewish girl was lucky. I was born in the one place Hitler had decided never to destroy. The Luftwaffe were ordered not to attack the city. He had earmarked it as the new British capital of his Thousand-Year Reich. I became aware as I grew up that although my parents had avoided the Nazis, they could not escape the small-minded snobbery, the insular prejudice, the intellectual pomposity of the English middle class. They were determined that I should not be shut out from middle-class achievement, as they had been. They knew they would never be accepted: they were determined that I should be. And I was.

The English judge people by their vowels, and mine are perfect. Mummy saw to that. Armed with elocution lessons from Miss Plowman and my confident personality, I successfully laid siege to Newnham College, Cambridge, and then the BBC.

So much was on offer to my post-war generation; when we left university, we knew there would be a job somewhere. Labour gave us everything, from the NHS to free education, social housing to employment possibilities. Young people today don't have that security. Everyone is fighting: old vs young, North vs South, town vs country, heterosexuals against the rest, rich vs poor. The rich have always won, but in the 1940s and 1950s it seemed for a tiny moment as if the poor had a toehold on a better life. But that has proved a chimaera: a ruse to put us off the scent.

Today the moronic and the wicked seem to be in charge, again. I hate it and I will continue to speak against it, railing perhaps fruitlessly like Cassandra, until I die. Of course, I am woke. And proudly so. When I am castigated for my 'potty mouth' I want to respond, 'Oh, so where do you stand on sending asylum seekers to Rwanda?' or 'Why has no one been prosecuted for Grenfell Tower?' And nowhere is this moral gap more clearly delineated than in language. Words have changed their meaning; rather than clarify they confuse and deceive. I wander, desperate, in a heartless, incomprehensible world. And realise I don't belong in this world any more. Take the term 'woke' itself. It is now used as a crude term of abuse for any liberal, left-leaning opinion – in the House of Commons, on the BBC, scattered throughout the comment pages of the *Daily Telegraph*. For the Tories, any opinion counter to their own is called 'woke'. For me, it's a high compliment. I want to be woke. I wish everybody were. What they dismiss so cuttingly as 'political correctness run amok' is actually the kindness, awareness and tolerance essential for an increasingly complex world.

When I was young, protesting was a holy duty. I marched for an end to apartheid, the abolition of the death penalty; against Trident missiles; for the repeal of Clause 28 (in my lifetime any discussion of homosexuality in schools was considered its 'promotion') – and we were listened to. Now the government attempts to criminalise the very act of protest. There has been a colossal change.

I never thought grammar would raise people's blood pressure, but the mild personal pronoun has now become a focus for insane violent opinion. As a person for whom grammar means honouring the structure of language, a member of the now-defunct Apostrophe Society, at first I struggled to accept the importance of being 'they'. But Zoe Terakes, the brilliant young transgender Australian actress, explained it to me: 'Why do you want to stop me from being "me"? Why is it so scary to acknowledge that gender is no longer merely binary?' And of course, I agree. What's the problem if 'he' becomes 'she' or 'they' – or anything else, for that matter?

More recently, when I was in Tasmania filming my *Australia Unmasked* documentary, I met Francine, an elderly transgender lady. It was in a place called Ulverstone, where there was a real loathing of homosexuality – or any gender difference, for that matter – and where there had previously been homophobic riots. Francine was eighty years old. After a stint in the military, she had worked as a teacher for nineteen years, dressing as a man during the day, and becoming a woman only in the evenings in the privacy of her own home. She'd had the sex-change operation only that year. She was fully now a woman and she wept as she told me her story. Francine said, 'My life is now complete. I am who I was always meant to be.' You couldn't fail to be deeply moved by her story. But I've known ever since I met my Latin tutor, Professor Tom Sargeant aka Agatha, when I was seventeen, that gender is a personal choice. Why should it unnerve and make furious those who describe themselves as 'M' or 'F'? Some people like Hobnobs, others Rich Tea; I'm easy. Relax, for Christ's sake! I just want to make sure that there are enough loos for everyone.

Now let's deal with 'cancel culture'. What is it, first of all? I rushed to Wikipedia: a phenomenon 'in which those who are deemed to have acted or spoken in an unacceptable manner are ostracised, boycotted or shunned'. A prominent example is J. K. Rowling. She has been cancelled for rejecting a definition of 'womankind' as merely 'people in possession of a womb' and is now described as a TERF (Trans-Exclusionary Radical Feminist). I'm describing myself as a Lesbian Without A Womb, LWAW. Any takers?

More recently, there was a huge fuss surrounding the host of *Match of the Day* Gary Lineker when he spoke out on Twitter about the Tory Home Secretary Suella Braverman's 'Stop the Boats' immigration policy. Whether you agree with his choice of language is a matter of opinion. And he's a football presenter, not the BBC's political editor, for God's sake! However, he received horrific messages on social media, culminating in a petition to get him sacked. And my beloved BBC buckled under and took him off the air. I am broadly in favour of the internet and of social media in general, but cancel culture is its injurious underside. If you're somebody who does or says something that people take offence at, the revenge can be swift and terrible. That is just wrong. It's bullying on a grand scale. What has become of us, that such vicious treatment is deemed acceptable? With Gary Lineker they bit off more than they could chew. He has almost nine million followers on Twitter but it still took a huge counter-campaign and his brave colleagues refusing to step in and present in his place before he was reinstated. But what happens to the thousands of people who don't have his platform, afraid to speak out in case they are cancelled too. Well, I am not afraid. If you see wrongdoing, you must speak out. The braver you are, the braver everyone else will be. It's the only way we're going to improve this shit world. Let's reserve rage for incompetence and true corruption.

Which leads me neatly into my next pet aversion: gaslighting. Remember that wonderful film, *Gaslight*, where Ingrid Bergman's sanity is undermined completely by her unscrupulous husband? That tactic is now in widespread use. Everyone, from bullying boyfriends to bullshitting politicians, is at it. Donald Trump's frequent dismissal of any criticism as 'fake news' is just one example of gaslighting – there are so many more. Be on the lookout and don't fall for it.

A useful and less dangerous piece of modern slang which amuses me is 'whatever', often accompanied by a two-handed gesture, using the index fingers and the thumbs joined together to form a 'W' – undiluted scorn squelching any further argument. Period, as they say in America.

Better Out Than In

I was once asked what my name would be if I was a Spice Girl. I didn't have to think about it. 'FARTY SPICE.'

My love of raw onions, radishes and cabbage may well have contributed to the quantity and quality of my gaseous explosions. But a good fart is nothing to be ashamed of. It can often break the ice – or even melt it entirely. My conversations are punctuated by short, fragrant (and fully acknowledged) interludes and they're all the better for it. Pretending that they haven't happened only makes you lose your train of thought.

In 2021, Alan Cumming and I went round Scotland in a somewhat cramped camper van for our documentary *Lost in Scotland and Beyond*. Before we set off, Daniel Radcliffe, whom I had met first in my herbology class at Hogwarts Academy some nineteen years earlier, had the bare-faced gall to warn Alan about my farting! As a budding actor, I don't recall he had any problems with them *then*. The other pupils clearly found them amusing. I kept to my two rules: try to direct the fart *away* from the nearest person and always warn up front.

I hate to name-drop but I think it's appropriate here to mention that in 1999 I was on the receiving end of a fart directed at me, in a moment of extreme vulnerability, by a well-known bodybuilder and politician, Arnold Schwarzenegger. We had been rehearsing a sublimely silly film, *End of Days*: Arnie was an ex-cop on a mission to stop Satan conceiving the Antichrist in the final hour of the millennium and I was playing the Devil's servant Mabel. In the anxiety of our rehearsals, I allowed a medium-strength fart to escape. The sound effect was inevitable, but there was no odourama, I assure you. Arnie however, leapt upon my transgression with frenzy. He couldn't stop talking about it, constantly referring to it, showing his shock and revulsion. A few days later, we were filming my death scene. Lying on the floor, my throat sliced in half by a glass table, Arnie had me pinned under him, utterly at his mercy. It was then he delivered the *coup de grâce* (or should I say, *coup de disgrace*?). He farted, loudly, purposefully and malevolently, directly into my face – and then laughed uproariously. He did it deliberately because he didn't like me, had no respect for me and knew he could get away with it. I was really cross and shouted, 'Fuck you, Arnie!' Well, at least he was exposed later, for adultery and fathering his housekeeper's baby. The fart, let's agree, was small beer in comparison.

I was later in *Wicked* at the Apollo Victoria. We'd all sit waiting in the wings – actors, costume and make-up artists – and I had a special place where I'd sit on my chair in my wig, bustle and voluminous skirts. Now, the Apollo wings are tiny. And we'd be all squashed tight listening for our cues – we couldn't go anywhere so we're trapped, basically. And then out of nowhere, I might feel one brewing, so I'd quietly announce 'Fart coming!', then I'd lift a cheek and let it slip out, usually equally quietly. But, if the others squished in there with me didn't hear it, they certainly whiffed it. I remember one night Nigel Planer was standing next to me when I did one of my farts; he was about to step out on stage, and there were suddenly tears streaming down his face – whether due to suppressed hilarity or the overpowering tang of my fart, who knows? 'Oh, Miriam!' he mouthed as he rushed onstage to his cue.

I do not understand the outrage with which my farts are greeted. Surely there are worse things than an expellation of wind from the arsehole, to relieve gastric tightness? Aren't lying, cheating and bullying (current government activities) more heinous than farting? Yet, whenever my farts are mentioned, there's a shudder of shock and disgust far outstripping the seriousness of the action. Maybe there's an *English* reserve about anything that happens below the waist. Farting is, I would say, a universal phenomenon – as animals too are famous co-farters, often blamed for what was actually a human's transgression. (Never forget that the levels of methane expelled from the rear ends of vast herds of cows is contributing to global warming.) I agree farting is usually a choice – but older sphincters cannot always be gainsaid. And it's uncomfy trying to contain a fart, and I like to be comfortable, so I 'let' a fart, almost with the same pleasure that I let a flat.

Our family was a farty family. My parents often farted and we giggled and enjoyed it. The dog was only blamed if it became a miasma. I was never reprimanded when we were on our own, but in public, it was regarded as rude. If I'm honest, I agree with that – it *is* rude to allow private gases to waft through public spaces. It is good manners not to fart in a lift – and I would only do that if I know everyone in it. The problem comes when the doors open and the lift takes in more people and the fart is still there. Here is another sign of my fundamental decency – I always own up. I claim the fart as mine; I would never expect another to bear the shame of a fart to which they didn't contribute. I have noticed others are not so scrupulous, pointedly staring at someone else, mutely accusing them of the something for which *they* should own responsibility. It's a test of morality and many are found wanting.

Oh Miriam!

I have never farted on camera live. Just before and just after, but live, never. The closest I have got was on ITV's *This Morning*. In the ad break before I came on camera, I felt the wind gathering. My firm belief is that it's always better to let a fart have its way, rather than try and sit on it. It never goes away. So, by then seated on the couch, I calmly lifted one buttock and released the fart. I propelled it, so it left in a hurry and, as it happens, rather loudly. A silent fart always takes time to prepare – time I didn't have. So, off it went and I could relax. But Holly Willoughby and Phillip Schofield couldn't. I had remained entirely professional. I had alerted them it was coming, with a discreet 'Fart!' warning. And I had done it off camera but I suppose the suddenness of it and the loudness, took them both by surprise. They dissolved into helpless giggles and went on giggling. I couldn't do anything, just looked a bit sheepish and hoped they would calm down. Even after they did, they kept referring to it and cracking up again and again.

The comic potential of a fart must be acknowledged. A fart is terribly funny and the longer and more drawn-out, the funnier it is. That's why fart cushions are marketed *and* purchased. But the way people carry on about farts is ridiculous. I am castigated as if I were ripping the Ten Commandments apart. I'm not murdering anyone, no one died from Covid because of a fart. So, pull yourselves together, accept it's a natural occurrence and LET IT GO!

266

Find Your Happy Place

I haven't always been in love with Italy. My first visit in the late sixties was with a trio of nubile Jewish girls looking for boys. I wasn't. They chose Cattolica, a shabby resort on the Adriatic coast. I hated it. While they flirted in bars, I crouched morosely on the packed, unlovely beach. I vowed never to go to Italy again. But that was before I got to know Francesca, our au pair from Vercelli – and before Heather. Together, they changed my mind.

Covid scared the shit out of me: I may seem a brave, confident person, but illness has always terrified me. My father was a GP and the realities of bad health were ever-present in our house, especially after Mummy's stroke in 1968. I never think I'm just under the weather; it's always motor neurone disease, ovarian cancer or Alzheimer's. In 2020, when I heard the shocking news from England about the incompetent handling of the Covid crisis, I decided to stay on in Italy and not risk a winter in London.

When we first saw La Casella, the old Tuscan farmhouse Heather and I bought with our friend Peter Lavery, it was still being used to house animals, and store wine, oil and tools. The front half was a warren of small, dark spaces, storerooms and rabbit hutches. The back half of the ground floor, where the cattle were kept, was lined with stone and old oak mangers. Steps led down to a vaulted *cantina*, with benches and huge green-glass wine containers, wrapped in raffia. (Think of the Chianti bottle at your local trattoria made extremely large.) But La Casella was a practical choice. Linked to Montisi by a *strada bianca* (a dusty primitive road), it was solid, with a sound roof (or so we thought) and, unusually, it had a corridor. Most old Italian houses had rooms which opened into each other, which meant little privacy. The house had been assembled over time by many generations; the corridor (added in 1955) was just the latest change. My favourite bit was the loo. Outside the front entrance at the top of a flight of worn travertine steps, half the loggia at the top had been bricked off. Inside was a wooden seat, the hole covered by a round piece of marble with a long handle. A pipe carried the shit down to an outside terracotta container. This would have been emptied into the *concemaia*, the compost heap. When we brought the plumbing into the twentieth century, the marble loo-cover proved an ideal doorstop. It was only twenty years later that Luca, our Sardinian builder and friend, felt he knew us well enough to express his horror at our keeping this thing in the house.

We bought La Casella with half a hectare of land, the old farm complex of a hay barn, piggeries and a circular flat area where oxen once turned the millstones to grind the wheat. There were also eighteen ancient olive trees. When the land-owning family began to sell their fields, a neighbour we were in dispute with was the first to buy. This shocked us so much we decided to purchase the olive groves to the south and west of the house and protect our peace. Altogether we now own about 280 trees. Producing olive oil is not a commercial proposition; finding someone to maintain our fields is hard, but it's worth the effort. We get about 30–60 litres annually. While this year's harvest lacked the peppery bite typical of the vivid green first pressing, it is still miles better than any oil available in an English supermarket. Alongside our olive grove, I must mention our cherry trees. A cloud of white blossom in the early spring matures into dark red, almost black, utterly delicious cherries – that is, if we can beat the bloody birds to them.

My bedroom in La Casella is the coldest room in the house. It's also Peter's bedroom. We both wanted the same one, because it's large, has a lovely view over olives and distant farmhouses, and is quiet, despite overlooking the farm track. Therefore, we always holiday at separate times. We're extremely fond of Peter, but once, when staying at the same time, we had a terrible row. I was being bossy and Peter has always loathed bossy women. He lost his temper and called me a fat cunt.[*] It took about three years to get over the row, but now we laugh about it.

It's a slow start each morning with the reluctant realisation that I'm awake, and I mean properly awake, because my nights are invariably broken with visits to the lavatory. I usually have to get up to pee twice in the night, and because I want to know what time it is, I have to physically restrain myself from looking at my watch, because even if it's three in the morning, that's it – all chance of further sleep is gone.

But if I don't turn on the lights, then I can go back to sleep for a few more hours. I love being in bed. I do a lot, but my natural mode is sloth. When I get into bed at night, I put my phone (which is my radio

---

[*] When I asked Peter for his comment on this incident, he suggested that I call this chapter 'Recollections May Vary'.

as well), my reading glasses, whatever book I'm reading and a box of hankies on the bed beside me. My bed is a *matrimoniale*, an enormous double with plenty of space for my nocturnal detritus. I now realise that I'm addicted to the screen. I carry my phone in a lanyard around my neck, which is obviously handy but also a manacle of sorts (or a 'neckacle', I suppose you could call it), a trap that I've chained myself to. This is something I've always despised in other people – I didn't notice I've become guilty of it myself.

Once I have finally looked at my watch, usually at five or six, then I think 'Fair enough.' I turn on my phone, I read my emails. Because I have another life in Australia, I get a lot of mail overnight from the other side of the world. Many are concerned with charities and pressure groups of various kinds; I am a spokesperson for bowel cancer and a spotted-tail quoll ambassador (that's a small marsupial nocturnal mammal in danger of extinction, only found in Australia). Whenever anybody asks me to help refugees, or to support the legalisation of euthanasia, or campaign to protect the environment, or raise money for a theatre at risk, I sign up. I should really include myself in the group of small mammals in danger of extinction.

I've joined many societies, not just political ones. In the old days, when I was young, I would have marched for them. But I can't do that now, so I march with my pen instead. I post their campaigning messages on my Facebook page, and sometimes forward them by email to friends.

Most often in the early morning, however, I go downstairs to the large living room and watch tennis on my computer. We don't have a television at La Casella. I subscribe to a tennis channel called 'Tennis TV', where you can watch matches all year. Last night, for example, there was the final of the ATP tour with Novak Djokovic versus the young Norwegian Casper Ruud. I watched the whole match. (Djokovic won in two sets: 7–5, 6–3. I LOATHE Djokovic; he's an anti-vaxxer, a liar and a bully. He just happens to be a superb tennis player.)

At school, I was hopeless at tennis. For fifty or sixty years I didn't think about the game. I certainly never played it. I've been a shaker, but I have never been a mover. People don't quite realise how difficult it is to serve: to throw up the ball and bring your racket from behind and hit it at exactly the right moment with enormous force and power. I prefer to sit back and enjoy the gladiatorial spirit of the game and the honed bodies of the players instead. It makes me forget that I've got things I ought to do.

Football is a newer pleasure. Previously, I had taken on the rather snobbish attitude of my parents who thought that football was only for 'yocks'. (*Yocks* is a rude Yiddish term for Gentiles, meaning 'Christians of no education'. It's a class-oriented insult, like saying someone is a 'chav', or in Australia a 'bogan', but definitely aimed at white-trash Christians. You could never have a Jewish *yock*.) Each morning, therefore, what with the tennis and my various email chores on my phone, I can easily be watching screens for two or three hours. Eventually, I log out of Tennis TV, and think, 'Right! Time to get up and get going.'

There is then a medical ritual to follow. I must take certain pills and drink a certain amount of liquid with them. I take three pills in the morning – my blood pressure pill, my blood thinner (which is red and easy to see) and something called bisoprolol fumarate (no idea what that's for) and with each one I'm supposed to down a whole glass of water. I hate it. A friend's grandmother always used to say: 'I don't drink water, it rots your guts.' Well, I'm with her, but my doctors have strongly advised that I should drink two litres a day. For some reason, I find that unbearably difficult. I'm not good at looking after myself. I resist the fact that I must be medically aware all the time. The realisation of age and gradual disintegration is what one is trying to avoid. So now I simply try to keep a bottle of water with me all the time, like all those joggers in leg warmers.

The bathroom window looks across the olive groves to the long, old farmhouse called Ginestrelle, whose lights stay on all night, now that it's been sold to Milanesi entrepreneurs. When I look at it, I think of its previous inhabitant, Signora Caboni, an impressive Sardinian woman whose husband had driven their flocks all the way across Italy after the war. I visited one of her sons, desperately ill with a potassium deficiency in Hammersmith Hospital. From that moment on I was part of their family. Whenever I came to Montisi, each time I walked past her house, I was plied with their *vin santo* and her delicious biscuits. Her sons Franco and Pepino still live in the village. I never spoke her language but I loved her very much.

I usually wear what I've worn the day before. It's difficult because in my bedroom here in Italy, I don't have a wardrobe, just a capacious chest of drawers. Of course, I should hang up my dresses, but I'm too lazy.

I'm always the first up, so once I'm dressed, I go downstairs and feed our cats, Abu and Tilly, and light the fire. It's one of the jobs I hate because I have to shovel the ashes into the bucket and fetch the wood from the woodpile in the back stable. It's too much like work. But the good thing is, when you get up early, the world belongs to you. Other than the cats, I have the house to myself. Heather doesn't get up till about lunchtime. She has suffered from chronic fatigue syndrome ever since she caught a respiratory virus on one of her research trips to Indonesia, and she doesn't get to sleep till about six or seven in the morning.

First thing in the morning, I'm supposed to get on the exercise bike. Lately, however, I've had recordings to make, Cameos to do and voice-overs for various documentaries to complete. It's odd: I've never been busier than I am now. And then, somehow, what with all my post-production and publicity commitments, the morning vanishes and yet again I've avoided the exercise bike! I know I should make myself go for a short walk. I used to go swimming every day, but after an attack of benign paroxysmal positional vertigo, I gave it up. Now, with my Blue Badge, I drive everywhere – which means more sitting down, not moving.

Usually, just as I'm dismounting the bike (if I've got on it), beetroot-faced and breathless, Heather will come downstairs. She makes herself some porridge and we have a chat about the rest of the day.

Then Rosa, Luca's lady, tidies and cleans up for us. This is a recent luxury. While Rosa is busy dealing with the mess, we take the opportunity to do our shopping and run various errands. We love Montisi. It has 300 inhabitants; the post office only opens once a week on Fridays, there is a small grocery shop, a bakery, a bar and a flower shop. When we first came, there were three grocery shops *and* three butchers. One of the butchers, Signor Cassini, who raised and slaughtered his own beasts, had customers from as far away as Rome ordering his meat and prosciutto. At least four generations of Cassinis had been Montisi butchers until the health department condemned the shop for having spotless marble instead of stainless-steel counters. How I miss the delicious all-beef sausages he made specially for me: no pork for this Jewish girl. He used to tell me about the Jewish families who hid in the farmhouses down the road from La Casella during the war. The village protected them and they survived. The castle tower at the bottom of our road was less fortunate; as the German army retreated, it blew up everything in its path. It was the dream of the Manucci-Benincasa family, from whom we bought La Casella, to restore its former magnificence.

The only remaining grocery shop is run by two sisters, who get on very well together. But while their produce is excellent, it is three times the price of the nearest supermarket, a twenty-minute drive away.

I prefer the Tuscan landscape outside the baking summer months. In spring, autumn and even in winter, it's more beautiful. I am continually delighted by the variety of colours, and the villages and fields receding in gently undulating layers to the horizon, broken up by lines of cypresses, marking the boundaries.

The old town of Sinalunga is up on a hill; at the bottom is the village of Pieve di Sinalunga, the downtown commercial area, with all the factories, the banks and the shops. That's where we do most of our shopping, principally in the Lidl, and the Co-op, which in this part of Tuscany they call the 'Ho-hop', because they don't pronounce the hard *c*. (It's an Arabic *h*, as in 'Huh'. So, you say '*h*aldo' for hot, rather than '*c*aldo'.) I love their *alici* (or pickled anchovies) and the fresh ricotta, which you can also get in the village shop, but only on Tuesdays. There is a bustle and cheeriness about the Ho-hop.

Every day there is a different market in a nearby town. On Wednesdays I love the vegetable market in San Giovanni d'Asso: three long trestle tables piled high with apples, artichokes, *cavolo nero*, and *cime di rapa* (a recent discovery, delicious with fresh pasta). Queue etiquette is strictly adhered to – each customer patiently waits their turn. Yesterday, an elderly gentleman shyly presented the lady behind the counter with a bunch of bright yellow mimosa from his garden. Everybody smiled.

Everyone has a nickname: mine is La Napolitana, which could question my reputation but I hope it's because of my dark flashing eyes. They can't believe I'm from England. Although my Italian isn't perfect, I won't let that hold me back from communication, asking which are the juiciest lemons or whether this celery is good for a *zuppa*. I come away, happy, with big bags of fresh ingredients for Tiziana, who still lives in the castle where she was once the cook. She is, I think, glad of the chance to cook again – delicious mushroom risotto, a big pasta *sugo*, and the most terrific ragus, *osso buco*, or a roast cauliflower or fennel – we like quite simple *contadini* (farmer's) food. Tiziana texts me (she loves the internet) when it's ready and I collect it from the side gate. Not to have to think about cooking is such a blessing. And because we have Rosa to look after us too, we don't do any housework either. I won't do housework. I simply won't do it. It's not on my list. That's what money is for; it makes life a lot less stressful than it used to be.

We sit in our armchairs near the wood-burning stove with the cats on two other chairs near us so they can be stroked. Our life here is without moment. It passes. There are no highs and lows and it's entirely selfish. However, I do find it irksome when it's not quite warm enough to go outside, to sit on the bench at the edge of my garden and bask in the sun like a lizard. It gets colder when the sun sets, quite early in winter around 3.30 p.m. We then start to prepare for the evening meal, deciding what to heat up and what film to watch. Then the cats have to be turfed out of the armchairs and their meal prepared. We build up the fire with logs from the woodpile in the back *stale* (stable).

After our film has finished, I take my evening pills and toil slowly upstairs with my sticks. I always go into Heather's room to say goodnight. She's often already back at her computer, writing her next book. My large bedroom is not as cold as it might be. Heather has turned on my electric blanket and my oil-filled radiator. And its cold floor is covered with rugs. I charge my phone and open my book. And after a bit, I turn out my bedside light. I feel blessed to be in Montisi. There is a gentleness in the place and a quiet which rests the soul.

Why Life is Like Cheesecake

Jews don't believe in reincarnation. We are *here* and *now*, and it's up to us to use what we have. To me, retirement is similarly meaningless. I've worked harder as I've got older. I don't like getting old. I'm not terribly fit. I've got a bad heart. I keep pissing myself because my bladder is weak. And I have spinal stenosis, so I can't walk without pain. *I* may describe myself as a knicker-soaked cripple, but don't you dare! My body is wearing out. However, for an octogenarian, I'm looking rather good. I see myself on Zoom and I am delighted to say that my skin looks fresh and youthful. And I've still got my marbles . . . I think. Being overworked and filling my life to the brim has kept me going.

I look outwards, not inwards. People stimulate me and there's a constant influx in my life of newness, seeing new places and learning interesting new things. I'm never bored, I believe that's the secret to a happy and fruitful old age.

Covid completely changed the way I live my life. I used to swim daily at my local Clapham Manor gym – now I never go near the pool. I used to go to the theatre three times a week. Now I never go. All crowded places scare me. But I'm still arranging lunch parties, seeing close friends, but now I ask people to come to me.

I thrive on their presence. But when they leave, old age catches up with me and I get tired again. Then I sit down and instantly nod into a slumber until something else happens – a Zoom call; the Thai takeaway or supermarket food delivery driver at the door – and I come back to life. I love an audience. If I have an audience, I can cope with almost anything.

Over the last three years, when most people were unable to work because of the global pandemic, to my intense surprise jobs were piling in. Making documentaries, recording books and podcasts in the 'duvet' studio, doing my Cameos, for me is more than work – it's enormous fun.

Perhaps I should explain the 'duvet' studio. Covid restricted my pleasure in going to various recording studios and, once settled in Tuscany, it was no longer possible. I decided to use the considerable space in the unheated back stable at La Casella. My friend, the musician Fabrizio Pagni, brought from the IKEA in Florence five single duvets and attached them with cable ties to five IKEA dress rails. Inside this tent structure, we arranged a seat, a microphone stand and all the accoutrements required for sound recording. I crouch inside the studio, reading the script from my iPad, and Fabrizio sits at the table-tennis table with his computer and twiddles the knobs. We have succeeded in achieving a remarkably pure sound.

I've never been a science-fiction fan – quite the opposite – but I have always loved the various Doctor Whos (or is it Doctors Who?) I've met. Some forty-six years ago, the delicious rainbow-bescarfed former monk, and fourth Doctor Who, Tom Baker, had requested me to play his assistant. But it was not to be. The BBC baulked at a bulky sidekick for the Doctor. Instead, they chose the lovely Louise Jameson as Leela and the robotic dog K9. (Fools!) But almost half a century later, things have changed and I've been allowed to join *Doctor Who* in November 2023.

While I may not be acting quite as much these days, I don't have time to miss it. I have become the poor man's Joanna Lumley, constantly heading off to different places around the world, meeting interesting people. I enjoy being able to infiltrate circles I wouldn't normally go into, and to have carte blanche to ask anybody about anything. Television is a great leveller. It seems I'm a natural documentarian (another word for being nosy). I relish intimacy and insist on frank exchange.

In 2022, I toured Ireland with Senator Lynn Ruane, for a TV documentary investigating the playwright and Abbey Theatre founder Lady Gregory – they called her 'Ireland's First Social Influencer'. Lynn expertly drove the camper van and we travelled all over the country – Wicklow, Dublin, County Clare and Galway. Everyone in Dublin has a nickname, so Lynn christened me 'Mimzo'. She gave me lessons in her strong (shall I say 'rough'?) Tallaght accent – one of the poorest areas in the south of the city – and posted them on Twitter. I enjoyed being recognised in the streets when people shouted 'Hey, Mimzo!' at me.

Then in winter 2022, Channel 4 invited me to revisit a Dickensian Christmas, for a documentary entitled (funnily enough) *Miriam's Dickensian Christmas*. I heartily dislike Christmas, as did my father – too much money spent buying silly presents you can't afford for people you don't really like. When I was little, I asked for a Christmas tree. 'Absolutely not,' Daddy responded. I was allowed to display the Christmas cards I received all over our sitting room, but very much under sufferance. But the TV programme forced me to adjust, to be less prejudiced than my father. I put aside his closed attitude and experienced the range of what Christmas can offer. Making a

Victorian Christmas wreath was thoroughly enjoyable; there was paper and glue, and I dipped my finger in the glue, put the glue on the ivy leaves, then stuck them on some paper, and finally I stuck rose hips all over it. I was gratified at how genuinely decorative my wreath turned out. My visit to a Victorian kitchen to learn some traditional Christmas recipes was less successful. The Victorians loved mock turtle soup; but if you knew what went into it, you'd run a mile! Much more appealing was the traditional plum pudding, wrapped in muslin and boiled in a copper mould, but my Christmas dinner of choice resolutely remains roast chicken, followed by a modern apple *tarte tatin*.

Just before my Dickensian Christmas, I'd been on my three-week road trip around Scotland for a documentary with Alan Cumming. I concede that a smiling and spritely Scottish-born Hollywood actor and an occasionally ill-tempered, large bosomed, practically disabled octogenarian might seem a surprising pairing to be fronting a documentary TV programme, but it was all Alan's fault – never would I have dreamed of such an impertinent suggestion!

We have known each other for years, although neither of us can quite remember exactly when and how we first met. We think it might have been in the early nineties, when Alan was acting in *The Last Romantics*, a BBC film based on the life of F. R. Leavis, played by the excellent Ian Holm. As Frank Leavis had taught me at Cambridge, Alan came with Ian to chat to me about my memories of him. We were 'showbiz friends', I suppose, and didn't really know each other terribly well, but it was thrilling to meet again on *The Graham Norton Show* in early 2020 and we really hit it off. Alan thought we sparred well and knew we'd be a good combo. And we are.

Scotland has a special place in both our hearts. Daddy's family were from Glasgow, and Alan was born in Perthshire, and grew up near Dundee. And so in 2021, we set off to journey through the Highlands and Lowlands together – in yet another camper van. The prospect of sharing long days cooped up together as we zoomed up, down and around Scotland's roads, was daunting.

That young pup Daniel Radcliffe had already warned Alan about my farting (cheeky sausage!). Having got wind of the problem, Alan made me promise to issue pre-trump warnings. There was much discussion about my high-fibre and raw onion diet and how that might impact on our onboard toilet. Well, let me assure you that my wind and my defecatory needs were dealt with in a safe, contained and always tasteful manner.

I had no idea if Alan would prove a competent chauffeur and I feared I might morph into the worst kind of backseat driver. I am *not* a natural passenger – I like to be at the wheel. Luckily, Alan's driving proved a great deal better than mine. And what's terrific is that he can talk, drive and be filmed all at the same time. Well, he is an international celebrity, you know! I soon trusted Alan enough to fall asleep when he was driving, even on the wildest and most perilous mountain tracks. So there were only a few little outbursts from me, the occasional 'For Fuck's sake! You're too near the edge!' or just '*Ooohhhh!*', but mainly it was road rage directed at other drivers.

We each took turns to decide the itinerary, Alan showing me parts of his relationship with Scotland and me showing him mine. Starting our journey in Glasgow meant taking him to the grim street in the Gorbals where Daddy was born.

Alan took me to his childhood home on the east coast. He felt anxious ahead of filming and didn't sleep well the night before. When we got there, he couldn't bear to go inside. Then he told me about some of the shocking things that he'd experienced as a young boy and I saw a different and serious side to him. 'It's something you never recover from. You just manage trauma,' he confided.

I never expected to be hurtling around Scotland with this much younger man as my companion. As Alan said: 'You don't often see intergenerational friendship on television. When I told people about it, they'd say, "What?! You and Miriam Margolyes in a van?" with varying degrees of horror and confusion but, actually, it was lovely.' And it was. Even if sometimes it felt like an audition for a touring production of *Travels with My Aunt*. I hope our experiences will encourage people to branch out. And let's be honest, a bit of farting never did anyone any harm.

Our age difference led to candid chats in the van, often hilarious, the topics remarkably random, ranging from being afraid of Madonna (not me!) to the history of Judaism in Scotland. Alan and I have come away from our two series with a special friendship which is still growing. So is our love affair with Scotland. I've come to know well a much younger colleague, and I've grown to be fond of him, to respect him. New friendships are one of the joys of our job and something that makes me forget my age.

It was a stark contrast to *My Happy Ending*, filmed in 2021 and where I played a patient on a cancer ward with Sally Phillips, Andie MacDowell, Rakhee Thakrar and Tamsin Greig, all serenely happy to wear bald wigs and be covered with tumours. Biddy, my favourite make-up artist and friend, compared me, egglike in my wig, to the Dalai Lama – I only hope in his pre-scandalous days. It's neither the strangest nor the least glamorous costume I've ever worn. I acted Beckett in a dustbin and I once did a photoshoot wearing only a large and spiky fish, tightly secured between my breasts. Life's too short for worrying about what you look like on camera.

Denise, my PA, who is blonde and gorgeous, will not be seen in a Zoom. She directs the camera up to the ceiling because she doesn't want to look at herself, or let others see her. She never will speak about her birthday. I know when it is – 14 January – but she never divulges her age. I'm not at all troubled about my age however, and I always insist on knowing how old people are.

Ageing is not a steady process: we lurch downwards in fits and starts. We look in the mirror and one day an old face stares back at us. Liz Hodgkin and Sophy Gairdner (my Cambridge supervision partner) are irritatingly spry. And Helen Andrews and Biddy Peppin, dear OHS pals, they're all great walkers – and in excellent shape. I used to be too, but not now, because my spinal stenosis stops me from walking. When Liz and Sophy came to stay in Tuscany about eight years ago, they used to go out for long walks together but I knew I couldn't accompany them. My knees wouldn't let me. I sadly said goodbye to them as they trekked across the fields and I remembered the times when I could've done that, but not any more.

When I was working on my first book and reflecting on my life and career, I admitted to regrets that I'd never played the National or the RSC. I felt my career had not scaled the heights I'd once hoped it might. I was delighted in be cast in the 2004 film *Ladies in Lavender* with Dames Judi Dench and Maggie Smith. They remained very much the Ladies while I was their aged retainer, Dorcas, comically obsessed with root vegetables and shoes being cleaned properly. Here's where I try to teach the shipwrecked Polish violinist Judi has fallen for how to peel a potato:

Andrea Marowski: [*speaks in Polish, subtitled*] You look like a potato.

Dorcas: What?

Andrea Marowski: [*speaks in Polish, subtitled*] Actually, you look like a sack of potatoes.

Dorcas: It's no good, I can't understand a word you's saying.

[*He shows her his potato, into which he has cut two eyes and a mouth.*]

He didn't get me either. It's true that I have seldom played the romantic lead, but maybe I never wanted it. I consider I've had a fair suck of the sauce bottle. No one triumphs in the way they expect, but when I look back I feel satisfied.

When you're young, you never think about death. You just think about your next fuck. Now I think about death a lot. Every morning when I get up, I think, 'Hmmm, another day,' which I wasn't expecting. I can't help but be aware that the amount of time ahead of me is less than the time behind. But I'm still ducking and diving. I'm still open to new experiences. I'm just very conscious that there is no light at the end of this particular tunnel. *Now* is the moment that counts. You've got to carpe that diem. So I keep resolutely looking forward and it's good to remain just a little greedy for the next challenge. Life is remarkably like cheesecake . . . You always want just one more slice.

How to Be in *Vogue*

Fashion never interested me, perhaps because most fashion designers are not looking for bodies like mine. I've always known that; I bear them no ill-will or rancour. Imagine my surprise, not to say consternation, therefore, when, in spring 2023 Giles Hattersley, the European features director of *Vogue* wrote to my agent, Lindy: 'The long and the short of it is that Tim Walker is dying to photograph her and so I wondered if we might be able to tempt Miriam to sit for a series of portraits for a feature in *Vogue*'s July issue? Edward [Enninful] totally adores her. As do we all.'

I was amazed as my wardrobe is undistinguished, even absurd. I have worked up a certain style of my own, which I would call The Summer Frock – made of highly patterned, cotton material, the sort of dress young girls wore in the 1950s. These are often run up for me by wardrobe mistresses in the various theatres and film studios in which I have worked, because I demand side pockets and these are sadly now under threat of extinction and hard to track down in the concrete jungles of Oxford Street. I have also developed a penchant (note the French) for enormous Aran cardigans, festooned with duffle-coat buttons which do up the front. Incidentally, I detest the word 'sweater', which not only has American connotations but is odoriferously redolent of exercise. My Aran cardigans are chunky, hand-knitted and very warm. Their patterns recall butch fishermen, a look I have long admired, and I wear my two favourites interchangeably, one dark burgundy, another in algae green. I also glory in a vomit-coloured yellow cardigan, donated from a previous production.

My other wardrobe staple, perhaps the most important, are my knickers. I like a sturdy and roomy undergarment, reminiscent of my former school knickers, always pure cotton. Luckily, the ideal plain white-cotton knicker is sold in my size by Zeeman, the Dutch supermarket chain, a bit like our Tesco or Lidl, I suppose. Heather buys them for me in bulk and then dyes them dark navy blue in the washing machine. When the elastic eventually goes, which, alas, inevitably it does in time, my wonderful London housekeeper Marina replaces it and the knickers spring back to life.

Shoes are easy. I only wear trainers from either New Balance or Skechers in dark shades. They are comfortable and dependable. I do impose orthotic insoles inside because my gait is uneven. Lord Byron, with whom I share a publisher, had a club foot, but I decided not to go that far.

My multicoloured socks are hand-knitted by my loving cousins Jenny and Catriona Cowen, who live in maidenly exclusivity in Melbourne guarded by their demonic cats. I visit them annually to refresh the sock supply and to hear their intriguing stories of the Solomon family, one of whom, a former convict, sold old clothes from a barrow.

Although I hadn't disclosed any of these details to *Vogue*, they wisely decided to bring everything with them. Many, many emails were exchanged. It became abundantly clear that a fashion shoot is a major production. Vivienne Westwood (my much admired near neighbour) may have died, but fashion was blooming in Clapham nonetheless.

—

Tim Walker has published books, had huge exhibitions, has work in the permanent collection at the National Portrait Gallery and retrospectives at the V&A. I couldn't believe that he wanted to take my picture. When he came to see me the night before, I was expecting noisy flamboyance but he is calm and quiet and still. He's very tall and slim, with a shaved head, and cool, casual dress – plain cotton shirt, dark jeans. He's always looking very carefully at the world around him and noticing the strangest things. Increasingly nervous about the shoot I was mainly relieved that he didn't seem at all 'fashion'.

It was to be handbags at dawn. That is, in fashion-speak, 8.30 a.m., but as this team were pros, I heard the sounds of the convoy of trucks containing the *Vogue* personnel, entourage and a frightening amount of gear gathering outside my front door a full thirty minutes before the arranged time.

Still in my slippers and nightie, I let them in, and soon at least twenty very young and beautiful people were swarming through my front door, carrying clothes racks piled high. First came the coats and robes – extraordinary sculptural creations from Martin Margiela and Marina Rinaldi. Then an entire shoe shop was laid out on my bedroom floor – pumps and platforms and kitten heels – in bright reds, jewel green and gold. Huge cardboard boxes were emptied onto my basement kitchen island – a mountain of extraordinary hats; fascinators with feathers, tulle and beads, perky berets, conical felt creations, and a chic little black felt pill-box. Most puzzling of all was some sort of white floppy foam-filled affair, which, when placed on my head, seemed to resemble a pair of white rabbit's ears.

A trestle table was erected to hold all the sunglasses of every size, shape and shade, about fifty small handbags, clutch size, and mostly in red and black leather, satin or velvet. Umbrellas, parasols, necklaces, brooches, watches, under slips, silk scarves, and stockings.

The basement rapidly began to resemble an exclusive Knightsbridge department store. But as more and more items and accessories were unloaded into the house, it became obvious that something was going to have to give. Much of my furniture was therefore trundled into the garden to accommodate them (eventually getting rained on as the hours passed). Looking out to the garden, one of the most fashionable of the crew asked with surprise, 'What are those lovely red flowers?' 'Tulips, darling,' I explained, realising that glam they may be, but they certainly don't get outside much.

Despite initial protests, a young female manicurist quickly filed my nails, then applied several glossy coats of vermilion. She was right. It did the trick; I instantly felt like a vamp. Then my hairdresser for the day sprayed and spritzed and combed and teased my short curls into a sort of up-do, adding a few choice hairpieces on top. Finally, my make-up artist expertly massaged moisturiser and foundation into my skin. I refused mascara – it makes my eyes water. Then a carefully applied crimson lipstick – and Miriam was ready to be dressed . . .

The house was full of clothes of all kinds, but in fact I only got the chance to wear a tiny proportion of what had been assembled by my stylist. (Whoever thought I'd ever use the words 'my stylist'!) Kate

Phelan was slender and fun and quick-eyed, clearly a know-all about clothes and which colours worked. Amazingly, she lives in Clapham too – so I took her address in the unlikely event of my needing her skills again. She was accompanied by a professional seamstress, ready to fix any split seams, darts or loose buttons on my various outfits throughout the day.

Back in the sixties I had met David Bailey at the first night party for *Orpheus Descending*. The elegant all-white Syrie Maugham room was filled with beautiful people and me. David was already a well-known photographer for *Vogue* and remained resolutely unimpressed by the preening around him. We had a funny conversation – perhaps because I was the only person in the room, male or female, who didn't fancy him. He said, 'You're an interesting bird. Come to my studio, I'll photograph you.' I always wished I had . . . until I read his autobiography and learned there that he only loved women who are thin and have small breasts – 'I don't like big udders.' Goodness knows what he would have made of mine! That was exactly how the fashion world had always made me feel: a scorned outsider looking in.

But now I was not just inside, but at the heart of things. It was a rare and beautiful experience after so many years of grumpy shop assistants, visibly horrified by the challenge of finding something that might fit me. This team were *my* people, and they clearly relished prepping and primping me.

I had always felt uncomfortable about having my picture taken – posing can feel so stilted and I've never liked either being still or silent – but this felt like that moment where the final curtain goes down and there is a deep beat of anticipation before the clapping starts. Finally divested of my nightdress and cardi, I was draped in the Dior 'New

Look'-inspired finery Kate had chosen. I stood there awkwardly feeling out of my depth. I've never been photographed for a fashion magazine before, let alone *Vogue*. 'I don't know how to do this,' I said. 'I don't know what you want. I'm an actress not a model.' Tim smiled. 'Act. Imagine you're playing a model. I want you to be Barbara Goalen.' Of course – that was the cue. I was ACTING. And suddenly I was striking all her poses, the cheeky moue, a saucy jut of the hips, as if to the manner born. Finally I was primed, prepared, and raring to go. Tim picked up his camera and we were off.

I had noticed three or four young men carting boxes and boxes of cream cakes, Victoria sponges and iced buns through the house. It looked like the entire daily output of Greggs the bakers had taken over my spare room. I thought that those were for the crew, not for me: please remember I am a Gail's girl – my cakes need to be of a markedly higher standard. So I was amazed when Kate suggested I strip to my knickers – and I mean strip, totally naked, from the waist up – and then the plate of iced buns with the glacé cherries on top appeared. I questioned, 'Should I do that?' It felt naughty to pose topless with two large iced buns just obscuring my breasts. And then I thought, 'Oh, fuck it. OK, let's do it.' *

———

I was overwhelmed by the power of Fashion, but I think they were also more than a little surprised by me. A video was made of the contents

---

* No photo ever taken of me has ever received such attention or praise. Bless you, dear Tim, for making this old woman very happy.

of my handbag. From their reactions I don't think they had ever thought of including a raw white onion in case of sudden hunger pangs. Let alone a capacious spare pair of clean dark-blue knickers. (You never know when you're going to need them.) Or that an entire beauty regime could consist of a small pot of Nivea and a pair of twee-zers. But now, thanks to them, I realise that lipstick has a place in my bag too. Madame Rubinstein was inspired by cartridge cases when, in Australia, she invented the lipsticks that made her fortune – hence their shape. It's indeed a useful weapon to carry round in your armoury. Watch out, world: here comes MM la Fashionista!

The Well, Well, Well of Loneliness

It's been a strange century to be gay. In my four-score years and two (glad to be out-Patriarching the Patriarchs) I have lived through great social change. It's been the best of times but also the worst . . . The HIV crisis was a particularly dark period. I lost thirty-four friends. I counted them one day, because there were so many who had died and they were all such beautiful, talented, funny, gifted boys. The nadir came while I was living in LA. I had to do something to help so I joined Project Angel Food, the charity which delivered meals to those with AIDS who were too ill to leave the house. I didn't always know their names. I just knew their addresses. They were on their own all day. It was as if they had already died. People were so afraid of infection that they pretended that the AIDS victims didn't exist any more. I still remember those haunted faces staring out of the windows, waiting for us. They haunt me now.

I had grown up in the shadow of another Holocaust and seen its effects on my parents. Conscious of it, they were determined that I should have the confidence I needed to live a larger life than they had. I know they were heartbroken I was gay. My mother made me swear on the Torah never to sleep with another woman again. I knew as I made the oath that it was a promise I couldn't keep. I was very very sad that they hated it so much. I have never had any shame about being gay. I knew homosexuality wasn't criminal whatever the Law said. I knew it was simply another way of being. You're in a strong position if you're not afraid to be who you are.

———

Gay people are very lucky to have escaped (or been rejected) from the conventional. We are a group slightly apart and it gives us an edge. We're good artists, we're good musicians. Gay people also have the luck to be able to fashion the relationship they want. Outside the strictures of the norm, we have more freedom than straight people. I love being gay. I wouldn't want to be straight for anything.

———

The *Vogue* shoot was a celebration of LGBT culture for the month of Gay Pride. I and other well-known queer figures were being interviewed and photographed. Of course, I wasn't going to turn down such a tempting offer, but I do feel the time has come to stop shouting out that I am a lesbian. No one should need my permission to do or be what they want. As Che Guevara (another lesbian!)[*] said: 'I am not a liberator. Liberators do not exist. The people liberate themselves.'

When I was young, I was a lesbian on fire, my cunt flew and danced. I adored being a lesbian, positive joy oozed from the main orifice I used and every other. I couldn't talk about it enough, I returned to its pleasures nightly, I thought about nothing else.

---

[*] Well, another lover of women . . .

Not so now. I am eighty-two, happily espoused for fifty-four years, but most important of all, I'M ALLOWED TO DO IT. My hope is that one day EVERYONE IN THE WORLD WILL BE ALLOWED TO DO IT. Of course, there are still countries – sixty-four at the time of writing – where homosexuality is forbidden and the fight must continue there. But for me, it is no longer a fight, an obsession. My lips are at rest – both sets!

The story that my heroine Queen Victoria intervened to ensure lesbianism was excluded from the relevant laws because she refused to believe such a thing existed, has always pained me. I am delighted to confirm it is a lie, although it is certainly true that lesbianism was long ignored by the law. Provided we were quiet about it, as long as we could stomach the assumption that it was only because no man wanted us, two 'tweedy' women sharing a house and a life could quietly get on with it.

And we did for centuries. Almost three thousand years elapsed between lesbianism's first two heroes: number one was Sappho, of course; the second was the odious Radclyffe Hall with her 'catamite' Una, Lady Troubridge. Catamite might not be the right word as it usually describes a male, but I like it! As they were racist, antisemitic, and very wealthy, their 'degeneracy' proved acceptable to the English upper class. They were safe breeding dachshunds and wearing male attire until Hall put her 'pen at the service of some of the most misunderstood people in the world' and wrote *The Well of Loneliness* in 1928. She outed herself. All hell promptly broke loose.

Sir Archibald Bodkin, the Director of Public Prosecutions at the time, wrote to several doctors trying to prove that Hall's novel would encourage female homosexuality and lead to 'a social and national disaster'. Keeping up the trend for ignoring actual lesbians, it was the book's publisher who was prosecuted for obscenity, not Hall herself. She was not allowed to speak and attended the trial in the spectators' gallery, flamboyantly butch in a leather driving-coat and Spanish riding-hat. But despite her many supporters, who included Virginia Woolf and Vita Sackville-West (whom we know now were 'friends in a big way'), her book was banned until 1949. *The Well of Loneliness* is not a work of great literature, but when I read it, I confess to a slight moistness. 'That night they were not divided' is the raciest quote I could find, but Radclyffe Hall herself does not elicit the same response. You have to be quite picky with your heroines – they can be cunts like anyone else.

Whenever I have found a taste I love, be it Big Tom tomato juice or Bendicks Bittermints (love the macho names!), I have always shared it with the world. Before I realised there was a better option, I kissed a lot of frogs (or penises as they are otherwise known). I roved open-mouthed and increasingly skilled in the art of fellatio through the halls of academe, not to mention the bike sheds of Newnham – and next morning I relished giving the post-prandial review, blow by blow to the breakfast table of my all-female Cambridge college. My friends were agog, a-gag and frequently hysterical at the latest instalment of my cock-sucking adventures. So, when I discovered clitoral joy in my late twenties, everyone had to be told immediately. I couldn't stay silent; there can never be Too Much Information.

Lesbianism did not stop my appreciation of men as people; the men I like, I like a lot. But the Patriarchs have no power over me. I need nothing from men. They cannot bully me. And if they try to threaten me in the street, I have a voice like thunder which I do not scruple to use. Men are harmless and usually irrelevant. But I always stay away from drunks – whatever their sex. Out-of-control people are dangerous.

Back in the late sixties, lesbians were usually shrinking violets. I was one of the few people that everybody knew was gay. I proudly wore my 'GAY YIDS' badge at the BBC and left my copy of *Gay Times* prominently displayed *pour encourager les autres*. I won't tell you who I saw reading it with interest: I would never out anyone – it's up to them whether they come out or not.

There's no end of adjectives – and pronouns – available which can be used to call up a person, a whole human being. 'Lesbian' need not be a definitive noun. It should be just another adjective. I'm lesbian, I'm short, I'm fat, I'm Jewish, I'm Dickensian. Many *different* things. I feel strongly that this government encourages separation of the strands of a people – that is not good. I slightly resist when gay groups want me to be their patron. Yes, it's a privilege to be asked – but I want some *straight* groups to ask me as well. I just don't think we need to be separated.

Being a lesbian is not the most important thing in my life *now*. There was a time when it was. And that's, of course, to do with sexual desire and the sexual instinct. At eighty-two, I'm not going to say my sexual instinct has been totally extinguished, but it's certainly been tamped down a bit.

I feel lucky to be gay; I have enormously enjoyed belonging to a subculture, a club. To be honest, it's not unlike being Jewish. It's a bit cosy, and the pluses far outweigh the minuses.

And now we have some more appealing icons – the Ladies of Llangollen, Gertrude Stein and Alice B., and the gorgeous Anne Lister of Shibden Hall, from whom we can all learn how to do it. As a result, dyke tourism has spiked in Hebden Bridge, the lesbian capital of Britain – it's all the rage and West Yorkshire is all the better for it.

I hope I'm not a threatening lesbian. They do exist – I knew one once. She was an antique dealer and had apparently been, at one time, Britain's most accomplished cat burglar, spending frequent periods at Her Majesty's Pleasure. She had a lithe body, a deep voice and a penetrating blue-eyed stare which held you uncomfortably transfixed, but sadly her chat-up line was: 'Let me guess your star sign.' If she thought that would be alluring to me, she was quite wrong. Two topics terminate any interest immediately – star signs and the telling of dreams. Apart from anything else, I've never been a predatory dyke. I just can't reach, for one thing.

Apparently, there is now a lesbian TikTok and a new phenomenon of straight women watching it and deciding that maybe they too would like to experiment in that area. I wasn't ever closeted, exactly, but when I was in America making a career in films in Hollywood, Susan Smith, my formidable agent said, 'Miriam, please. Don't talk about being gay.' But of course I *did*. It didn't matter whether I was gay or not for the sort of parts I auditioned for, and I don't think it's ever had an impact, quite honestly. It's like saying, 'Do you think people with brown hair always like tomatoes?' Some do and some don't.

There *are* certain lesbian giveaways; a kind of masculinity in someone's walk or hairdo – something about them that gives you a signal. There's a stiffness and uncertainty, sometimes a sort of dourness. But often it completely surprises me. I'm thinking of a good friend of mine, very nearly my age. And for a long time, she had a secret relationship with a woman that nobody knew about. Many people have confided in me about gay relationships they haven't felt able to tell anyone else about. But they tell me. I don't know quite why; perhaps they feel that they can because they know I'm gay and I won't care.

If I hadn't come out then, I couldn't be the person that I am. I think it's impossible and damaging to conceal such a fact, because your sexuality, and whom you love, are central to your life. I can now dismiss it, because it doesn't need to be talked about, it's not worthy of comment. But if I'd had to conceal that, my whole life would have been about the concealment. And then it assumes a position of importance that it shouldn't have. That is deforming. But equally important: consider those who receive the information. Some simply cannot deal with it. And their inadequacy must be recognised. It's selfish and indulgent to spray your sexuality where it's not wanted.

I have often talked about my regret at coming out to my parents. But everybody's different, everybody's caught in the web of their own family and friends. I wanted to strike the cobwebs away and be my own person. But if you live where people loathe homosexuality, or worse, where being gay is outlawed and forbidden, when you find out that that's who you are, you carry a terrible burden. To be able to release yourself from that burden you need to be able to talk about it. Susan Smith always said you have to know with whom you're having the pleasure; you have to know who you can tell and who is unable to deal with it. But what would have happened to me if I hadn't come out? I think much of the energy that makes me who I am would have been channelled into playing the part of the virtuous daughter, who sadly just never met the right Jewish doctor. I would have been forced into untruthfulness. I could never have sustained that.

Maybe, in the long run, it was a case of them or me; every child has to reject their parents to a certain extent, because that's how you become yourself. I couldn't stay silent, but in coming out, I damaged the people I loved most in the world.

There's no doubt in my mind that I dealt my parents a lasting misery. Of course, I enjoyed my sexual freedom, but it came at a price. If society could be a little more giving and understanding, this hurt could be prevented. And I hope that most parents now let their children realise that they can be whoever or whatever they want.

Life has become more complicated. There is no longer a binary solution to gender.

Nature isn't simple. We've always told ourselves that it was. Actually it isn't. And not only are some people homosexual but they're also transgender and fluid and several other choices on the spectrum. Does it matter? Yes, it matters to *them* terribly. In time, I hope it will matter less. I can remember often commenting on someone in the street, saying, 'I don't think that's a woman.' Such an uninformed judgement one day none of us will ever make.

I'm not exclusively in the gay world. I'm happy for anybody who wants to be in a gay world to be in it. Be in the world you want. But I want to be in THE world, the wider world. And I say to you, as I will say to God – should He turn out to exist: 'Thanks so much for waiting. HERE I AM!'

Other people can define me as they choose. *I* don't define me. I'm Miriam Margolyes. End of story. 'Nuff said.

Acknowledgements

Sometimes people enter your life and make such a difference that they become essential; my editors Georgina Laycock and Rose Davidson are just such angel benefactors. From our almost daily conversations I have learnt to be a writer. Mistakes happen – and they are all my fault. But the joy of knowing them and being given the confidence to risk another book has been a blessing.

Thank you also to: Lenore Abraham, Mahnaz Ala'i-Vaillancourt, Stefanie Alboretti, James Albrecht and the Fane team, Sarah Arratoon, Eileen Atkins, Rowan Atkinson, Juliet Brightmore, Lorraine Brown, Rachel Brown, Momo Brubeck, Martin Bryant, Kathy Burke, Steve Buscemi, Ellinore Busemann Sokole, Jimmy Carr, John Castle, Paul Cheifitz, Katerina Clark, Emily Cook, Laurie Critchley, Alan Cumming, Tim Curry, Sophie Dahl, Lucy Darwin, Luca Deidda, Diana Eden, Ros Edmunds, Barnaby Edwards, Serena Evans, Francesca Franco, Stephen Fry, Richard E. Grant, Nicky Hall, Jocasta Hamilton, Liz Hodgkin, Olivia Holman, Drew Hunt, Charlotte Hutchinson, Dr Tito Kabir, Lindy King, Tom and Kate Kinninmont, Robert Kirby, Jeremy Lanson, John Lawton, Iain Leighton, John Lloyd, Sylvester McCoy, Ruth McVey, Sara Marafini, Steve Martin, Deena Mavji, Mojtaba Moji, Katharine Morris, Jimmy Nail, George Naylor, Mark North, Graham Norton, Biddy O'Brien, Ruth O'Neill, Rohan Onraet, Catherine Pasternak Slater, Mark Pawsey, Biddy Peppin, Matthew Perry, Kate Phelan, Siân Phillips, Nigel Planer, Joan

Plowright, Mark Raymon, Jay Rayner, Sandy and Dianne Rendel, Charlotte Robathan, Tony Robinson, Zoe Ross, Pam St Clement, Phillip Schofield, Arnold Schwarzenegger, Paolo Seratini, Dr Ranil de Silva, Maggie Smith, Nick de Somogyi, Carmen Tabanyi, Diana Talyanina, Marina Thurairatnam, Jill Townsend, Anna Truelove, Stanley Tucci, David Vaillancourt, Tim Walker and the *Vogue* team, Ouida Weaver, Justin Webb, David Westhead, Caroline Westmore, Ellie Wheeldon, Will.i.am, Holly Willoughby, Stella Wilson and last – but by no means least – my wonderful assistant of twenty-two years, Denise Wordsworth.

Credits

Text

Extract from Natalie Anglier, *Woman: An Intimate Geography* (Little, Brown, 2000), used with permission. Extracts from *Blackadder* © Rowan Atkinson, Richard Curtis, Ben Elton and John Lloyd. Text of Anusol advertisement © Church and Dwight, Bum's The Word campaign for Anusol. Introductory quote to chapter, 'When Did You Have Your First Fuck?', by kind permission of Carey Harrison.

Pictures

Author's collection: 1, 2, 9 above left and centre right, 14 above left, 15 above. Image courtesy of The Advertising Archives: 6 above left. Alamy Stock Photo: 5 above left/Cinematic Collection, 5 centre right/Photo 12, 7 above left, 8 above/Vuk Valcic, 9 below left/PA Images, 11 below/Landmark Media, 12 above/TCD/Prod.DB, 13 centre left and below right/PA Images. BBC Photo Archive: 6 below left/Dave Pickthorn, 7 below right/Chris Capstick, 13 above left/David Clarke, 14 below. Courtesy of Daniela Cesarei: 15 below left. Ken Hively/Los Angeles Times/via Getty Images: 11 above. © Graeme Hunter: 10 above left. Courtesy of Francesca Gualtieri: 15 below right. ITV/Shutterstock: 3 above left, 6 centre right, 13 above right/Ken McKay.

Marilyn Kingwill/ArenaPAL: 12 below. Kobal/Shutterstock: 5 below. Melbourne Theatre Company, 2019, Miss Shepherd in *The Lady in the Van*, photo by Jeff Busby: 10 above right. Radio Times/Getty Images: 3 below left. Don Smith/Radio Times via Getty Images: 4. © Southern Pictures: 10 centre right and below. © Alexandra Tandy Photography on behalf of Oxford High School: 8 below. TV Times via Getty Images: 3 centre right. © Prudence Upton: 7 below left. British *Vogue*, July 2023, Miriam Margolyes: 16. Photographer Tim Walker/Stylist Kate Phelan/Hair stylist Ali Pirzadeh/Make-up Bea Sweet/Manicurist Simone Cummings/Set design Miguel Bento/Production Zoe Wassall and Jamie Spence. © Tim Walker Studio: 16.

Every reasonable effort has been made to trace copyright holders, but if there are any errors or omissions, John Murray will be pleased to insert the appropriate acknowledgement in any subsequent printings or editions.

Index

Index